Fabrications

OXFORD STUDIES IN DANCE THEORY
Mark Franko, Series Editor

French Moves: The Cultural Politics of le hip hop
Felicia McCarren

Watching Weimar Dance
Kate Elswit

Poetics of Dance: Body, Image, and Space in the Historical Avant-Gardes
Gabriele Brandstetter

Dance as Text: Ideologies of the Baroque Body, Second Edition
Mark Franko

Choreographies of 21st Century Wars
Edited by Gay Morris and Jens Richard Giersdorf

Ungoverning Dance: Contemporary European Theatre Dance and the Commons
Ramsay Burt

Unworking Choreography: The Notion of the Work in Dance
Frédéric Pouillaude

Making Ballet American: Modernism Before and Beyond Balanchine
Andrea Harris

Choreomania: Dance and Disorder
Kélina Gotman

Gestural Imaginaries: Dance and Cultural Theory in the Early Twentieth Century
Lucia Ruprecht

Dancing the World Smaller: Staging Globalism in Mid-Century America
Rebekah J. Kowal

Moving Modernism: The Urge to Abstraction in Painting, Dance, Cinema
Nell Andrew

Choreography Invisible: The Disappearing Work of Dance
Anna Pakes

The Fascist Turn in the Dance of Serge Lifar: Interwar French Ballet and the German Occupation
Mark Franko

One Dead at the Paris Opera Ballet: La Source 1866–2014
Felicia McCarren

When Words Are Inadequate: Modern Dance and Transnationalism in China
Nan Ma

Body Impossible: Desmond Richardson and the Politics of Virtuosity
Ariel Osterweis

Fabrications

Dance, Costume, and Material Culture

Rachel Fensham

OXFORD
UNIVERSITY PRESS

OXFORD
UNIVERSITY PRESS

Oxford University Press is a department of the University of Oxford.
It furthers the University's objective of excellence in research, scholarship,
and education by publishing worldwide. Oxford is a registered trade mark of
Oxford University Press in the UK and in certain other countries.

Published in the United States of America by Oxford University Press
198 Madison Avenue, New York, NY 10016, United States of America.

© Oxford University Press 2026

CIP data is on file at the Library of Congress

ISBN 9780197699607 (pbk.)
ISBN 9780197699591 (hbk.)

DOI: 10.1093/9780197699638.001.0001

Paperback printed by Integrated Books International, United States of America
Hardback printed by Bridgeport National Bindery, Inc., United States of America

The manufacturer's authorized representative in the EU for product safety is
Oxford University Press España S.A. of Parque Empresarial San Fernando de Henares,
Avenida de Castilla, 2 – 28830 Madrid (www.oup.es/en or product.safety@oup.com).
OUP España S.A. also acts as importer into Spain of products made by the manufacturer.

For Christine, once a child in a mill town, who taught me to sew; and,

for Peter, whose thesis studied the effects of automation on workers in a garment factory.

Contents

Series Editor's Foreword

With this book, Rachel Fensham offers us a strikingly new and productive approach to dance history and theory. The unitary focus given to movement in studies of modern dance, where "embodiment" itself seems to be not only the form but also the content of choreography and performance, has obscured how costume contributes to our perception of movement. The world of modernist modern dance of the twentieth century was distinguished from ballet in part by departing from the latter's conventions, which prior to the Diaghilev era had presented nothing new in terms of the presentation of the human form and human expression since Romanticism in the 1840s. Coco Chanel can serve as a paradigm case, as her *haute couture* of the 1920s brought together high fashion statement with sportswear and inexpensive utilitarian clothing on the avant-garde ballet stage. And, of course, Chanel's contributions to costume design in both dance and theater of the French interwar period are well known. But attention to the modernist innovations of modern dance has rarely extended to costume except in the case of the "technological avant-gardes" represented by Loïe Fuller, Oskar Schlemmer, and Alwin Nikolais. Specific attention to costume in terms of its materiality and the relationship of its materials to modes of mass production in the clothing industry, as well as to the ever-changing modes of fashion itself, is therefore an undeniably rich and revealing new entry point to the history and theory of dance modernism of the twentieth century. In fact, it is arguably a paradigm shift in dance scholarship today.

Fabrications: Dance, Costume, and Material Culture deals a blow to the myth of dance's ephemerality, one whose predominance has tended to keep dance within an idealized sphere of cultural production far from the material and social factors that condition it. Claims for the materiality of dance cultures—not only through fabrics that collaborate with the bodies wearing them to create an effect that neither could have managed alone but also through other material remains of an archival nature—have recently been advanced by studies in danced re-enactment that also stress the non-ephemeral, durable qualities of choreographic performance.[1] By emphasizing and analyzing the aesthetic and semiotic role of costumes created for and worn in twentieth-century modernist and post-modernist choreographic repertoire and by understanding costume itself as a form of dress that is determined by specific modes of fashion, fabric manufacture (in particular textiles), and design techniques, Fensham not only puts the ephemerality of dance into question but also reexamines the material/immaterial culture binary itself. The acknowl-edgment of salient material factors in choreography's "fabrications"—this term serving to stress the theatrical nature of choreography—suggests that dance is not immaterial but instead material culture or that at the very least dance can no longer be entirely divorced from material culture and sequestered in the domain of immateriality. This claim is a major achievement with wide-reaching implications. Moreover, Fensham's discussion of the limitations inherent to the idea of clothing points to the importance of a theatricaliza-tion of clothing that itself moves us far beyond materiality as solely a conditioning factor economically, socially, and politically. In fact, the intervention of this new materiality, far from being a critical epiphenomenon divorced from the realities of artistic creation, is shown to be aesthetically and semiotically at the heart of performance's materiality.

Fensham's focus on the technologies of fabric construction and costume design also places a slice of dance history in the domain of the archive: costumes remain, where they can be interrogated after the fact as the participants in the conception and formation of innovative movement discoveries. After their use, costumes retain movement traces, and the texture, color, and weight of fabrics enhance languages of embodied movement. Modernist and postmodernist choreography is here revealed to be part and parcel of ma-terial culture because embodied movement is seen to be a dialectical relationship to a form of materialism: it is inseparable from the literal and sustainable existence of fabric. The entanglement of dance with material culture, until now more familiar to Africanist dance aesthetics, is here extended to Western cultural expression. The word costume itself al-most risks underplaying the scope of Fensham's project, but this is where the astuteness of her analysis opens a different way to understand materialism in the context of embodied movement. The idea of dialectical costume, adapted from Walter Benjamin's concept of the dialectical image, plays an important role in her analysis, as does Roland Barthes's idea of the fashion silhouette, as well as insights imported from the new materialism.

One also finds in this book a recognition of the multiplicity of costume artifacts inhabiting archives as opposed to the museal exhibition of some costumes in a more singular and/or elitist sense. In this way, the costume archive works against the idea of unique and singular presence that has also for so long been the hallmark of dance mod-ernism. This book encourages us to read both dance history and dance historiography against the grain, and it offers a distinctive turning point in the received methodologies of dance scholarship by enriching the interdisciplinary potential of dance research, which is one of the goals of this series.

Mark Franko
Series Editor

Acknowledgments

This book began more than a decade ago when I decided to think about costumes in dance archives. Since then, given the vicissitudes of demanding jobs, relocation, stolen computer, and other book projects, followed by the pandemic, the research and completion of this book have become indebted to many.

First, I would like to thank the editorial support team—Gillian Butcher who has brilliantly and relentlessly assisted with managing the images and permissions that grace this book's pages; Jenny Lee who has provided capacious and insightful copy-editing; Angela Conquet who has been my guide and translator through the French collections; and, Bronwyn Kidd, who ensured that the costume photographs were consistently beautiful. Thanks also to Gil Dwyer who undertook an early editorial reading of the manuscript, and Wil Villareal, the Copyright Services Manager at the University of Melbourne, for his advice.

Second, I must express my immense gratitude to all the curators, archivists, and librarians who have made my short visits productive and responded to innumerable queries and requests with grace and speed. They are the precious custodians of our shared cultural heritage and the real heroes of books such as this: Norton Owen, Director of Preservation, Jacob's Pillow Archives; Patsy Gay, Associate Archivist; and Caroline Hamilton, Dance and Costume Historian; Adam MacPhàrlain, Curator of Clothing and Textiles; and Lauren Sallwasser, Associate Archivist, Missouri Historical Society, and in 2016, Shannon Meyer and Amanda Claunch, Missouri Historical Society; Leverne E. Backstrom, Katherine Dunham Museum, East St. Louis; Matthew J. Gorzalski, Morris Library Special Collections Research Center, Southern Illinois University; Jill Vuchetich, Archivist, Head of Archives & Library, Kova Walker-Lečić, Assistant Registrar; and Mike Lind, Collections Management Coordinator, Walker Art Center, and in 2016, Mary Coyne, Curator, Walker Art Center; Jessica Pushor, Chicago History Museum;

Allison LaPlatney, Alex Ross, and Janine Biunno, The Noguchi Museum; Kathleen Sabogal, Director, Rose Archives and Museum, Carnegie Hall; Francine Snyder, Director of Archives, Rauschenberg Foundation; Angélique de Labarre, Manager and Owner, Château des Milandes, Castelnaud-la-Chapelle; and Delphine Pinasa, Director, Centre National du Costume de Scene, Moulins.

Busy people in dance companies have assisted with providing documents, photographs, important information, and personal accounts: Joyce Herring, Director of Martha Graham Resources, Martha Graham Company, who shared her unique experience of working with Graham and made access to the costumes possible; Jennifer Goggans, Merce Cunningham Trust, who understands how costumes shape the feeling of movement for a dancer; Beth Rudig, Company Archivist, Trisha Brown Dance Company (TBDC); they all most generously contributed to this research. Thanks also to designer Anna Finke, and Patricia Lent who opened the amazing Merce Cunningham Dance Company capsules for me, and especially the writer, Nancy Dalva, whose "eyes" for the poetics of the Cunningham repertoire are a gift to his legacy. Designer Marsha Skinner shared rich correspondence from New Mexico that echoed the depths of *Ocean;* and David Bolger warmly contributed resources from his late partner, the designer Mark Lancaster. Marie-Christine Dunham Pratt was generous in her response to this research, which recalls both her father, John Pratt, and mother, Katherine Dunham.

The visual documentation of costumes has been a priority, and I would like to acknowledge photographer Hibbard Nash, assisted by Quinn Czejkowski, who documented the Martha Graham costumes with great finesse, and Karen McLeod who captured valuable images from the Milandes collection, as well as the photographers Cameron Wittig from the Walker Art Center and Cary Horton from the Missouri Historical Museum. Many dance and studio photographers granted permission to use their works in this project, and we recognize that without them, dance would lack its visual memory. As they are particularly numerous, please recognize them through their attributions in the list of illustrations. Other sources of images include Tate Britain, the Library of Congress, New York Public Library, Archives Monte-Carlo Société des Bains de Mer, Imogen Cunningham Trust, UCLA Library Special Collections, Kunsthistorisches Museum Wien, Greg Gorman, Reiko Kopelson, MKUM Hungarian Museum of Trade and Tourism, Tenement Museum, The Metropolitan Museum of Art, Smithsonian: National Portrait Gallery, Hagley Museum, Stedelijk Museum, The Museum at FIT, Scala Archives, Getty Images, New York Aikikai.

As a dance historian and performance theorist entering the field of costume studies, I would like to thank the Costume Research Reading group at Melbourne, who shared their expert insights into costume, fashion, and dress history; in particular, design colleague Emily Collett who assisted me with linking costume details to photographs in the Katherine Dunham archives. Theater and dance colleagues have also provided critical input; feedback from the Theatre Studies reading group sharpened the proposal; and dance professor Sherril Dodds, Temple University, who always encouraged my "fashion" interests, generously commented on a first draft. An unexpected invitation from dance historian Lynn Garafola to contribute a paper to the Columbia University Seminar "Studies in Dance" was a wonderful opportunity to speak and get feedback on a chapter. Carol Brown, Head of Dance at the VCA, artfully programmed a recreation by Melissa Toogood, supervised by rehearsal director Nicole Corea, of Merce Cunningham's *Ocean*, that added immeasurably to my public pleasure in that work. Peter Eckersall, City University of New York, shared my journey to the Berkshires for research at Jacob's Pillow, and Ien Ang, University of Western Sydney, and Ian Johnson, University of Sydney, introduced me to the Baker collection in the Dordogne and provided local connections at a critical juncture.

This book was not externally funded, so I am immensely grateful for the support of the School of Culture and Communication and the Faculty of Arts at the University of Melbourne for the publication grant support. Given the pressures on academics to provide the advanced work and costs of publication, the necessity of institutional support for scholarly work becomes ever more essential. Without university funding, this book could not have been completed, particularly in relation to copyright in images.

The intellectual acumen of series editor Mark Franko, the keen interest of publisher Norm Hirschy, and the two anonymous readers for Oxford University Press have sharpened the focus of this book, but its omissions or elisions are obviously my responsibility. I imagine there are other hidden narratives somewhere.

Of course, the book has also weighed heavily on my personal life. I want to thank friends who have kept me sane by calling me out for a walk and family who have foregone my attention. And throughout, Adrian's care and ongoing love make all things possible.

Illustrations

Covers

Front Cover
Detail of dress with silk plaid patchwork, *Honky Tonk Train* (1941). Photograph by Cary Horton. Katherine Dunham Collection, 1991-077-0115 a. Courtesy of the Missouri Historical Society, St. Louis.

Introduction

Chapter 1

Chapter 2

Chapter 3

Chapter 4

Chapter 5

Chapter 6

Introduction

In my formulation: "The eternal is in any case far more the ruffle on a dress than some idea." Dialectical Image.

Walter Benjamin, *The Arcades Project* (1999: 69)

This book begins with the claim that dance is "dressed." Dancers are (almost always) wearing clothes, and these clothes are mostly fabricated in the form of costumes—particularly for stage choreography but also in popular dance. These costumes, as material artifacts, are items of fashion representing the modes of their contemporary culture. This claim means that any dance garment is dependent on the available materials and technologies of textile and garment manufacturing in a given historical time. Costumes are therefore things that have been worked; they involve the imaginative repurposing of textiles and styles of dress by dancers, designers, and choreographers who enhance their potential on the moving body. The artist imagines how dancers will be seen and how the stage picture might appear by making costumes useful and of value to the expressive gestures and stories of choreography.

The book's focus is therefore on how the manufacture, art, and symbolic effects of costume have informed aesthetic and social transformations in twentieth-century dance history, specifically American concert dance. Inasmuch as clothing invokes contemporary fashion, any dance garment will be dependent on its construction as textiles and in forms of dress tied to its own epoch. This aspect of a costume introduces an important thread in this study—the material aspect of dance. Costumes are always fabricated in relation to resources, and it is the imaginative use of garments by dancers, designers, and choreographers that makes it more meaningful or dynamic. In this sense, the historicity and materiality of the costume are recuperated and animated by the body in motion, and the costume and the choreography weave themselves together as complementary modes of creative production. This interplay between the material work of costume and the presumably immaterial work of dance-making is what this book calls *fabrications*.

In this introduction, I outline the theoretical and practical methods that enable us to examine the dance costume as an artifact that materializes dance labor in relation to

Fabrications. Rachel Fensham, Oxford University Press. © Oxford University Press 2026. DOI: 10.1093/9780197699638.003.0001

the received status of dance performance as immaterial culture. My approach is largely historical, an attempt to think through the ways in which twentieth-century costumes produce meanings in dance that accumulate expressive power. They do so as tangible things that accompany embodied movement, but they also have a value and durability that precedes and exceeds the performance. The entanglement of dance with material processes, on and off stage, requires a somewhat museological focus that can extend discourses on dance concerned with the specificity of choreographic ideality within a given sociopolitical context, alongside the phenomenology of the dancing body. Moreover, as a project concerned with the materiality of dance, it has involved locating dance costumes in a range of archives and engaging with their economic and political history, by detailing how innovations in the textile and garment industries influence the design, construction, and fashioning of dress. Beyond its manufacture, the transformation of the crafted object into a costume takes place through its role in dance representation, and therefore, this book is also concerned with the imaginative, affective, and corporeal aesthetics of garments as worn in and manipulated by performance.

Before I expand in this introduction on the critical discourses that shape a materialist analysis of dance as costumed—including my conception of the dialectical costume and the dance silhouette—I want to address two principles that are important to our understanding of dance costumes. First, the remains of costume disrupt and contest the much-vaunted ephemerality of dance, and second, an attention to the multiplicity of costumes is required rather than the exceptional instance.

Dance Ephemerality and the Multiplicity of Costume

A focus on how dancing bodies (gendered, racialized, differently abled) produce meanings has been one of the distinctive contributions of contemporary dance studies.[1] Yet, despite decades of inscription, decoding, and recoding of dancing bodies, the primary condition of much dance and choreography, even when recorded, is that it is haunted by its disappearance, an ephemerality Peggy Phelan has theorized as the "ontology of performance," leaving "no visible trace" (1993: 149). Often, we barely know what we have seen or experienced of a dance, a gesture, or a rhythm in a choreography before it has escaped in all the fullness of its spine-tingling presence. Afterward, we feel suspended, already forgetting. Andre Lepecki, a scholar of European conceptual dance, continues this line of argument when he writes, "The whole project of dance theory can be summarized as follows: dance vanishes; it does not 'stay around' (for such is the unfortunate condition of its materiality)" (2004: 130). With no trace, we would rely only upon memory and speculation rather than historicizing the immediacy of dance as both an immaterial and material event, one capable of leaving behind archival remains as well as mental images.

Nonetheless, Lepecki in *Exhausting Dance: Performance and the Politics of Movement* is also attuned to materialist cultural history when he cites the Greek cultural anthropologist Nadia Seremetakis and her concept of "historical dust" as those moments in choreography "when the buried, the discarded, and the forgotten escape to the social surface of awareness" (2006: 15). From the perspective of this book, dance costumes are objects that have had lives in a performance, like domestic artifacts in a household, but they may have been buried, discarded, or forgotten in histories of dance modernity. Their very materiality recalls, and can disrupt, how we think therefore about the historical forces that determine subjectivity, mobility, and representation for dancing bodies.

Diana Taylor, in her ground-breaking study *The Archive and the Repertoire*, makes another important distinction about the live event and its traces or records, which may be embodied as repertoire and/or "archived," respectively.[2] Rather than a disjunction between diverse methods of transmission for performance, she proposes a generative conception of materiality that incorporates the reality of everyday performative actions alongside those constructed as artistic events with distinct temporal and spatial boundaries. "Performances," writes Taylor, "are, in a sense, always in situ: intelligible in the framework of the immediate environment and issues surrounding them" (2003: 3). Moreover, research on performance that engages with cultural memory will bring together practices, in this case, the fabrication of costumes, which "have historically been kept separate as discrete, supposedly free-standing, ontological and epistemological discourses" (2003: 3). If we adopt an understanding that respects the material conditions that give rise to performance, the costume can be located as both "live" in the evanescent immediacy] of choreography and as a "constructed" object, long after the dance has vanished. As many artists have shown, past costumes can also become potent resources for dance re-enactment, retrieval, and reconstitution; animating the afterlife of objects thus activates important reminders of an absent, yet embodied and situated, choreography (Connolly 2024; Matomoros 2021). In this book, rather than ponder their disappearance, the residual matter of costume and their role as legacy objects have ramifications that further extend discourses of dance history and cultural interpretation.

My own research on dance costumes began in the Natural Movement archive at the National Resource Centre for Dance in the United Kingdom, when I read handwritten labels on cardboard boxes:

Childrens Tunics: 19 Various dyed tunics, pants and girdles; Large size.
Toil: 11 skirts—(hand-dyed) 2 brown, 2 purple 2 green, 3 blue, 2 red.

The description identified a collection of costumes for children, with designations both general and particular—"Tunics. . . Large size"—and the color-coding indicates various garments were worn by different dancers: Who wore which dyed ones? These modest and evocatively sensual costumes—"pants and girdles"—piqued my interest: How did the pants, or bloomers, move around the legs, and how was the girdle knotted? These

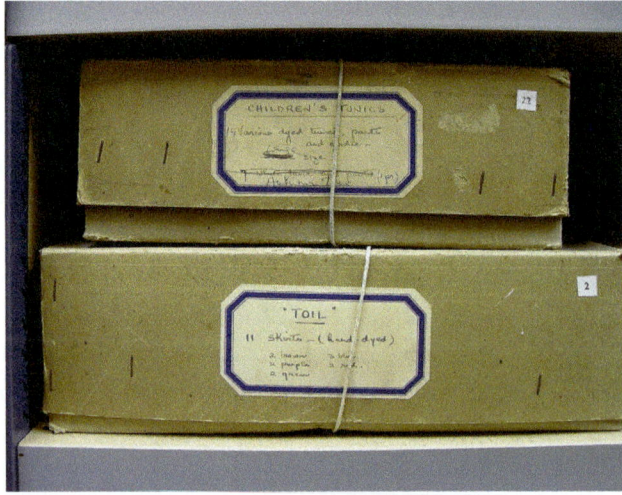

FIGURE 1.1 Archive boxes for children's tunics at the National Resource Centre for Dance, University of Surrey, UK. Photograph by Rachel Fensham.

delicate objects preserved in a dance archive bore the traces—labels and hem-lengths, as well as sweat-marks and tears—of the many young female dancers who had crafted or worn them.

With fading knowledge of "natural movement" in early twentieth-century dance, these tunics revealed details about embodied habits, as well as insights into the choreography in which these outfits were worn (Fensham 2015). The fabric, for instance, was a lightweight silk that fitted loosely around the body, and the dye-patterning produced a visual ensemble that caught the light much as would an impressionist painting. Their soft colors added a novel dimension to the familiar black-and-white photographs of expressive modern dance. Given the artifacts' lowly status—they were only student costumes, after all—their loving preservation was also a potent reminder of a free-flowing movement style transmitted through schools and communities. Initially retained for future reproduction on dancing bodies in new choreographies, these legacy objects held the past, evoking memories of a distinctive choreographic and social formation. My attempts to understand these remains of a historical performance culture led to a close engagement with these costumes as an archive, indicative of past repertoire and of a cultural milieu. But they most provocatively insisted that I consider costumes as a multiplicity, objects that rarely exist alone when seen on stage and that have multiple variations across a repertoire.

When performing or watching a choreography, we almost always encounter sets of leotards, masses of tutus, or hundreds of T-shirts shaping the past or present experience of dance. At the level of fabrication, these dance garments also represent a multiplicity of processes involving fibrous cloth, decisive cutting, pieces of elastic, and linked threads. Once assembled by dancers or choreographers, an arrangement of costumes may express an abstract or narrative concept by establishing a particular visual or kinesthetic design for the ensemble. The effects of such a multiplicity thus include the complexity of each costume as well as the look or shape of the whole; in turn, the repetition of a costume style becomes intrinsic to a choreographic pattern in performance, with the most obvious example being that of a tutu in ballet. However "natural" a costume appears for a particular dance or choreography, even when not designed or highly intentional, this constructedness involves choices about how the costumes will move in a given dance or choreographic genre.[3]

Most studies of costume in dance, however, focus on a singular unique object, usually identified with a character, perhaps a celebrity artist, or on outfits that display some quality of excess, such as Vaslav Nijinsky's ornately embroidered tunic by Léon Bakst for *Le Dieu Bleu* (Buckle 1989: 36).[4] Later, when the costumes are preserved, documented, and stored for posterity, they are removed from the dancer's or company's wardrobe and given enhanced status as museum artifacts. Displayed on mannequins, these iconic costumes represent mystery and glamor, inviting fascination with their symbols and sensory meanings for both the past wearer and the present spectator. But all too often, these strange or beautiful items of dress from a past choreography stand alone, their historical significance interpreted simply as an instance of exceptional dance artistry or design.[5]

In this book, I am less interested in the singular instance than in the multiplicity—the accumulation of experience that accrues from the repetitions of a costume—creating patterns on the moving body and changing perceptions of space. The repeated uses of a given type of costume, therefore, contribute to the evolution of choreographic aesthetics and provide a methodology for identifying both dance habits and motifs (Fensham 2014). I follow here a distinction made by Allan Sekula, who points out that one item in a class of objects is not "emblematic," like Nijinsky's costume, but can be "typical." Sekula argues that systems of archival classification must be able to sort items that were "circumstantial and idiosyncratic" into types that enable them to be more scientifically and practically retrieved and interpreted (1986: 17).[6] While my study of typicality in the use of costumes is not intended to produce a scientific system for ordering meaning, costume inventories can become ascribed to specific dance genres or ways of moving (Fensham 2023). Some "typical" costume objects may be easily identified—the "fetishisation" of the tutu and toe shoe in relation to ballet or low-hanging baggy trousers and sneakers with hip-hop dancers (Chazin-Bennahum 2005: 224–5). Over time, their distinctiveness as objects of a particular shape or fabric becomes identified with a specific choreography or dance genre. They can be copied and reproduced with variations and cease to draw attention to their specific function in performance; for instance, the toe shoe designed to elevate the female dancer *en pointe* or the baggy trousers to fall with the moves of the break-dancing b-boy. At the same time, the object itself—tutu or tracksuit pants—has a semi-independent history as a product of fashion, its own contemporary appearance in a social time and place. It is this dual functionality of the costume as a material thing that requires a critical analysis through historical materialism.

The Dialectical Costume as Historical Method

The literary critic Walter Benjamin is of particular importance to this book, because he was one of the first to recognize the significance of fashion, including the "boom in the textile trade," to the modernity of Paris in the late nineteenth century (1999: 6).[7] In doing so, he expanded upon Karl Marx's interpretation of the commodity form in capitalist economies. For Marx, the weaving of linen and the tailoring that produce the value of a coat were his central examples of how human labor enters into a system of exchange.

> The body of the commodity . . . always figures as the embodiment of abstract human labour, and is always the product of some specific and useful concrete labour. . . In the expression of value of the linen, the usefulness of tailoring consists, not in making clothes, and thus also people, but in making a physical object which we at once recognize has value. (Marx 1990: 150)

Given this insight into the bodily labor that manufactures not only the coat but also the personhood of those who wear the clothes, the role of commodities in dance culture provokes close consideration of the values attached to the uses of costume within a given artistic and social milieu. For Benjamin, these questions of commodity form were best approached through their circulation rather than in the abstract mechanics of production modes and systems, and this is what he identified as "fashion."

Fashion, for Benjamin, was a value system that reflected the popular sensibility of everyday consumption, and hence an approach to capturing, in a fleeting way, the dynamics of a present time that has now passed. The commodities that circulate within modern capitalist societies therefore have, in addition to their role as the products of human labor, an afterlife in places and objects, which can be recuperated for interpretation:

> being past, being no more, is passionately at work in things. To this the historian turns for his subject matter. He depends on this force, and knows things as they are at the moment of their ceasing to be. (1999: 833)

To read the past, therefore, the historian undertakes a work of immersive consciousness, returning to "things" that have been overlooked in order to revitalize or "do justice" to the conceptual force of their contribution to a once present reality.

In *The Arcades Project*, his monumental unfinished work, Benjamin assembles and annotates a range of texts on the cultural productions (exhibitions, shopping arcades, mirrors, and modes of lighting) of the late nineteenth and early twentieth centuries; "Convolute B," his chapter on "Fashion," covers twenty pages (1999: 62–81). In this Convolute, a conception of fashion becomes elaborated by diverse, yet astute, observations on bourgeois forms of dress, artifice, fabrics, shopping, and theatrical style that demonstrate the rapid, dreamlike, and unpredictable changes of modernity. For

Benjamin, bringing such disparate ideas into conjunction, however disruptive, produces the "dialectical image," a constellation of a "now-time" that represents "the smallest gestalt" of recognition that a thing has happened or that it has coincided with a change in the human condition (1999: 867). This approach differs from that of Marx and Hegel, in which contradictions in the machinery of historical progress were only dialectical if they could reveal the structural and economic forces of capitalism. With regard to fashion, however, Benjamin identifies a process in which the historical and psychological aspects of dress produce a demand, by fabricating (or transforming) a future expectation of a new subjectivity or potential social liberty (Wollen 2003). When explaining the dialectical image as a form of praxis, Benjamin writes:

> The dialectical penetration and actualization of former contexts puts the truth of all present action to the test. This means however: the explosive materials latent in fashion (which always refers back to something past) have to be ignited. (1999: 857)

From the perspective of dance history, the dialectical image enables therefore apparently insignificant objects (such as items of clothing, shoes, or makeup) to be considered as historical processes, leaning toward the future with a capacity for recycling and reinvention, while looking back at the remains of past uses and associations.[8]

Such a capacity for recycling coheres in fashion and art around certain items of dress and modes of comportment, as the design historian Ulrich Lehmann explains in his Benjamin-inspired book, *Tigersprung: Fashion in Modernity*. A specific instance of a fashionable item of clothing, as seen in dance rehearsal clothes, can be detached from participation in the flow of time in order to "reflect the social circumstances of its creation by repeatedly referring to its own past" (2000: 300). In this sense, a sartorial object not only exists as evidence of a past performance for an individual subject (the dancer, the designer, the choreographer) but also incorporates changes in social movements and economic conditions—the availability of cheap fabrics in urban America, for instance—that may differ from present-day ideologies and desires.

For Benjamin, such objects are neither fully demonstrative of individual ownership nor representative of historical patterns of change as commodities. Instead, what he terms the "dialectical image" is a perception of history that is always estranged, because it ruptures the horizon of material reality as continuous progress. The accumulation of details, perhaps the micro-historical moments that constitute an event, the parlays that move both backward and forward between the environment and the movement of persons, and the incommensurable nature of things that exist in a given time are the ingredients of a dialectical image. In dance, the dialectical image is saturated by the effects of labor, discourse, power, and imagination in modern societies, even as the "image," of a costume and its material form, can be torn from the narrative or pictorial frame to look back at the past afresh.

Given this book's focus on dance in the twentieth century, which marked an extended period of ambitious capitalist modernity in American culture and society, Benjamin's observations on "fashion" in the emergent modernity of nineteenth-century Paris may seem distant, but his writings on the dialectical image give this book a significant conceptual method for the historical analysis of dance costumes as artifacts or representative material fragments of a mode of dancing. What I am calling the "dialectical costume" is the body of a commodity that has a given use and exchange value in dance. Every costume has been woven, cut, and stitched to deliver a consistency of perception for the choreography of its own now-time. In this context, a return to the fragment, the costume as a material trace, becomes a means of reconfiguring the process of dance narration to excavate its historical materialism. By disordering and reassembling the parts, a coat, a tutu, or a tunic, can be located within the temporality and economic conditions of its appearance; at the same time, as Lehmann writes, it also becomes available for a "contemporary rendition" in a "fashion to come" (1999: 301).

Benjamin himself did not regard the work of art as a semi- autonomous system but as a partner to cultural transformations—collective ideologies, patterns of consumption, and the everyday practices of a rapidly evolving society. If we adopt the concept of the dialectical costume as a principle of analysis, then dance clothing is partner to modes of production that transform material objects into commodities while simultaneously opening the garment to the immanent potential of embodied performance, both now and in the future. While not concerned with dance as an art form, "Benjamin is explicit that any particular aesthetic phenomenon—be it painting, sculpture, photography or film—emerges at the collision of representational and material orders" (Mieszkowski 2004: 49). Nowhere can this collision of the aesthetic and the political be more intimate, and perhaps more disturbing, than in the phenomenal realities of costumed bodies in choreography.

The Silhouette and the "Fashion System"

To orientate the reader to this collision between different orders of meaning in one example of mid-twentieth-century choreography, I will advance here the understanding of the costume silhouette as a sign, albeit a cluster of material signs, that is exchanged within performance. That silhouette, as we will see, resonates outward into another system of representation constituted as "fashion."

In his solo *Junkie* (1966), part of a longer dance suite entitled *Blues for the Jungle*, the choreographer Eleo Pomare wears a pair of loose but fitted denim trousers, a singlet top, peaked cap and sunglasses, scruffy sneakers, and a light-colored, long-sleeved bomber jacket.[9] On a sparse stage, he dances frenetically, unfolding the experience of an addict roaming the streets of Harlem, and encountering the dispossession and tragic meanderings of a young black man in 1960s New York. Both an individual and a universal story, the dance scholar Charmian Wells argues that the choreography of *Blues for the Jungle* has a "vitality [that] conveys a knowledge of structural violence . . . from the perspective of black social life" (2020: 6). The dancing itself is intense, informed by Pomare's formal dance training and yet translated into a new idiom through the finely honed methods of expressive modern dance.

My interest here is in what his dress signifies and how it concentrates and encompasses a highly specific world. On one level, Pomare wears casual clothing that could as easily be worn on a train as on a stage, but its flexible fitting is amenable to the exertions of his body. The trousers fold and bunch around his legs, allowing him to leap or to roll across the floor, while the jacket falls off his shoulders and flops as his muscles jerk and lunge. The outfit complements the dramatic quality of Pomare's actions; it shows his vulnerability to the painful contradictions that exist in a city, "the jungle," that thwarts his very existence. Later, after a strenuous sequence in which his body quivers with violent desperation, he turns away and unthreads his belt. In Figure I.2, the singlet reveals his exposed and waiting arms, and we, the spectators, feel the hurt experienced in his body and the sense that there is no escape. From a poverty of means—items purchased in discount stores or found in clothing bins—Pomare's dancing transforms this fabricated costume

FIGURE I.2 Eleo Pomare performing Junkie in *Blues for the Jungle*, 1966. Photograph by David Fullard. © Dr. David Fullard, PhD, LMHC 2024.

into a vanguard stylization of modern black masculinity—exploiting its local currency as fashion from the likes of James Brown and funk music—to devastating effect.[10] In this performance, then, the historical potency of a distinctive stylization of dress is magnified by Pomare's ravaged embodiment of a harsh but vibrant street culture.

The combination here of the slim-fit jeans, jacket, singlet, and cap by Pomare is what Roland Barthes has called a "silhouette," a representative typology of dress that might be repeated or added to with variations in the "fashion system."

By way of contrast to Benjamin, Barthes was less concerned with the circulation of material things than with identifying the vestimentary system that encodes a complex pattern of ideals in relation to gender, class, and commodity culture. His reading of the semantics in French fashion advertising produces some acute insights into how items of dress and adornment also begin to function as a form of language.[11] For Barthes, a fashion typology provides the units of signification that make the communication of dress codes possible. Throughout this book, I adopt two of Barthes's key ideas—the silhouette and the logic of combination. In his inventory of key components of dress, Barthes defines the silhouette as follows:

> It contains the very essence of Fashion, it touches the ineffable, the "spirit," and lends itself to the sublime, inasmuch as, by unifying diverse elements, it is the very movement of abstraction; in short, it is the garment's aesthetic meaning. (1990: 109)

The silhouette is the embodiment of the garment's abstraction, while it is also "like the operations of a machine that result in an *idea*" (110). The silhouette of a garment can therefore be equated with the perception of "ideal" bodies in dance, although as we can see with Pomare's costume, there are many ways in which clothing will define the shape of a dancing body or form its movements. Together, a choreographer and dancer will attune themselves to the abstraction of a costume silhouette in order to elaborate an idea and the combination of variants available in the garment. When choreographers position bodies in space and time, an assemblage of costume variations might include size, color, volume, texture, surface, pattern, and decoration. These concepts will be further explored in the following chapters.

For Barthes, the inventory of variants constitutes another order of meaning, in that they can be combined to render a garment anew each season, as the rhetorical features of fashion require (1990: 111). Presentation on the catwalk, however, is very different from the fashioning of a costume in choreographic repertoire. Unlike fashion models, who standardize the display of a design's silhouette by posing and using a standardized walk, dancers inhabit their clothing in ways that accentuate or transform the possible range of movement. Whether dancers of natural movement, ballet, or street culture, they experiment with the silhouette while encased by the particularity of a given material style. We might note again that dance silhouettes are rarely seen in isolation on a stage; rather, they most often consist of arrangements that formalize dynamics, building contrast and adding lines of adornment.

These arts of combination in choreography do not always conform to the expected patterns. For example, when the Japanese minimalist designer Rei Kawakubo was commissioned to make costumes for Merce Cunningham's *Scenario* (1997), she produced a series of boldly striped and draped leotards stuffed with padding that added prosthetic extensions to conventional body shapes (Meade and Rothfuss 2017). Cunningham, who preferred his dancers to show sleek lines, was initially horrified, but later he accepted that these unusual silhouettes might enable the permutations of his choreography to be enjoyed in new ways. Unpredictable dress assemblage can thus be a source of delight, while other arrangements might reinforce normative expectations about dancing bodies and their visual appeal. Either way, the choreography will exist across a spectrum of agreements about how a costume silhouette may be danced.

Another aspect of the costume's multiplicity emerges from its capacity to be reproduced at scale as part of mass culture's "massive mode" in relation to dress and textile production (Mieszkowski 2004: 50). Inevitably, the twentieth century is aligned with the advent of many forms of mass production and reproduction and with the circulation of imagery designed to stimulate mass consumption.[12] Rather than regarding the culture industry with hostility or suspicion, I consider dance costumes as representative, often at the forefront, of novel manufacturing processes that have created new forms of leisure and consumption. While the massive mode of industrial production "standardizes" the availability of dress as commodities, it also ensures that what is worn becomes highly differentiated by gender, class, race, and age; in turn, this informs its use in dance.

A multiplicity that originates in production processes is therefore a vehicle for connecting to an experience of performance as one that was fabricated—not only manipulated by individual artists, but crafted by the very real labor that makes the production of material objects contemporaneous with the embodied work of dance. These social dimensions of material culture are then interpolated with discourses on work and pleasure, fashion and anti-fashion, art and craft, through their appearance in choreography. In this sense, dance costumes contribute uniquely to the material cultural history of certain modes of manufacturing, design innovation, and popular commodification of dress before they become articulated in and as a choreographic idea.

The New Materialisms of Costume

An important theoretical development in material cultural studies has been toward what has been termed the "new materialisms" (Coole and Frost 2010). While this book is oriented toward those questions of materiality—production, style, and meaning—that enrich historical understanding, the new materialism has drawn attention to the ways in which matter reorientates our focus away from individual narratives and subjects toward the vitality of objects. In her book *Vibrant Matter: A Political Ecology of Things* (2010), Jane Bennett rethinks the distinctions between animate and inanimate objects, aiming to understand how things might "act as quasi-agents or forces with trajectories, propensities, and tendencies of their own" (2010: 9). Bennett's discourse draws equally on the actor network theory of science and technology studies (Latour 2005) and on histories of vitalism in phenomenology; her attention to matter also turns focus away from subjectivity toward an active relationship with the objective nature of things.

For Bennett, the corrective to human exceptionalism in its command over the earth, other species, and resources is the affirmation that there is an "agency of assemblages," so that a "specific arrangement of things," in our case, the arrangement of fabrics, style, dynamics, and fittings within a costume "owes it agentic capacity to the vitality of the materials that constitute it" (2010: 24). The density of attributes, including tactile and visual qualities, that, for instance, constitute the children's tunics or Pomare's leather bomber jacket, adds to knowledge of the transmission of dynamics and energy in performance. In these costumes, the distinct "felt" aesthetics of the fabric—its slipperiness, its stiffness, or its weight—add to the euphoria of the quick, rhythmic movement.

As the example of Pomare shows, tangible things—the sweating chest of a man wearing a thin singlet—are palpable, if fleeting in performance. But the ordinary jacket and pair of everyday trousers, washed regularly to remove stains and replaced if torn or worn out, is an adaptive silhouette, a representation that explicates the political forces in a situation, and a localized fashion. In Bennett's terms, the ontology of the costume helps to "induce in human bodies an aesthetic–affective openness to material vitality" (2010: 11). Through this material "vitality," the costume "assemblage" modifies the choreography and is simultaneously modified by the actions of performance. And, whether it is worn for one night or many, the costume lingers on, carrying with it residual effects—the sweaty patches or torn seams—of its fabrication as history and embodied memory.

For Diana Coole, writing on the new materialisms, "folds" in "fabric" are like the "involutions" of an "embodied humanity," because they generate these embodied and haptic dimensions of experience (Coole and Frost 2010: 110–113).[13] For the dance historian as costume researcher, this potential for a dense, embodied vitality in the animated costume extends beyond its representational logic in the choreographic work; it encourages us to consider also these affective and sensory qualities and their agency within dance. In terms of the new materialism, the potential for variability in alignment between material effects, collective action, and affective excitement will always ricochet in unexpected spatial and temporal directions. The dialectical costume, and its density of attributes, is therefore one part within a larger constellation of meanings attributed to the garment by an artist or spectator. In practice, any given arrangement of materials generates alliances that must account for the effects of appropriation—the endless copying, the unlicensed citation, and the inventive recycling—that are integral to the interactions between dance and other art forms. Indeed, understanding the communicative labor of costumes as objects in networks of production and co-production expands the means and ends of dance practice. And those networks extend from the role that fabric plays in clothing and fashioning of the self outward to the cultural and economic practices that influence the representation and accessibility of clothing, textiles, and fashion in a given culture or society.

Costume Studies: From Clothing to Fashioning

To understand the complex weave between the material costume and artistic production, it is useful to consider developments in the burgeoning fields of dress, textile, and fashion studies, but let us begin with the significance of clothing.[14]

Clothing is the generic term for any item that covers the body for reasons of modesty, warmth, or display; but as the art historian Anne Hollander suggests in her groundbreaking book, *Seeing Through Clothes*, "objects made of fabric [that] convey messages beyond the power of the cloth itself to convey" (1975: 2). Across an entire history of Western art, she insists that visualizing clothes in figurative paintings is not only a way to consider "social custom, economic pressure, or psychological emphasis" but is an invitation that foregrounds the world-making aspect of a picture. Hence, through the ways in which subjects dress in paintings, we become conscious of the "temporal changes and contemporaneous differences" in artistic form and of how subjects choose to be seen (1975: xv). Each chapter unpicks a key theme—such as the role of drapery, nudity, and theatrical costume—but throughout and importantly for this study, Hollander examines how clothes are embodied. In this sense, as she continues, dress also becomes a mode of wearing the self that is related to performance: "Dress has clearly much to do with peoples deep theatrical impulses, their desire to be costumed characters, especially because it functions only in wear and in motion" (1975: 451). Following from Hollander, a wide range of clothing histories have evolved that include studies in political and social economy as well as recording personal stories, artistic practices, and community specialisms; however, her aesthetic focus on the wearing and mobility of clothing as represented in art over time remains formative.

More recent narratives of textiles and design, a prolific contemporary publishing genre, extend the picture of clothing as a social formation to that of the materials from which they are made.[15] In *Worn: A People's History of Clothing* (2022), Sofi Thanhauser chronicles the manufacture of different types of cloth, whether produced by ancient looms or high-end industrial production lines, as advances in technology. Connecting stories to "tangible things" is also an increasingly popular approach to narratives of material culture in museums, and yet many items of clothing are subject to deterioration or disposal. In *The Golden Thread: How Fabric Changed History*, Kassia St. Clair writes of this dilemma: "the objects that most commonly survive, and from which archaeologists infer larger-scale textile production, are the tools that were used to make them" (2018: 30). The sewing machines may persist, but the scraps of fabric on the cutting-room floor have been lost. Developments in design, during the twentieth century, also require knowledge of industrial methods and identification of any distinctive shaping introduced to increase a product's desirability.

An important strand of this book examines how the cultural mobility of twentieth-century dance often masks inequalities in the exchange of goods and services required to produce costumes. The dance scholar Priya Srinivasan provides a notable example of costume appropriation in her book, *Sweating Saris: Indian Dance as Transnational Labor* (2011). She argues that a specific type of dress, the sari, which has featured in global North representations of Indian dance, was often predicated on a "division of labor such that the poor working class women and men who created the dance accoutrements from raw materials never encountered the shopkeepers who sold them at marked-up prices to middle-class and upper-class female dancers" (2011: 154). Making visible the "sweat" of sari-makers and merchants, according to Srinivasan, as well as documenting the narratives of Indian dancing bodies absent in the colonial archive, demonstrates "moments of resistance" that change our conceptions of modern dance history.[16] For the museum curator, Anita Herle, many non-Western clothing artifacts are materials that were "collected in circumstances of great inequality, at times stolen or seized as part of colonial loot, [at other times] . . . readily exchanged, sold, or gifted" (2016). Comparative cultural analysis of dance dress therefore requires a degree of specialist knowledge to unpick how global flows of capital and goods have been exchanged between "classes, genders, roles, groups, and nations," and hence modified clothing practices and social attitudes (Appadurai 1996: 12).

Critical fashion studies also highlight the uneven relations between clothing production, consumption, and waste, and the growing literature covers everything from African style to punk design, from haute couture to sustainable dress. With fashion itself often a form of performance, the combination of dance and fashion often features on stage, in shops, on screens, and in the scholarly literature.

Dance historian Judith Chazin-Bennahum, in *The Lure of Perfection: Fashion and Ballet*, was one of the first to recognize that the "performance uniform" of ballet depended on a dance–fashion nexus: "My perception is that we cannot track the progression of costume design independently from the study of fashion on the streets" (2005: 1). In her seminal text on *Dance and Fashion* (2014), the fashion historian Valerie Steele attended to more contemporary intersections between expressive dance and the fashion statements that appear in parades, magazine photography, and designer clothing. Steele identifies the migration of novel dress styles from the stage to the catwalk or magazine in "looks" that accentuate the fashioning of an artistic identity. The commodity form of the costume is thus enhanced by its wider adoption in popular culture.

Museum culture has accelerated this convergence between fashion and dance, with the moving body often incorporated into the display of more static objects. Exhibitions have, however, diversified from the static cases of ballet fantasy to installations of hip-hop fashion, while museum collections, like those at the National Gallery of Art or the

Victoria and Albert Museum, have supported major histories of dance costume design through large-scale exhibitions and catalogues. They often feature a singular designer or artist, such as Pablo Picasso's *Parade* designs, Elsa Schiaparelli's surrealism, the work of Jasper Johns and Robert Rauschenberg for Cunningham, or the costumes worn by a star dancer such as Rudolf Nureyev.[17] These elite exhibitions contribute to increasing recognition of well-preserved iconic costumes, often displayed theatrically on mannequins that allow the museum visitor a close-up view, although the awkward poses often contradict the absent gestures of a dancing body. Presenting the costume as a specialist art object, with accompanying illustrations, celebrates the influential contribution of dance to developments in stage and costume design, but they often do little to represent or animate the costume as a mobile artifact.

As the above discussion suggests, constraints upon museum display culture often fail to realize the potential of the dance costume to offer novel insights into how choreographic aesthetics may have fashioned the object, or indeed, how that costume might depart from a conventional narrative of dance history. Too often, the costume is rendered as an illustration of the seamlessness of the dancing body with its past appearance, and such convergence between object and subject reinforces hierarchies of meaning about the dance event.

In contemporary live performance, the dance–fashion relationship often features the designer's signature in the making of outfits for new choreographic commissions, and in turn, designers ask choreographers and dancers to curate the performance of fashion shows. Such connections between the portability of clothing and looks between the fashion industry and dance culture are significant for contemporary choreography; this, however, is a topic for a different project. More critically, the competing ideas of "fashion" may be interrogated in choreography, since fashion is both an industry (organizing dress manufacturing from production to consumption) that determines the precise value of clothing, and an ideology or mechanism for communicating subjectivity, change, and collective social ideas.

In the wider context of interest in style, one of the most enduring legacies of choreographic form—even in works for which only the bare attributes of clothing apply—is the fashioning of dress. As a result, I understand the costume worn for dancing as a compound of ideas about dress that accumulates weight or meaning through the many stages of fabrication into choreography. But to approach dance costumes, one must also locate them in the practices of an archive and as an archive.

Costumes as Performance Archive

For this book, the dialectical costume is not only a method for excavating the historicity and contemporaneity of dance, but it is also the thing itself, the costume as worn, and retained as the artifact of choreography in a collection or archive. An archival costume is decidedly different—not least in its bulk—from other forms of documentation such as photographs, videos, programs, or notated scores. Costumes suffer particularly from the heavy impact of use, the obscurity of their manufacture, and their devaluing as a record of performance. Whether made from organic or inorganic composites, they are frequently modified during performances or between shows. These problems are exacerbated by the volume and care required for storage and preservation. Preservation also militates against some material objects being seen and their curation often limits the circulation of potential meanings. And, as I have suggested, museum culture is often caught between the fragility and impermanence of the artifact (a topic I will return to in my conclusion) and the centrality of the emblematic item's relationship to the spectacle of exhibition.

Contemporary work in theater and performance studies, however, is developing valuable models for research and analysis of scenography, design, and costume as "theatrical objects" that archive the practices of performance (Schweitzer and Zerdy 2014). On stage, the more mundane characteristics of dress are transformed by a degree of artifice. Theater historian Carol Chillington Rutter describes the costume in a narrative drama as providing "an intimate scaffold for building a character"; it might provide clues to a social or professional type, or, as a garment from another era, it makes a historical statement (2001: 107). More imaginatively, Aoife Monks' book *The Actor in Costume* observes how specific costumes have influenced the reception of characters in memorable stage productions. Since an actor is attempting to recreate a believable, if idiosyncratic, reality, Monks recalls the mnemonic function of costumes, which can "act as a literally material memory of the performance, permeated and formed by the work of the performer" (2010: 140).

Dance costumes, by way of contrast with theater, not only represent characters but are designed to draw attention to the "embodied life of materials" on moving bodies as energetic, perhaps abstract, expressions. Leading costume curator Donatella Barbieri extends the analogy of the costume as a corporeal sign, arguing that the "costume in performance" is also a method of interpretation that "embodies histories, states of being, and previously unimagined futures" (2017: xxii). In her visually arresting volume on *The Costume in Performance*, she identifies these abstract dimensions with the performance's affective potential:

> In the visceral connection with a group of performing, dancing, or singing bodies, costume plays a significant role: the affective material performativity projected by the dress of the performer is extended through the numerous bodies on stage. The perception of the body as felt, a body wearing, is multiplied, emphasized, and woven across other bodies. . . . As a surrogate participant, it draws attention to its own corporeal and material here-and-now reality, shared with the present, sentient, and dressed spectators. (2017: 30)

Attending to the "material here-and-now" significance of the costumed "body as felt" during performance complicates the relationship of the curator to the narratives associated with the archival costume. For Barbieri, a museum costume can also resist interpretation, because it may have been altered, mislabeled, or displaced, and she describes the "encounter" with each artifact as a form of "quest" (2013: 284). Detecting modifications in the outfit of a famous clown, she writes that the costume becomes a "complex, charged object" because it continuously appropriates materials in popular circulation. If few clues are left about its provenance in design or its history of use in performance, then it is potentially an "unreliable narrator" of the past (Barbieri 2013: 282). Even when dance critics, diarists, photographers, or audiences have recorded their perceptions of an arresting costume image, or when dancers have vivid memories of wearing a specific outfit, an actual costume has required me to carefully examine its constructedness as a partial, if once-embodied, artifact of the choreographic work and to reconsider its significance as an historical trace of past events.

Given the ascendancy of collecting institutions in the twentieth century and a heightened interest in the material culture of performance, many dance costumes still exist in personal collections, company storerooms, or museum archives, but in most situations, they are fragmented and partial collections. Nonetheless, as I have argued throughout this introduction, the material dynamics of archival costumes will stimulate novel ways of thinking about the choreographic repertoire as systems of transaction involving textiles, clothing, and industries of fashion and fashionability that mitigate against the ephemerality and disappearance of dance itself. These material exchanges of dance also enter into a dialectical relation with the meaning and values attached to the choreographic event.

The Structure of This Book

The epigraph from Benjamin that opens this chapter aligns a costume detail with the experience of historical duration: "the eternal is in any case far more the ruffle on a dress than some idea" (1999: 69; B3, 7). This aphorism is his most concise, if curious, formulation of the dialectical image, and it resonates throughout this book: In what ways can a ruffle be more powerful in generating an immanent temporality than another kind of historical trace? How can a humble piece of fabric lead us to contemplate limits beyond history and the singularity of the individual? Does the "eternal" ruffle and its distinctive form allude to the transient status and autonomy that accompany the adorning of a dress? Perhaps Benjamin writes with irony, provoking his readers to query our notions of what makes meaning or indeed what marks out the common sense of clothing in modern societies.

Each chapter in this book begins with another text fragment from Benjamin, and collectively they chronicle his observations on the evolving experience of dress that he identifies with capitalist modernity. They sit in contrast to the intensified sense of mass culture and capitalist hypermodernity we have come to associate with twentieth-century America. But if we take the "fashion," fashioning, and fashionability of the "ruffle on a dress" seriously, the dance costume becomes one of the constellations through which choreography ruffles the empty historical time of capitalism in the twentieth century. By rupturing our knowledge of dance as a smooth, repetitive, semi-autonomous process of embodied movement, how a dancer is dressed therefore has the potential to show how commodities can be transformed. This dialectical costume is an object whose fabrication is immanent within the complexity of a specific historical time.

Fabrications are the creative products of human labor, a making of the garment that is indicative of the imaginative work embodied in dance, and it is a principle that I return to in the coda of this book through the writings of Hannah Arendt. Throughout the book, however, this concept of fabrication evolves across several analytic layers, focusing on the materiality of cloth, the garment silhouettes, and how choreographers, designers, and collaborators have fashioned costumes in repertoire. While informed by broad theoretical concerns, the narratives of each chapter are vividly tied to costumes as archival objects. Distinctive costumes have been researched across a range of dance archives and collections from which discrete discourses, practices, and memories can be selected and woven together. A primary question is that of provenance—who made each item and where? Of what was it made, and how? And how does the material form of the artifact influence the artistic work of dance? At one level, these are very practical and personal questions; as the design scholar Llewellyn Negrin writes, "often it is the texture of the material and the cut of the garment, rather than simply its look, which attracts us, such as the warmth and feel of a wool jacket or the voluminous nature of a skirt that swirls around our bodies as we walk" (2016: 123).

Given the new materialist focus on each costume's tactile qualities, I have identified specific fabrics with different stages of manufacturing history, beginning in Chapters 1 and 2 with silk and wool production in the early twentieth century, moving on in Chapters 3 and 4 to the expansion of cotton and synthetics in the mid-century, and in Chapters 5 and 6, which focus on the postwar period, returning to a contrast between mass-produced cotton and decorative feathers and sequins. The formal properties of each textile imply varying degrees of texture, malleability, and ease that influence the movement qualities of dance. And often, a specific thematic of embodied mobility arises from techniques used in fabrication, such as drapery, cut, torsion, color, stretch, surface, and ornament. Their modes of manufacture range from the artisanal to the industrial, ensuring their mass production as dance costumes. Indeed, one might argue that the very success of textiles as a commodity form has universalized their use in the dance genres that circulate globally to, from, and around the United States.

Reviewing the silhouette's functions in the fashion system leads me to consider the typicality of dress for the choreographic system. Denaturalizing relations with dress and dressing enables us to identify their rhetorical and connotative functions in choreography and in dance more generally. The silhouette is not static but gives form to the objective reality of the costume, as in this example (Figure I.3) of the black and white unitards

FIGURE I.3 Marsha Skinner, costume design for Beach Birds, 1991. Walker Art Centre.

in Marsha Skinner's design for the Merce Cunningham work, *Beach Birds* (1991). The unitards are standardized, and repetitive, but the patterning of color on the surface of the textile adds connotation.

A unique mode of manufacture thus activates the shaping properties of the item of clothing under scrutiny. In the approximately chronological structure of the chapters, differences in silhouette provide the next layer: the silk tunic and trousers from 1911 to 1930; the jersey wool skirt from 1920 to 1940; the cotton petticoat from 1930 to 1950; the lycra unitard from 1940 to 1960; the cotton T-shirt and loose trousers from 1960 to 1980; and the feather-and-sequin sheath dress from 1920 to 1990. My choice of these twentieth-century dance garments depends on their categorical consistency. Often, the selected genre of clothing contributes to claims about corporeal politics that might be realized through choreography, such as enhancing free, dynamic, and flexible movement. In each chapter, the specific form of a typical garment within dance therefore represents ideas and values that determine its appearance on a stage or preservation in an archive. Where it has been possible to rupture time by leaping forward to subsequent, especially more rebellious, instances of a costume's use or repetition, I have included contemporary examples.

Finally, the chapters discuss costumes in association with canonical figures of American dance—the silk tunics and trousers of Ruth St. Denis and Ted Shawn; the knitted woolen skirts of Martha Graham; the cotton petticoats of Katherine Dunham; the lycra unitards of Merce Cunningham; the cotton T-shirts and trousers of Grand Union and Trisha Brown; and the embellished dresses of Josephine Baker and Line Renaud.

These artists were pioneering innovators in dance form; their choreographies have been much appreciated and studied for their contributions to the history of twentieth-century Western concert dance. Each of these chapters refers to the relevant scholarly literature, but there is limited biographical narrative or choreographic cataloguing; I assume that readers will be able to elicit more detailed information from other sources. At the same time, given these choreographers' extensive repertoire, their creative use of typical costumes expands to include historical references to other artists and often disrupts choreographic conventions. A singular performance "uniform" may become a source of variations, adaptations, and modifications that will see a choreographer slip into garments from another mode of production—for instance, Cunningham wearing woolen leggings or Brown dancing in draped silks. In other cases, vestimentary codes that mark class, gender, or race have been harnessed, adapted, or used resistively in specific dance practices, as when black male dancers in Dunham's repertoire wear zoot suits. I read these imaginative contributions as distinctive to each choreographer while also reflecting on the anomalous gaps revealed when the study of choreography accounts for the actual availability of material resources.

In pursuing this study, I have examined all the costumes as physical objects in company archives, museums, and art institutions in New York, Minneapolis, Florida, St. Louis, Guildford (UK), Melbourne (Australia), and southern France. Their tactile realities have excited my imagination and informed my research. Such unique costumes hold memories of desire and resistance, as well as reveal the dynamic forces that were at work in the dancing bodies. Given the rich variety of costumes—with many unknown or rarely viewed—I have sought to include numerous photographs, often commissioning them myself. It was important to show how repetition and variations in a style of dress situate fabric and design histories, as well as indicate the involuted nature of the object–subject relations, as well as sketches, annotations, and ancillary photographs, which document the exchanges that contribute to the dialectical potency of these dance costumes. For the most part, I have eschewed using reviews as source material, preferring instead to use the immediacy of my encounter with the costume, as Barbieri suggests, to activate a form of quest.

The potential for the study of costume to inform historical understandings of dance and performance is therefore a core argument of this book. It is intended for a diversity of readers—dance artists, fashion lovers, and cultural historians—and situates the sensuous realities of typical dance costumes in the wider context of their meanings as artistic, social, and historical artifacts. This book represents more than a decade of wondering about costumes in dance, and the historical and theoretical research has evolved peripatetically, taking on new turns and directions. Writing the book has fundamentally altered the way I think about dance as material cultural production without diminishing my pleasure in responding to the sensory potential of a costume being worked on the dancing body. I hope you enjoy this encounter as well.

From Silk Tunics to Workwear
Ruth St. Denis and Ted Shawn

It is an undulating musical extravaganza, an opera made of
draperies. . . . This revolt . . . appears as a prelude . . . to a revolution that
was indeed no more than drapery covering a slight reshuffle in the ruling
circles.
  Benjamin (1999: 71)

A rectangular length of woven fabric—long, short, square, plain, or patterned—can be wrapped, knotted, twisted, tied at the waist or neck, hung, draped, or waved on and around the body as an item of clothing. Many variations appear around the world in different forms of dress: sarongs, saris, dhotis, kimonos, tunics, towels, or simply scarves. A woven scarf belonging to Isadora Duncan can still be seen in a display case at Carnegie Hall in New York (Figure 1.1). Three feet wide and made from silk crepe, with a base color possibly once cream but now slightly discolored, the scarf has been block-printed in shades of brown, rust, and gray—colors that were probably from natural dyes extracted from onion skins, mussel shells, or weeds. With its art nouveau detailing of crisscrossed rows and patterned sections depicting animals, plants, and naked women, it is less like a dance scarf than an evening wrap. Notably, it carries the mark of its designer, Raymond Duncan, Isadora's brother; beyond this signature in the Carnegie Hall Susan W. Rose Archives, the narrative provenance of the scarf is limited.

A different long scarf, in red batik, was the cause of Duncan's untimely death by strangulation after it caught in the wheels of a car in 1927.[1] The floating scarf, almost synonymous with the free-flowing movement and loose garments of expressive dancing, therefore reminds us that modern dance is haunted by many forms of tragedy. The trace memory of the dangling scarf creates a ripple, as if the dying dancer's bravado eclipses the dance, bringing this early phase of dance modernity to a conclusion. While these images, gestures, and narratives remain compelling enigmas, this book departs from mystification in favor of a materialist history that reframes the ways in which woven textiles,

Fabrications. Rachel Fensham, Oxford University Press. © Oxford University Press 2026. DOI: 10.1093/9780197699638.003.0002

FIGURE 1.1 Isadora Duncan's scarf by Raymond Duncan. Photograph by Chris Lee. Courtesy of Carnegie Hall Rose Archives.

specifically silk, used by modern dancers were produced, worn, circulated, retired, and returned as embodied life. So how does this conception of a Duncan scarf situate the history of Isadora's presence on this New York stage?

In 1898, when she was only twenty-one, Duncan was one of the first dancers to perform at Carnegie Hall, appearing alongside eccentric opera singer Julie Wyman and Ethelbert Nevin, a modern composer.[2] Later that year, Isadora traveled to London with her mother and siblings and went on to find fame in Paris; she did not return to Carnegie Hall for more than a decade. By 1911, Duncan had become famous for her interpretative modern dancing to symphonic music, and she performed a Bach repertoire supported by the influential conductor Walter Damrosch.[3] Her costume was most likely a handwoven silk tunic, replete with decorative scarves like the one shown in Figure 1.1.

For many European artists and intellectuals, as the musicologist Samuel Dorf writes, "the act of performance and the idea of antiquity shaped the modernist project in the first decades of the twentieth century"; and, as chief exponents of this revivalist philosophy, the Duncan family wore primitive tunics in daily life fabricated using ancient weaving and dyeing techniques (2018: 4).[4] Given the light weave and detailed block printing, this Carnegie Hall textile thus functions like a draped emblem since its illustrations suggest the diverse artistic and poetic influences informing modern dance. Along with plant and animal motifs, the naked dancers who form rows across both ends resemble the five bulbous bodies in Matisse's 1910 collage, *La Danse*, which the Duncans may have seen in Paris or St. Petersburg.[5] These figures alternate with panels of loose-haired women in draped tunics, freely turning; the print therefore registers as a hieratic device reminding us that Isadora's dance was inspired by Grecian statuary. When Duncan knotted and draped a tunic to ensure a minimum of modesty, she claimed direct inspiration from Greek vases in the Louvre, although her dancing, according to historian Artemis Leontis, was at the "ragged edge of exposé" (2019: 43). A decade later at Carnegie Hall in 1923, young women from the Duncan school in Berlin (Figure 1.2) were still wearing drapery that fell in folds from their shoulders as they dramatized archaic gestures.[6]

The solitary Isadora scarf, unremarkably placed in a crowded display case, marks the significant if fragile legacy of Duncan's career in the United States. If she was the first "modern" dancer to grace Carnegie Hall's stage, the multi-layered historicity of this handmade object provokes complex strands of inquiry, including how the scarf was worn and modified by dance, and why it has survived. The scarf becoming tunic, as we will see, is an example of a dialectical costume: on the one hand, it desires a relationship to the past by evoking associations between domestic craft traditions that run counter to modern life, and on the other, it seeks to represent the radical transformations of European, particularly that of middle-class female, subjectivity at the turn of the century.

In this chapter, the initial focus is on silk textiles and the silhouettes of dance tunics and trousers in modern dance. It will examine their artisanal construction from basic fabric squares and their relationship to "expressive movement" in the naked and gendered body. In the shift from the improvised to the reproducible, from personal item to commodity form, it considers their modification in the formation of an industrial model for American dance dress. It argues, more concretely, that choreographic practice was an

FIGURE 1.2 Program advertising Duncan dancers at Carnegie Hall, November 3, 1923. Courtesy of Carnegie Hall Archives.

active participant in the social transformations of a material culture evolving from the colonial marketplace to the manufacturing enterprise. Indeed, the utility, or use value, of costume is a constituent and essential part of the dialectical conditions for creative practice in early modern dance.

The chapter closely examines a selection of costumes in the Jacob's Pillow Archives, which holds records of the companies created by Ruth St. Denis and Ted Shawn, both together as The Denishawn School of Dance and Related Arts, and as independent artists. As with many dance collections, the costumes are housed in two repositories, one at Jacob's Pillow, a dance center in Massachusetts, and the other at Florida State University—places that echo Shawn's complicated biography.

Shawn was St. Denis's romantic partner as well as her male dancing muse until 1930, when he left to create his own dance company, Shawn and his Men Dancers. At that point, the two divided ownership of the costumes according to which roles they had created. According to Barton Mumaw, a leading Shawn dancer, the remaining props and sets were burnt—"armloads of shoes and wigs, of scarves and garlands, of leotards and nautch skirts, of Egyptian masks and Viennese ball dresses"—in a literal conflagration of their past together, entangled as it was with exotic fantasies (Murphy and Hamilton 2023: 36).

For decades, the Shawn costumes were kept in traveling trunks at Jacob's Pillow. Some were used for remounting works, while others were refashioned into new items for summer performances. According to Jacob's Pillow archivist Norton Owen, "some costumes were borrowed and returned thirty years later," but he diligently began the process of identifying and preserving them for the Pillow archives by consulting former dancers Mumaw and Jane Sherman.[7] Other costumes that had belonged to Shawn were sold at auction in Florida after his death, and they became The Killinger Collection of Denishawn Costumes.

St. Denis's costumes, on the other hand, traveled with her to California, where they were donated to the University of California (UCLA). In 2000, the UCLA library, unsure about storing these 2500 items, returned the costumes to Jacob's Pillow, so four collections were reunited in one location. In 2017, the costume and dance historian, Caroline Hamilton, was commissioned to catalogue and rehouse the diverse pieces in archival boxes, as well as co-curating a major exhibition in 2018.[8]

This modern dance costume archive is significant in both volume and range, and its multiplicity reveals and disrupts complex issues of costume provenance. For this chapter, the "full company sets and multiple iterations of some costumes" provide a vital record of social and economic exchanges occurring between dancers, designers, and domestic industries in interwar America (Murphy and Hamilton 2023: 45). The replication of generic dance garments illuminates how modern dance companies experimented with the materiality of silk textiles in choreographic form and indicates how emerging technologies of dress production and consumption shaped the localized communities of American dance modernity. At the same time, the chapter illuminates the making, wearing, and inventive energies located in the costumes used by Denis and Shawn as pioneering choreographers in the first decades of twentieth-century American dance. The legacies of Duncan's scarf as woven textile and revolutionary garment therefore recur throughout the chapter.

Silk Fabric and *A Legend of Pelée* (1925)

The St. Denis collection holds many fine silk scarves (Figure 1.3) in bold, pearly, and iridescent colors—peach, gray, lilac, lime green, and yellow tinged with red—often attributed to an "Unknown Work." In Shawn's Killinger collection, such items are labeled "Miscellaneous Fabric" along with "sashes, belts, scarves, shawls, and remnants" that have multiple functions (Young and Killinger 1997: 135). Silk panels could be knotted around a performer's waist, draped over a shoulder, folded over the head, tied around the hair, or given to young dancers to swirl at certain moments in the dance. Apart from performance, some remnants may have been used to repair or make new garments, but those in the archive are folded neatly into squares, big and small.

Such scarves may have been worn by the Denishawn dancer Jane Sherman when she reprised the "Valse, Ribbon Dance, and Butterfly Étude all to the music of Chopin" (Mumaw 1984: 1–2). Or, they might have appeared in St. Denis's performance of *Salome*, a popular subject for concert dance, with seven fabrics of different "weight, color, and design." These silk lengths of no firm provenance represent elements used adaptively in the choreographic repertoire, and their ongoing archival presence attests to this versatility of purpose.

The prevalence of silk in modern dance costumes was also a product of changes affecting silk as a commodity. Photographs from the turn of the twentieth century

FIGURE 1.3 Five fine colored silk scarves worn by Mary Howry, c. 1920s. Photograph by Patsy Gay. Courtesy of Jacob's Pillow Dance Festival Archives.

frequently depict wealthy women, such as the American heiress Natalie Clifford Barney, with squares of silk fabric, either decorated or simply hemmed, draped across their shoulders.[9] Even in black-and-white, the sheer qualities of silk display the female body in a distinctive way, and the "tactile pleasures of silk" were talking points for cinematic stars (Conor 2004: 121). Sitting lightly on the shoulders, silk frames the body as if through a veil, creating a seductive drape and intimacy.

This fascination with silk in fashion, design, and dance was facilitated by changes in the economics and politics of trade. Most accounts of sericulture begin with the "silk road" and the secrecy surrounding the ancient manufacture of this fabric through the cultivation of silkworms in China. By the sixteenth and seventeenth centuries, however, silk was being made in the Middle East and Europe, and there were flourishing silk industries in France and Italy (Schoeser 2007: 17–55). According to textile scholars, silk fiber evolved in quality and diversity as new scientific and industrial techniques were applied to its production (Schoeser 2007: 50). In her study *Silk and Empire,* Brenda King documents how Bengali weavers, who specialized in a range of silk products including velvets, taffetas, and satins, were unable to keep pace with the impact of European modernization (2005: 66–81). British, French, and American control over the silk trade in East and South Asia became even more rapacious after the 1900 Boxer Rebellion in China.

For Walter Benjamin, "[w]orld exhibitions glorify the exchange value of the commodity" and were a primary site for immersion in the "phantasmagoria" of trade in an expanding modernity (1999: 7). Indeed, American world fairs in Chicago (1893) and St. Louis (1904) introduced commercial innovations and promoted the circulation of local and foreign novelty goods. From the late nineteenth century, American industrialists opened hundreds of mills in New York, Philadelphia, and Paterson, New Jersey. Known as "Silk City," Paterson produced "large quantities of inexpensive standardized fabric" (Postrel 2020: 36).[10] This increased scale of production relied on protection of foreign, largely European, skilled labor. As one industrialist reported to a 1919 inquiry, "the hands of the silk worker are one of his most important assets. ... Machinery does not do away with the use of hands in silk manufacture."[11]

Markets in Europe and the United States began to favor the refined silks produced by Japanese growers and weavers. By 1929, more than 520,000 bales of this imported silk were traveling across the American continent annually (Finlay 2023: 372–373).[12] As a result, bolts of fabric suitable for making clothing, known as "broad silk," became more readily available in the domestic market. Silk also became increasingly diverse and durable and was used for an expanding range of functions, from industrial sailcloth to parachutes.

During World War I, the raw silk imports continued but disruption to supply lines accentuated the demand for locally manufactured goods in the expanding department stores of the cities. Mass clothing production was in full operation by the 1920s, and local silks of varying quality entered the expanding market for middle-class American women who wanted the appearance of luxury without the price of the imported fabric.

At the same time, the fashion for clothing that minimized the surface friction between the dress and the skin helped foster new forms of performance. Layers of distorting garments or elaborate confections added for theatrical or dramatic effect were removed in favor of clothing that moved with the body. Silk, being readily available, was adopted by professional actors and dancers, particularly female performers such as Ruth St. Denis.

René St. Denis, also known as "Brother Dennis" or "Buzz," was a supportive partner to his sister Ruth's stage career. He ran a business in Hollywood known as the St. Denis Asia Bazaar; as its name suggests, it imported goods from China and Japan (Figure 1.4). Through his connections, St. Denis had access to a wide range of textiles and ornaments, which were a source of fascination for artists in search of new ideas. Overtly linked to the thriving commerce in silk, the Denishawn Company entered into a sponsorship deal with the Robinson Silk company, and its principal dancers extolled the virtues of silk for use in their choreography in press interviews (Scolieri 2020: 155).

One unusual item in the St. Denis collection is a "huge silk cloak" consisting of many meters of heavy silk, tie-dyed in bands of vivid color. This cloak is the performance costume for *A Legend of Pelée, the Hawaiian Volcano Goddess* (1925), a ballet that toured widely but is sparsely documented.[13] Drawing inspiration from the American dancer Loïe Fuller, whom St. Denis saw dancing in Paris in 1900, the choreography relies on the manipulation of this parachute-like garment by the soloist, St. Denis herself, who is standing on a platform or stage.

Fuller's own dancing in Paris is renowned for its fabrication of illusion from colored lights playing on the surface of undulating silk, and poets, film scholars, and dance historians have celebrated these experimental spectacles (Albright 2007; Brannigan 2011). As the dancer whirls her props consisting of large lengths of silk joined to bamboo poles, she transmutes into a flame, butterfly, or orchid. With gestures extending beyond the partially obscured body, the volume of volatile fabric becomes an aesthetic membrane to ignite the spectator's fantasies of non-human motion. Fuller's choreography, as Ann

FIGURE 1.4 St. Denis Asia Bazaar letterhead banner from correspondence, September 7, 1948. Courtesy of Jacob's Pillow Dance Festival Archives.

Cooper Albright suggests, hence simulates both the "absence and presence" of a fleeting embodiment (2007). Silk, as a tensile material that resists the air, retains an almost transparent flexibility; once in motion, the silk costume becomes a dance partner mirroring the metamorphosis of self in a choreography.

St. Denis was also involved in propagating "skirt dancing"—manipulating capacious skirts illuminated by electric lights—having performed for the impresario David Belasco at Worth's Family Theater and Museum in New York between 1900 and 1904.[14] Throughout her subsequent career, the aesthetic maneuvering of fabric was central to her choreographic art. In group works, such as *Soaring* (1922) at Mariarden (Figure 1.5), young dancers moved gracefully in and around long lengths of billowing silk, resembling birds or clouds in an animated sky.

In addition to the fabric, exotic silk garments—whether kimonos from Japan or saris from India—informed St. Denis's vision of herself as a "guru" or "goddess" and dictated the quality of movement practiced by Denishawn dancers (Mumaw 1984: 3).[15] While on tour in Asia, St. Denis, Shawn, and Pearl Wheeler, the company costume designer, would shop avidly in local markets in search of novelties such as fabrics, beads, fans, and headdresses. The dance scholar Priya Srinivasan has rigorously critiqued this "ethnic tourism," particularly in representations of the nautch, a temple dance popular in India before and after colonization.[16] Srinivasan argues that the signature choreography of St. Denis's *Radha* (1906) granted her a professional identity in American concert dance while denying her Indian co-creators, who were teachers and dancers themselves, the right to visibility and financial remuneration (2011: 72). By way of contrast, the company's

FIGURE 1.5 *Soaring* at Mariarden. Photographer unknown. Courtesy of Jacob's Pillow Dance Festival Archives.

history of involvement with silk merchandise, locally and in their travels, indicates that most fabrics were purchased at source before being recrafted into dance materials.

The lineage and misrecognition of occluded traditions and practices remains however problematic when we view the full range of Denishawn costumes identified with India, Japan, and precolonial America.[17] Whether authentic (direct purchases) or inauthentic (made in the costume workshop), the narratives associated with such outfits require reassessment. At the same time, their existence traces the variety of ways in which clothing commodities entered modern dance through invention, purchase, appropriation, and creative adaptation.

To return to the choreography of silk in *A Legend of Pelée*, the title misnames, or perhaps deliberately conflates, two different volcanoes on islands at different borders of the national imaginary. Mt. Pelée, a mountain in Martinique in the Caribbean, had a deadly eruption in 1902, while a different volcano in Hawaii is associated with the goddess Pele, believed to be the creator of the islands. Also known as Pelehonuamea, "she who shapes the sacred lands," Pele embodies fire, lightning, wind, and dance (James 2010). In spite of this misspelling, the ballet's full title connects the work to Hawaii. Annexed to the United States in 1898, the islands were made a US territory in 1900 and featured in the Panama–Pacific Expo in San Francisco in 1915. This "exhibition," like the other world fairs, led to a craze for Hawaiian tourism, and the commodification of novel clothing, as well as the popularization of dance forms such as the hula.

Exposure to the "Hawaii craze" in the United States may have stimulated St. Denis, but her embodied interpretation of the powerful female fire deity was not mimetic. After inserting herself into the neck-hole of the parachute poncho (Figure 1.6), a seated St. Denis could withdraw her head via reinforced slits at the apex and slowly allow the "mountain" to compose as she drew up to full height. As she shifted her weight and turned her shoulders, massive streaks of tie-dyed color—reds, browns, and purples—would cascade around her. This movement required considerable effort, as the fabric was immensely heavy; as she shook, the molten lava and burning clouds of a volcanic eruption were conjured by the impressions of the costume spreading out and over the ground (Figure 1.7).

With the fabric as a choreographic score, her dancing made a dramatic statement about the terrifying effects of a destructive eruption. Shockingly, Martinique's Mt. Pelée had caused 30,000 deaths in 1902, and residents had to flee further eruptions between 1929 and 1932. Apropos of Hawaii, global news reports regularly featured articles about the volatility of its main islands by announcing the return of the fire goddess Pele.[18] While the *Volcano* Goddess dance repeats some of the elisions associated with St. Denis's interactions with non-Western cultures, mythologies, and dance genres, the abstract choreography of real natural disasters is her own. Her attempt to manifest the planetary in the amorphous shape of a silk textile with tie-dyed patterning must have had its own peculiar ecological force.

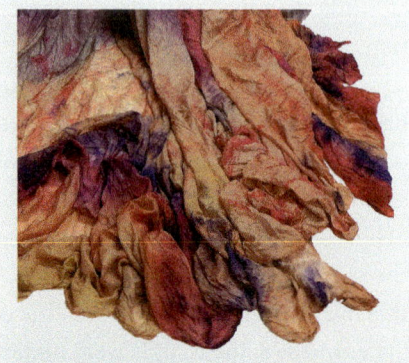

FIGURE 1.6 Huge silk cloak, *A Legend of Pelée*, 1925. Photograph by Patsy Gay. Courtesy of Jacob's Pillow Dance Festival Archives.

FIGURE 1.7 Detail of huge silk cloak, *A Legend of Pelée*, 1925. Photograph by Rachel Fensham. Courtesy of Jacob's Pillow Dance Festival Archives.

With creative imagination, St. Denis transforms Fuller's mutability of fabric into a dance that embodies the emerging American consciousness of environmental awe, which was in turn inextricably tied to territorial expansion.[19] This performance could thus be aligned with the mission of *National Geographic* magazine, a household name in the early twentieth century, which aimed "to increase and diffuse geographic knowledge while promoting the conservation of the world's cultural, historical, and natural resources" (Crooks 2024). In line with this ideology of extractive beneficence on the part of the United States, dancing in the multi-colored cloak becomes simultaneously documentary event and fabrication of corporeal presence.

While exotic garments are frequently identified with St. Denis in fascinating if confronting ways, these many meters of parachute silk also served as a personal symbolic theater. St. Denis purportedly wore the "volcano" costume, which completely covered her body, on ceremonial occasions. The ironic duality of silk, which is both light and tensile, and this presumption of originating power sets the scene for a new medium of dance, one that abstracts fabric as a commodity while recognizing its potential to project meanings beyond the self.

Drapery for *The Prophetess* (1931)

In choreography, the silhouette of the tunic has repeatedly appeared as a formative design. Wearing a tunic for dancing does not necessarily signify scandal or impropriety; rather, it is also a practical, somewhat utilitarian form of basic clothing. Made from two rectangles of fabric, secured at the shoulders and fastened around the waist with a tie or belt, a tunic does not require cutting, shaping, or sewing; the belt can be used to adjust the drape and folds, depending on the length or volume of fabric. In ancient Greece, variations of this garment—differing in length, in textile (linen or wool), plain or patterned—were worn by both men and women (Laver 1995: 25). Its mode of reproduction persists in the history of drapery—the manifold ways in which cloth has fallen over chest and hips in classical and religious art imagery. According to Anne Hollander, "the dialect of cloth and body is the secret of Greek art" because it transforms the human form into an idealized figure that has become "an abiding source of aesthetic satisfaction" to artists ever since (1975: 5). In the world of fashion, according to Barthes, such an "ideal body" shifts meaning by design processes that "lengthen, fill out, reduce, enlarge, take in, [and] refine" the artifices of a silhouette; hence, through endless citation, the contours of a tunic presuppose a vaguely defined classical past (Barthes 1990: 260).

From the Empire period of Napoleonic France through to the Paris couture houses of the early twentieth century, the properties of the tunic multiply. Around the turn of the twentieth century, European and North American museums avidly collected Greek statuary and illustrations, having been alerted to their existence by archaeological discoveries. A widely read book, *The Ancient Greek Dance, After Sculptured and Painted Figures*, by French scholar Maurice Emmanuel, published in 1896 and translated into English in 1916, provided popular access to classical dance imagery (Smith 2010: 81). In fine art schools, draped figures extended from Greek heroes and goddesses to various uses of sheeting in life drawing. Hollander suggests that the appearance of fabric "obeying the law of gravity as it hung about the body seemed again to express some kind of eternal truth unadulterated by either excessive drama or prosaic modern fact" (1975: 63–64).

The alignment between the French Republican values of noble democracy and the intellectual disciplines of European philology and art history was a feature of late nineteenth-century neoclassicism. This fed into a fad for "poses plastiques," which Carrie Preston has suggested came to be particularly embodied by wealthy women posing for portraits wearing light tunics (2011: 38). There was also considerable fluidity between popular and high art entertainment genres. In satirical plays based on classical Greek mythology as well as in melodrama and burlesque shows, women frequently played male parts wearing tunics and tights.

For modern dancers, however, the tunic was less risqué if wrapped up in loftier ambitions. A significant influence here was the spiritual, social, and physical training regime devised by François Delsarte, the French movement instructor, whose methods of teaching oratory and performance were transported to the United States by several women including Anna Morgan. Adherents believed that respectable forms of "artistic statue posing" as dramatic tableaux gave the performer a sense of subtle inner motivations in expression (Preston 2011: 73–9). Morgan, for example, appeared wearing the "usual Greek robes," and the movement lecturer Genevieve Stebbins encouraged all her students to wear "a long white sleeveless gown resembling a Greek tunic or chiton" (Preston 2011: 71).[20] With this representation of the modern muse as statuesque woman, a congruity of interest emerged between expressive movement and the politics of dress reform, adding legitimacy to the tunic's public role as simultaneously a progressive and retrospective aesthetic.

An early devotee of Delsarte's teachings, Ted Shawn used similar methods to sculpt attitudes for bodies draped in cloth and subsequently published his own teaching manual called *Every Little Movement* (1954). In 1916, as a young man collaborating with St. Denis, he choreographed "all manner of ancient dances—veil dances, urn dances, a Pyrrhic dance, and a bacchanal" for the Greek theater at the UCLA in Berkeley (Scolieri 2020: 104). Producing this pageant-style work with a large outdoor movement choir developed Shawn's power as a choreographer, and several of the dance segments, including the *Pyrrhic Dance* (1928), persisted into his later career (Scolieri 2020: 102–105).

The Jacob's Pillow collections contain several examples of Denishawn drapery. A set of cotton tunics was donated by dancer Jane Sherman (1979: 13), who wore one in a classroom dance called *Sculpture Plastique* (1924). These delicate white chitons (Figure 1.8) are shaped with three rows of elastic extending from under the bust to the waist; below that, they spring out joyfully into a short skirt.

In a costume note, Sherman describes their construction:

> Off-white silk chiffon was slit a short distance at one corner of each of two squares of material. This created a bias cut which made a circular skirt when the four ends of the opposite corners were sewn together into shoulder straps to form a V neck. Space was left for armholes, and then the opposing seams were sewn together.
> In order to give the resulting loose shift some shape and a definite bosom, three bands of narrow elastic were tacked two inches apart to the chiffon right under the breast. These bands were hooked at one side to allow the costume to be put on or off over the head. The skirt was cut evenly at mid-thigh and left unhemmed.
> (Sherman 1984: 38)

This "loose shift"' with "some shape and a definite bosom" contains a girlish delight in the freedom of skipping across a grassy plain. An archival photograph of St. Denis in exactly this costume shows her somewhat older and plumper than her students, but still with a spring in her step.

In another photograph (Figure 1.9) taken outdoors at the Denishawn summer school at Mariarden in 1922, members of the company pose in various dance tunics,

FIGURE 1.8 Selection of Denishawn chitons, c. 1920s. Photograph by Patsy Gay. Courtesy of Jacob's Pillow Dance Festival Archives.

ranging from St. Denis's *himation* to Shawn's *Doric chiton*; the nymphs include a teenage Martha Graham at center. The heightened artifice of the photograph shows the dancers adopting various attitudes toward their costumes while St. Denis displays a statuesque nobility.[21]

The St. Denis collection also houses a long hand-sewn chiton, in the iconic shape worn by many modern dancers, consisting of two lengths of deep teal chiffon seamed down the sides and tied at the shoulders.[22] Of unknown provenance, this teal tunic was possibly worn in a choreographed work called *The Prophetess: An Allegorical Dance Drama* (1931), and it retains a certain grandeur even in its forgotten state. The fabric is gathered under the bust and again at a low waistline; the hem is raw. Depending on the range of movement required, the skirt could be bunched around the buttocks or left long and flowing. This evocative dress (Figure 1.10), with its beautiful silhouette and faded color, resembles the sculptural columns known as caryatids that depicted Greek maidens beneath the entablatures of ancient temples. These figures embodied female

FIGURE 1.9 Ted Shawn & Ruth St. Denis at Mariarden, 1922. Photographer unknown. Courtesy of Jacob's Pillow Dance Festival Archives.

grace, and the image of "the body wrapped in pleated fabric" has retained an extraordinary power, appearing variously in Athena's statue in the Parthenon, the Statue of Liberty in New York Harbor, and Eugène Delacroix's revolutionary painting *Liberty Leading the People* (Leontis 2019: 44).

In modern aesthetics, from visual art to dance, the flowing tunic comes to symbolize freedom of movement and a loosening of prohibitions on sexual expression. This form of dress celebrates the semi-naked body and is responsive to the curves and folds of "natural" bodily movement. Both the short and longer Denishawn tunics hide little, nor are they meant to. They are worn to give the feeling of semi-nakedness—the shoulders bearing minimal weight, the air running between the legs, nipples lightly grazing the fabric, and the froth of silk making its own energetic dance. Their erotic charge was as much for the wearer as the beholder. The dancer Jane Sherman has reflected on the mnemonic properties and affective afterlife embodied by such delicate garments:

FIGURE 1.10 Sea green silk crepe chiton or "tunic," possibly for *The Prophetess: An Allegorical Dance Drama,* 1931, Denishawn. Photograph by Patsy Gay. Courtesy of Jacob's Pillow Dance Festival Archives.

We might even believe we see in those costumes the actual shapes of those long-ago dancers. Their ambitions and hopes did strain every seam. Their tears and perspiration did blot the silks and satins. Their joy in applause did permeate the very fabric, to leave behind in these lifeless bits of material an aura of a bygone era as definite as dried rose petals. (1984: 1)

These tunics are loved objects, but there is no record, written or visual, to tell us when these "bits of material" were worn or by whom. And yet we owe an entire epoch of modern dance romance to the tunic, for spiritual communion with nature and among women was once a site of potential joy and revelation. Whether the tunic is made of diaphanous silk or perhaps sturdy cotton, wearing this costume invokes a classical Greece pursuing ideals of freedom and aligns modern democracies with ancient forms of the polis. Wearing the tunic is a dance fashion that also ushered in a novel form of experimentation with relations between fleshed bodies and their liberated potential.

Whether conscious of this history or not, the artistic repudiation of conventional dress informs many subsequent costume choices in modern and postmodern dance. Basic costume choices often resist normative everyday clothing while also instantiating conventions associated with a repeated fabric, shape, or stylization of the body. This desire for increasingly fluid dress in early twentieth-century concert dance remains the material sign of new attitudes toward movement and points both backward and forward to a reclamation of nudity in choreography. In the subsequent and more masculine phase of modern American dance that sought to engage with the living variability of the muscular and skeletal apparatus that animates choreography, the clothes were to be further stripped down, or off.

Tights, Fleshings, and Trunks

For early twentieth-century dance, apart from the tunic, there were limited comfortable dress options. Rehearsal clothes were often derived from the modest outfits of the imperial ballet studio, which included short black tunics for women and light shirts for men, both worn with woolen tights (Buckle 1989: 70). These were adapted from new types of knitted men's swimwear with straps and trunks, sometimes belted for definition, but they tended to sag and stretch and became hot and smelly as the body sweated. Later, German expressive dance began to stylize cotton tunics and bloomers for rehearsals, but these could be awkward and scratchy.

The proximity of skin and costume in choreography is however intimately affected by the undergarments of dance. In this section, I will consider the role of silk thread and fabric as a coveted, if expensive, alternative to the wearing of knitted leotards, singlets, or pants. By examining items of clothing that are often hidden, we can glimpse how it might feel to dance naked, and the eroticism of costume choreography comes to the fore.

Knitted silk is an extraordinary fabric. It often has a sheen, and while it can be sheer when worn for fashion, it has an inbuilt elasticity that responds to the mobility of musculature. A sample of Denishawn undergarments reveals a range of different silk items: a pair of pale pink tights with shoulder straps and elastic stirrups at the foot; some flesh-colored, high-waisted shorts owned by dancer Mary Howie; and a distinctive pair of opaque blue-green tights with a cotton gusset and sequin detail on the foot and calf. These tights were worn in St. Denis's *The Legend of the Peacock* (1914–1949), where they were accompanied by an elaborate beaded and feathered cloak and headdress, creating a highly theatrical choreographic ensemble (Hamilton 2023: 20–23).[23] The grandiose design, fabricated by Wheeler who was devoted to the service of St. Denis, included sequined eyes appliquéd on the tights embroidered with carefully segmented toes (Scolieri 2020: 236–237).[24] The Peacock costume was worn for many decades, and Mumaw recalls St. Denis "strutting and preening in her inimitable way." At the suggestion that the train might need cleaning, he reports that St. Denis exclaimed: "For heaven's sake, dear, it would fall apart!" (1984: 2). Material testament to the value accorded these silk tights lies in the extensive darning of now-ragged heels, with the holes in the claw-like feet amplified by age (Figure 1.11).

In general, pairs of tights are rarely retained in costume collections, not least because they need frequent replacement. The Denishawn dancers, however, mostly danced

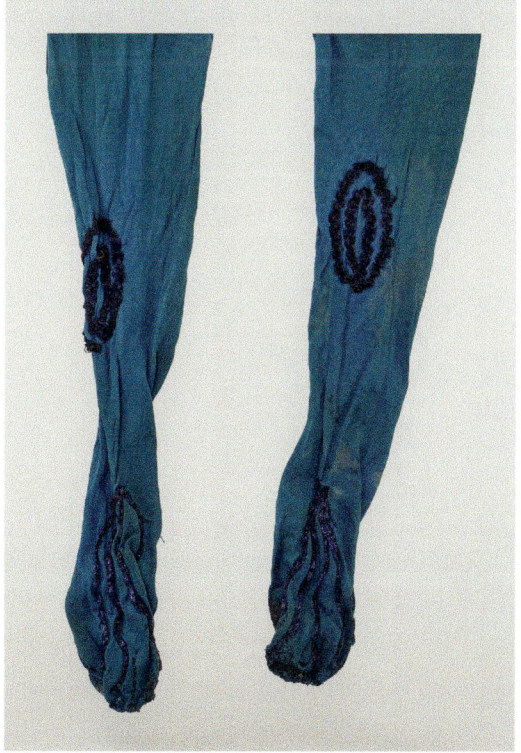

FIGURE 1.11 Tights from peacock ensemble, *The Legend of The Peacock*, c. 1914. Photograph by Patsy Gay. Courtesy of Jacob's Pillow Dance Festival Archives.

barefoot, only wearing tights when performing in places where local regulations demanded that their fleshy legs be hidden. Fully fashioned silk tights for dancing were also expensive, although the Killinger collection includes silk knit leotards and trousers worn by Shawn's men dancers in a performance tour of *The Dome* (1940); made in fine white silk, this costume tested the visibility of the male body (Young and Killinger 1997: 106–108).

An unusual find in the St. Denis collection was two full sets of women's "fleshings" in two color ranges—ivory and tan, or more precisely, pale cream and boot-polish brown. More intimate than tights, they were made of cotton net rather than silk and fastened at one side and shoulders with hooks and eyes. The thin straps scoop toward a low neck, and the hems and outer seams were rolled and stitched by hand.

The addition of nipple and crotch modesty pads made of matching georgette enhances these delicate constructions (Figure 1.12). Such highly personal artifacts, as Mumaw recalled, "were carefully fitted individually to each dancer [so] that there was the illusion of complete nudity underneath any overlying costume or material" (1984: 2). The dancers' own minor modifications include tying the straps more tightly with ribbons or

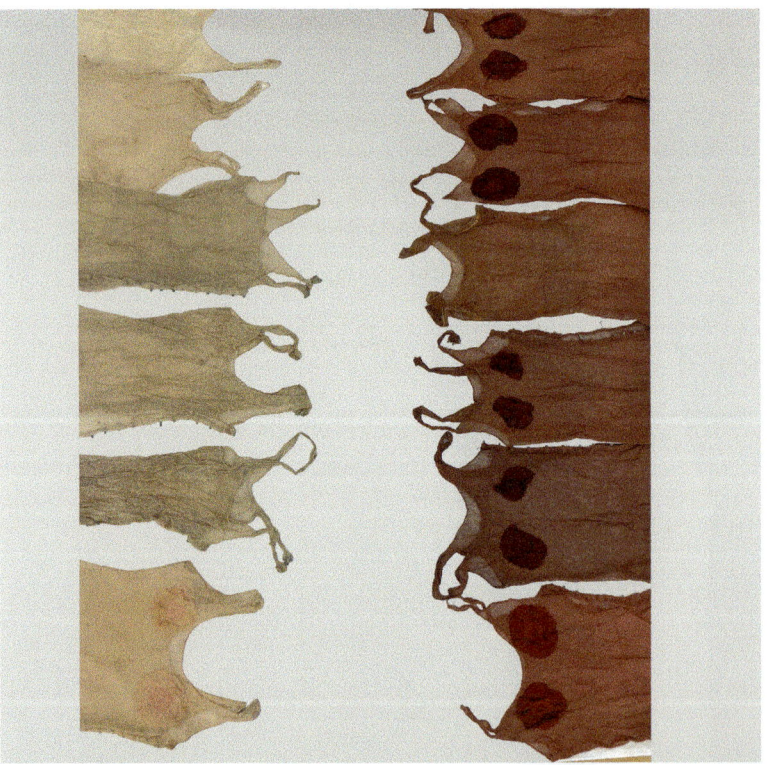

FIGURE 1.12 Pink and brown net leotards, unknown work, Denishawn. Photograph by Rachel Fensham. Courtesy of Jacob's Pillow Dance Festival Archives.

supplementing the breast pads with chiffon. While the net provided flexibility, in time, each costume has become a shape molded to a particular body.

These early forms of "body stocking," transferred from the use of net in ballet and cabaret, are both rare and remarkable for their uncanny appearance.[25] According to Mumaw, "the requisite flesh tones" were created by steeping the net suits in strong tea. The Denishawn dancers who wore them also used makeup powders and creams that allowed them to "pass" as "Asian" bodies in performance (1984: 3). These undergarments thus exist on a continuum with the misrepresentations of blackface, in which white performing artists have appropriated, mimicked, and distorted the appearance of brown bodies and their histories. Shriveled into these skin-like sheddings are therefore the ghostly traces of many bodies that were absent, ignored, or abandoned, as modern dance started to take its first steps. Fretful, uncanny, and in strange dialogue in the dance archive, these bare silhouettes look more like desiccated mice than Sherman's "rose petals."

Beneath the choice of undergarments worn by modern dancers lies a changing relationship to the body. Influential European social movements were validating the psychodynamics of a "natural state," and nude bathing and dancing were viewed under the umbrella of "naturism" (Ross 2005). In terms of artistic representation, Hollander interprets nudity as a potent interplay between artful clothing and the naked body. "Nakedness," she writes, "with its meaning enhanced by clothing, has lent itself to notions of ideal beauty and of natural reality, and it can express not only the loftiest abstract concepts but the most personal physical feeling" (1975: 87). In dance as in visual art, the eroticism of the naked body as sculptural form elicits this relationship between "two kinds of ideal nudity—the one created by clothes directly and the one created by nude art" (Hollander 1975: 87).

Paul Scolieri, Shawn's biographer, notes that Shawn asked his male dancers to perform "entirely nude" in a performance for the journalist Lucien Price, rather than in mismatched trunks. Price was so impressed by this neoclassical choreography that he responded as if "the whole being is permitted to speak, and no false and artificial horizontal lines [exist] to cut the harmonious vertical lines of the erect human body" (2020: 310). Indeed, the question of "dancing naked," as Scolieri explains, was a subject of open debate and philosophical contention for Shawn's male dancers and avid followers, as well as a daily reality at Jacob's Pillow (2020: 307).

In his work for Denishawn, Shawn had performed many character dances, appearing as an ancient warrior, a Native American "brave," or an exotic "god" stripped down to a loincloth or tunic. Yet he also resisted his persistent objectification. When he split from St. Denis to form his all-male troupe, an established health and hygiene movement was shaping physical education, and young men were encouraged to perform strenuous exercise, whether hiking in mountains, skinny-dipping in cold lakes, ballroom dancing, or athletics (Foster 2011: 102).[26] In popular culture and film, it also became accepted for showmen and male actors to show muscle or sweat under duress.

In sports clubs, university dormitories, and at gay parties, a greater range of visual, haptic, and kinesthetic relations between men found expression, and Shawn's male dancers were on a continuum with these changing ideologies of corporeal masculinity. He recruited his company from Springfield College, a sports academy, choosing candidates for their physiques rather than their inscription by coded dance forms such as ballet. Many were athletes or swimmers, and others had some degree of dance training. Central to Shawn's preoccupation with these new modes of male sociality was the interplay between the virile body and costume.

At Jacob's Pillow, a farm in Becket, Massachusetts, he founded a school and home for his new company, which he called Ted Shawn and His Men Dancers. An afternoon summer pleasure there was to offer "tea dances" for the local community. Conspicuously lithe young men in white terry toweling robes—already a Hollywood symbol of decadent flirtation given the ease with which the waist-tie could be loosened—would serve tea to local patrons, particularly "shocking the ladies" (Sherman 1984: note 6).[27] When "exercising," however, the male dancers wore tan-colored underpants fastened with hooks and eyes down one side.

Twelve pairs of these trunks have survived, most of them still bearing the names of their owners. Like the female body stockings, these scanty clothes have often been personalized—some have tightened waistbands, others have less fabric around the hips, and almost all have been repaired by hand. The smaller pairs appear rather risqué, while Shawn's more bulbous silk trunks, marked T.S., in Figure 1.13, befit his mature physique.

One can only imagine how the men who wore these garments or others who touched them experienced their feel. The crumpling silk must have played a notable role in producing the effect of the "natural," with its organic form conducive to feeling "naked" and freed of restriction. Even today, the sensory response to finely woven silk justifies its preponderance in the sophisticated underwear industry. When the men danced on the lawn

FIGURE 1.13 Tea garden silk trunks worn by Ted Shawn. Photograph by Rachel Fensham. Courtesy of Jacob's Pillow Dance Festival Archives.

during their "tea dances," the short pants clung to their buttocks, and their bare torsos were exposed. Their chests were often depilated to appear smooth and shiny, and they were tanned from working outdoors, rippling with muscle on bone. These semi-naked dances with their focus on educational themes provide a decadent contrast to the constraints imposed by the Depression on much of the American population.[28] They were however testament to Shawn's liberating experimentation with male sexuality; he simultaneously invited attention to the exposed flesh of his troupe and asked the audience to look beyond the costume choreography to its "higher purpose" as art.

Making Trousers: Dance of the Ages (1938)

Shawn's repertoire work, *Dance of the Ages* (1938), offers a valuable comparison between experiments in the shape, style, and movement of numerous sets of "shorts" or "trunks" and the appearance of long trousers in modern dance. This full-length dance was choreographed in four parts, with each episode representing one of the four elements—Fire, Water, Earth, and Air. In keeping with Shawn's interest in theosophy, they also represented various stages of human evolution. The choreography progresses from hunter-gatherers in "Fire," held together by the powers of a shaman, to the evocation of "Air," in which the creative individual aspires to flight and enlightenment through art. With gestural tableaux, the men personify types in the life cycle rather than individuals. Likewise, the costumes rely heavily on color symbolism as an accompaniment to the choreography.

In addition to their shorts, Shawn's Men Dancers frequently wore leotards, which had been used by circus performers since the nineteenth century. They also collaborated with the emergent dance manufacturer Capezio to test "designs from new materials to see how they stood up under the rigors of one-night stands" (Mumaw 1984: 3). For the "Earth" episode, the men wore fitted stretch jumpsuits with tight-fitting long-sleeved T-shirts, creating an overall impression that presaged a slim, abstract, and uniform representation of the figure in dance. These outfits were in earth tones ranging from russet to browns, ochres to blacks. Their construction exemplifies two technologies of early twentieth-century costume design: first, a metal zip fastener, patented in 1926, is attached by overlocking stitches at the trouser hip (Figure 1.14).[29] And second, the tape measure represented a new tool for standardized garment fitting with one label including vital measurements that identify Mumaw as their owner (Ross 2008: 55).

Shawn's royal blue leotard for "Water," on the other hand, is decorated with stripes of cream silk hand-painted in green. Made of silk cellulose, the leotard is sewn with robust seams, crotch gusset, and closed at the rear with strong hooks (Figure 1.15). Such fasteners feature on many other close-fitting dance garments, often at a scale that contrasts with the fine fabric. Indeed, the delicate appliqué of Shaw's watery costume design is infinitely more vulnerable than the base molding.

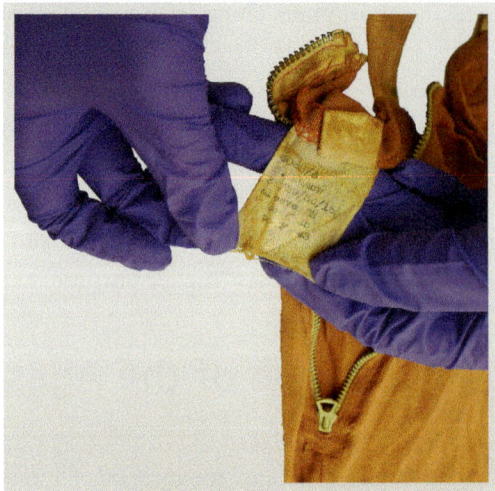

FIGURE 1.14 Detail of label from silk and synthetic jumpsuit, *Dance of the Ages*, 1938, Earth Movement, worn by Barton Mumaw. Photograph by Rachel Fensham. Courtesy of Jacob's Pillow Dance Festival Archives.

FIGURE 1.15 Reverse of blue leotard decorated with green hand-painted silk, *Dance of the Ages*, 1938, Water Movement, worn by Ted Shawn. Photograph by Rachel Fensham. Courtesy of Jacob's Pillow Dance Festival Archives.

In an audio recording, Shawn himself describes the costumes for the Water choreography: "The men [are] costumed in green, tight-fitting slacks." Constructed from a silk-synthetic blend dyed jungle green, the pelvic area was supported by a sheath; an early example of the internal cotton belt used as protective covering (Figure 1.16). The garment label indicates manufacture by Aldrich & Aldrich, a newly established Chicago-based athletic clothing company that was producing pre-made industrial designs for sports and dance.[30] Flared in the legs, worn tight, the trousers fall unevenly from the hips, but give wide scope for energetic, flowing movement. Since viscose has little stretch memory, the trousers in the archive appear baggy and carry the tell-tale scuff marks of strenuous dancing.

If the gauzy tunic revealed the female dancer's swelling breasts and offered a glimpse of her legs, the tiny waists and slim hips of these trousers with their skirt-like covering of the lower body serve to focus attention on the naked torso. This male sensuousness acts indirectly as a stimulus for the uncanny desires of the fluid medium represented in the choreography. In his taped remarks, Shawn reflects further upon the dance:

> There is less story-line, more like an archetype of fluidity, everything enquiring, everything progressing, growing. It shares a concern with rhythms and forms of water, brooks and rivers, the ocean in its calm moods and turbulent moods and the vortices and whirlpools that water makes.

The dancing features the men rocking on their heels, swirling around, leaning in and out, with their "slacks" hanging from their hips; the flowing movement in the bell-bottomed legs, as Shawn suggests, echoes the rhythm of ocean currents.[31] The men are wearing dark skull caps—they dance a rotational patterning, twisting, and spinning, with counter-movements from the whole ensemble—and as the caps bob, they form peaks on the waves. When Shawn enters as the "spirit of the ocean," wearing his blue leotard and a white skull cap, the dancers flirt with him, turning and flicking, making responsive skips with uplifted arms. By harmonizing the diagonal gestures and upper body torsion, Shawn embodies a large wave enhanced by the twisting of his costume (Figure 1.17). Stripped to the minimum in their trousers, with their sweating bodies touching and rolling together, the male dancers arch around Shawn to present an intimate portrait of aqueous emergence.

Weaving, as an act of creative textile making, provides yet another connection between modern dance and its costumes. Woven fabrics have an ancient history, not least in *The Odyssey*, where Penelope spends decades weaving, shuttling back and forth, and unraveling thread from a complex loom while she waits for her husband Ulysses to return. A loom is a dual structure that includes the warp, the long vertical threads, and the weft, the cross-threads that are shuttled between alternate warp threads to create the patterns of woven fabrics. A fine weave consists of many threads per square inch, while a looser weave opens space between them. A highly skilled weaver will manipulate the design with

FIGURE 1.16 Selection of green silk and synthetic trousers from *Dance of the Ages*, 1938, Water Movement. Photograph by Patsy Gay. Courtesy of Jacob's Pillow Dance Festival Archives.

FIGURE 1.17 *Dance of the Ages*, 1938, Water Movement. Photograph by Shapiro Studio. Courtesy of Jacob's Pillow Dance Festival Archives.

mathematical precision. Although the machine looms of the Industrial Revolution accelerated the production of woven textiles for everyday use, artisanal weaving continued for customary purposes or catered to elite markets that desired highly prized forms of cloth and distinctive patterns.

European men had only begun to wear trousers regularly during the nineteenth century, but once trousers served as uniforms for work in the metropolis, their construction reflected both necessity and fashion. Like the tunic, a pair of trousers begins as two equal rectangles of fabric, each seamed into a cylinder to form a leg. Cutting, gathering, or adding fabric to the crotch produces a tapered fitting around the waist; the trousers can then be hemmed, rolled, or cuffed, and may be tied or fastened by more complicated means. This two-legged garment can be wide or tight, sculpted or draped, and made in an endless variety of fabrics. Cloth woven tightly is more durable but stiffer, and hence requires more careful shaping than looser fabric. As the United States approached World War II, technologies of industrial production began to determine the shape and values of men's clothing, and perhaps not surprisingly, the

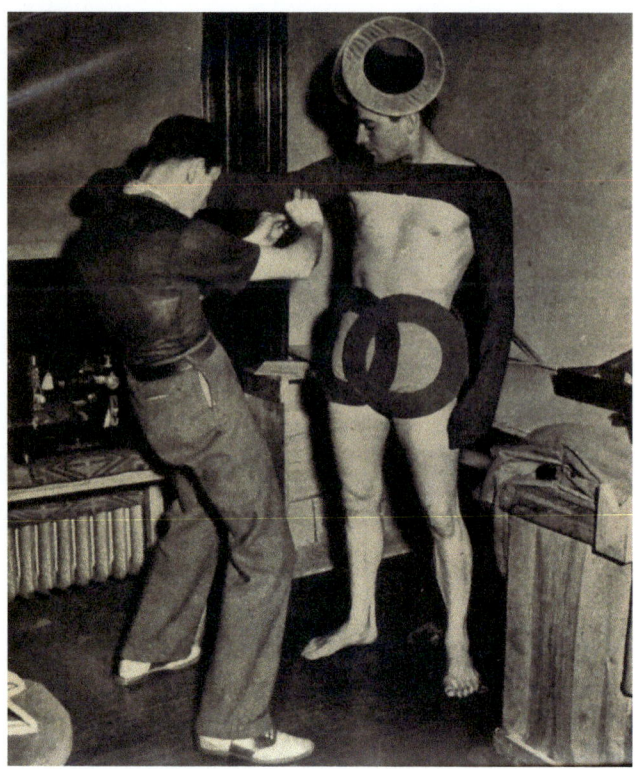

FIGURE 1.18 George Horn fitting Frank Overlees for *A Dreier Lithograph*, 1938. Photographer unknown. Courtesy of Jacob's Pillow Dance Festival Archives.

structure of woven cloth became most contingent and vulnerable in relation to the function of trousers.

Given the tight budgeting for Shawn and His Men Dancers, all the company's costumes, as Mumaw put it, "had to be worthy of time and money being spent on them" (1984: 2). Many of the trousers in the archives highlight detailed variations in construction: some are fashioned more simply on domestic sewing machines and designed with side fastenings and overstitched waistbands for ease of access and robustness. George Horn and Denny Landers were two dancers responsible for fabricating costumes, under guidance from Shawn, although all members of the company were expected to make and repair "outfits, accessories, and head-dresses" (Sherman and Mumaw 2000: 105). Figure 1.18 shows Horn wearing dapper cuffed trousers and two-tone shoes while fitting sleeves for Frank Overlees, who is wearing a pair of decorative trunks and a headdress adorned with theatrical hoops (Figure 1.18). On Horn's left is a Singer sewing machine, another invention that transformed domestic dress production when patented in 1896 (Ross 2008: 58).[32]

Domestic weaving as an enduring practice of textile production however looks back to tradition, and its slow design methods appear to formulate and embody ethical and spiritual values. In addition to the stretch silk slacks worn in the "Water" episode, the

FIGURE 1.19 Selection of green raw silk trousers from *Dance of the Ages*, 1938, Water Movement. Photograph by Patsy Gay. Courtesy of Jacob's Pillow Dance Festival Archives.

archive contains a second set of trousers made from woven raw silk and hand-dyed bottle green. The curators believe that this cloth was produced at Jacob's Pillow by the American heiress Eva Palmer-Sikelianos, the sister-in-law of Raymond Duncan.[33] Estranged from her Greek husband and caught in the crossfire of World War II, Palmer-Sikelianos was drawn to the Jacob's Pillow community in 1939, hoping to mount future artistic collaborations and continue her work exploring ancient Greek theater aesthetics. With great diligence, she mastered the "popping levers, thudding peddles, clicking shuttle, and thumping batten" of the loom and taught some of the men, including Landers, to weave (Leontis 2019: 190).[34] The resulting raw silk garments form an impressive ensemble (Figure 1.19). Despite faded knees and wrinkles from having been kept in storage, the varied green tones of organic dyes on the rough weave of these trousers create a subtle effect like strips of kelp or sea grass. Moreover, the intimate values of the handmade are embodied in the irregularities of each pair's difference from the other. The weaving techniques also create the conditions for conceiving the workings of organic materials with the body in the choreography.

Workwear: *Kinetic Molpai* (1935)

In one of Shawn's most distinctive choreographies, *Kinetic Molpai* (1935), the tensions between design structure and dance produce a robust, work-like representation. This extended abstract piece is organized as a series of physical studies based on Delsartean exercises, with segments such as "Strife," "Solvent (divine love)," and "Resilience," all characterized by a dynamic flow of motion. Given Shawn's absorption with Greek philosophy and poetics, he believed the translation of "molpai" as "embodied expressions of meaning" could be performed on "mountain tops, threshing floors, and altars" (Scolieri 2020: 317). Located choreographically between the pastoral and the sacred, *Kinetic Molpai* became a celebrated work; it toured widely and was maintained in repertoire.

The dance had a powerful effect on its audiences. One spectator wrote that the ferocious display of physical energy conjured the "masculinity of grief" (Price, quoted in Scolieri 2020: 318). But its focus on kinetic movement, punctuated by forces in the body, required the costume to perform a new role in modern dance. It was no longer allegorical but asserted a collective uniformity in which fabric and choreographic design prepared the stage for an industrialized masculinity.

Again, two different sets of trousers for eight dancers have been retained from *Kinetic Molpai*. The first is in woven hessian-like fabric, and the second in handsome moleskin. Like the trousers for *Dance of the Ages*, the handwoven silk trousers were created on site. Palmer-Sikelianos and Horn produced "ninety-six yards for new pants for him [Shawn] and his eight dancers in the *Kinetic Molpai*" (Leontis 2019: 185). Now wrinkled, with worn patches caused by kneeling or bending, these russet-colored trousers are shaped like denim jeans. They were lined in cotton to the knee with side hooks and bar fastening and a tight waistband. Shawn appreciated the rugged fit of this silhouette and used these trousers for reconstructed performances of *Kinetic Molpai* under his instruction in 1962.

The other set of hard-worn moleskin trousers in the Men Dancers' collection is dialectical toward American culture in a different register; they have an "intention that ignites" further debate (Benjamin 1999: 868). Moleskin is a densely woven, durable cotton that is shorn and brushed to produce a soft nap. Long worn by farmers and hunters in mid-century agricultural communities, it was increasingly linked with trades in which a worker needed additional protection from sharp or hot materials, or where there was a high risk of injury. For example, cattlemen and rodeo riders wore moleskin trousers as rigid coverings to protect their legs; they were a form of industrial shield for the working body.

For added resilience, the moleskins for *Kinetic Molpai* were overstitched on the seams and waistband, and their bell shape was adapted for movement with panel insets that widened the lower leg circumference to 16 inches (Figure 1.20). Given the stiff fabric, the dancers had realized that a deep plié in these trousers risked splitting them between the legs; so triangles were added at the crotch with similar inserts in the underarms of shirt-tops (Mumaw 1984: 3). Even so, several pairs of moleskins have heavy stitching across the buttocks where repairs have been needed.

Since *Kinetic Molpai* experimented with the mechanics of forces at work in human joints to achieve motility, close analysis shows how the wide-legged trousers and wrist cuffs wove together a sturdy and adventurous performance. Designed by Shawn himself

FIGURE 1.20 Two pairs of flared moleskin trousers from *Kinetic Molpai*, 1935. Photograph by Patsy Gay. Courtesy of Jacob's Pillow Dance Festival Archives.

and custom-made to achieve the "sculptural forms of the overlapping flared trousers," the garments "hung heavily on the limbs and bodies of the dancers" (Mumaw 1984: 2). Indeed, given their solid form, the trousers functioned like props to be sculpted by the choreography.

The piece begins with Shawn entering stage left to strident piano music, composed by the pianist Jess Meeker. Shawn walks forward, turns right, makes some small kicks backward, then holds his fists clenched, with a wide leg stance and bare chest expanded, head erect. He pivots into a semi-plié, the wide trouser leg sculpting the air like a bridge as his fists draw down. A series of sweeping arm rotations becomes opening salutes, summoning eight dancers, who enter two by two. They form a V around him, their open stance echoing his silhouette, then they lift their heels and pull the arrow shape of the closed trouser legs into focus. As the dancers peel away into two clusters, Shawn leaves the stage, while the men turn and rotate, with fists clenched, trousers folding and creasing at the knees. They turn, stepping forward and back, wheeling around the stage. One man falls, and without pausing the machinery of movement, they carry him on their backs and stretch him out, first in the air and then on the ground.

The choreography is in keeping with Shawn's interest in heroic masculinity and men's labor, especially in rural life. The dancers sweep along the fields, and in one sequence, they work together, perhaps loading hay. When Shawn returns, the mood becomes more lyrical. He parts the horizon, pushing them gently away, and folds his body like a bird, making scooping and sweeping gestures. Then his arms flick forward, rotate, and ascend, while the dusty brown trousers reassemble like stubble left behind in the dry ground.

At other punctuation points in the score, Shawn stands still, surveying the scene, his trousers folded beneath him like a skirt, while the other men squat, their muscled arms bent at the elbows, showing off their wrist bands. Then suddenly they whirl across the stage, forming two lines, while Shawn reaches toward them. Not unlike the actions of a loom, one group pulls slowly backward with pointed toes and scooped feet, while the second group bends forward like slow-moving wheels. The brown trousers fold across one another like ropes, each swaying step carving out a bounded space (Figure 1.21).

These formations were designed to unify different forces, with the costumes binding the men together; their sweeping open arm gestures and fleshy chests are counterbalanced by the heavy weight below. The tension between the costume and the rhythmic formalism of the dance adds to the drama, particularly in Shawn's final admonition, when he reappears center stage, gesturing with locked fists, then thumping to the ground. One dancer returns to collect his prone body, while the others form a cortege, piling up their bent torsos into a ritualistic timber pyre for his departure. The moleskin trousers rise and

FIGURE 1.21 *Kinetic Molpai*, 1935. Photograph by Shapiro Studio. Courtesy of Jacob's Pillow Dance Festival Archives.

fall, hiding Shawn's exit from view. With mourning duties performed, the men progress off stage in pairs—their rocking chests exaggerating the composition of the ensemble.

The Delsartean patterns of the dancing focus on the abstraction of figurative attitudes, but the brown garments support an earthiness that supplements the erotic tonalities of torsos, hips, and swaying legs. The choreography thus turns away from romantic or pictorial illusion, instead celebrating the efforts of muscular activity and transforming the men into workforce commodities. In this dance and other "spectacles of labor," Scolieri describes the Men Dancers as the "ideal embodiments of Taylorism—efficient, reliable, durable laborers" (2020: 301). From the farm to war, from the studio to the factory, the modern dance costume now modeled a form of robust work, since labor power in the industrial nation was an honor to be valorized and protected.

Conclusion

In the epigraph for this chapter, Walter Benjamin writes of the fashion for theatrical drapery in 1828. He describes it as an "opera" that appears to cause a revolution, but in fact makes little more than a "reshuffle in ruling circles." According to the dance historian Mark Franko, when movement technique became harnessed to political ideology in the modern dance of the late 1930s, a revolutionary body appeared. But one might assert that the fabrications by St Denis of the Volcano Goddess and Shawn of Kinetic Molpai equally demonstrate how "movement's flow and the implication of self-conscious power worked as a glue, allowing dance to simultaneously address pre- to post-revolutionary situations" (Franko 1995: 32). This "flow" and the effects of "self-conscious power" are, I am suggesting, stitched into the representative costumes worn by the early modern dancer as choreographic form. The chapter has thus documented the dance costume types that evolved in the first three decades of the twentieth century. It has drawn out significant changes in the uses of fabrics from silk to moleskin and examined the silhouettes created when modern dance experimented with new ideologies of gender and sexuality, abstraction, and eroticism.

For both St. Denis and Shawn, the movement of fabric became an integral aspect of dance composition. Mumaw writes, "The manner in which materials behave in use was always a prime consideration and interest" (1984: 3). Whereas dress in ballet or opera denoted characters or types, these modern choreographers viewed the weight, cut, and stylization of the garment as a source of movement potential: "a life waiting to be released by the wearers or handlers" (Mumaw 1984: 3). While their idealization of "traditional" or "ethnic" cultural forms was problematic, the immaterial effects of these costumes facilitated the artistic and economic flows associated with modern modes of dress, shifting the stylization of the body from artisanal design to industrialized fashion.

In this respect, the Jacob's Pillow archives can be seen as doing double duty. On the one hand, they include the Denishawn School costumes, which provide a remarkable record of the multiple, malleable properties of silk while also demonstrating how dance gestures that rely on little more than the delicateness of silk drapery against the skin can transport the dancer and her audience to exotic locations. On the other hand, the archive records the developments that took place when Shawn gave full expression to his delight in the male body—its torso, pelvis, and muscularity—which took him from exploring minimal coverings with his Men Dancers to expressing the rugged masculinity exemplified by the cut and construction of workwear in woven textiles. He also ushered in the first all-over stretch fabrics that moved with the body.

Perhaps the most significant change in early modern dance derives from the democratization of domestic dress production through new technologies. Rather than costumes being dependent on seamstresses or expensive wardrobes, dedicated friends and family members could purchase a growing range of textiles and produce adaptable, reproducible costumes for smaller ensembles. Notably, from 1918 to 1931, St. Denis had the constant assistance of Wheeler, an artisan able to construct original costumes using research and ideas presented by St. Denis or Shawn (Sherman 1984: 3). From a storeroom filled with exotic fabrics and notions, she found novel ways to incorporate the beading or braiding, pleating or layering to dance garments that would ensure the maximum effect. The dressing room prompts of this "anonymous choreographer" were dance instructions, such as "Do a slow turn . . . [or] flip the material with a small kick to the other side" (Sherman 1984: 4).

Both the Denishawn dancers and Men Dancers were also responsible for laundering tunics, leotards, or trunks nightly, as well as repairing and ironing their own costumes (Sherman 1984: 4). Shawn, on the other hand, relied heavily on "making do" for his company's wardrobe. Apart from the late 1930s when Palmer-Sikelianos contributed expertise in weaving, Horn and Landers oversaw costume production, while all the men could be found "sitting around the fire sewing." Where necessary, Shawn purchased clothing from mail-order catalogues, especially durable, ready-made sports and work wear. Most importantly, the commodity form of the dance costume as mass production began during this period, with Shawn identified as an early collaborator with Capezio, the first dedicated dance manufacturing firm in the United States.

Informed by these shifts in costume fabrication and circulation, some enduring patterns in the imagination of diverse choreographers emerge from this warp and weft. The natural fibers of silk are often used in performance as wraps or sculptural drapes, even as modern dance costumes became increasingly gender differentiated. For women, the scarf retains the symbolic residue of an archaic femininity, while the tunic reifies the voluptuous nakedness of female form. For men, shorts and sculptured trousers reveal the bare torso and exalted pelvis. Once textiles include stretch materials, the intimate relations of handmade and measured dress items could be replaced by an industrial model of costume design. At this juncture, the reality of consumption at scale begins to define the ethos of an "American" dancing body.

Undoubtedly, many aspects of modern dance liberated the dress and movement of the female body, with the shock of Duncan's scarves and the silky manipulations of

St. Denis claiming an enhanced freedom and exotic nobility. Such corporeal transformations were however exclusive to a class of white, bourgeois women able to reap the benefits of modern capitalism, with new goods, opportunities for travel, and a material culture producing the labor-saving devices that gave them time to pursue dancing. The "revolt" of Shawn and his male dancers in adapting underwear and experimenting with trousers also prepared a select group of men for a society transitioning away from agriculture toward the production processes of a civic, industrial, and service society.

Drapery, in the sense of loose, moving fabric, was soon to be discarded in a fashion revolution that would pragmatically harness resources, labor, and creativity for an expanding economy of innovation. In the decades that follow, the industrialization that supported the production of fasteners, robust fabrics, and standardized patterning would also construct the new clothes required for a post-war choreography. From drapery to workwear, the costume forms fabricated by the "ruling circles" of mercantile capital in a modernizing America represent therefore a shuffle and a reshuffle of the corporeal values at work in dance.

From Wool Tube to Bias Skirt

Martha Graham

The dress is thus cut diagonally across the body and stretched
over . . . the belly.
F. Th. Vischer, in Benjamin (1999: 70)

When Martha Graham taught at the Cornish College of the Arts in Seattle in 1930, the dancer Dorothy Bird recalls a distinctive memory of costume:

[Martha] taught us how to make leotards. . . . We got white wool and dyed it in tea or coffee, and with three-quarters of a yard we put a little diamond here under the crotch in a little insert, and then we got into this piece of tubing and put safety pins up the sides. We cut out a little bit here and there and then put elastic in the legs and that was it. We barely ever hemmed it or anything, and it was wool fabric and it shrank right away. And we danced in them with bare legs. (Bird Villard 1984)

Like Ruth St. Denis and Ted Shawn, Graham was preparing her young dancers for the experience of moving in undergarments. This intimate, improvised clothing was made of brown wool knit, tightened to the shape of the body and clipped as required for decency around the crotch. In these skimpy costumes, Graham would ask them to run down a grassy hill as fast as they could, attempting to crush a rock in their path with "tremendous energy." Bird's account has powerful material traces: the attributes of stretched wool and its shrinkage; the dramatic shaping of the body; and the dynamics of a choreographic action shaped by the imagery of an internal force colliding with an external obstacle.

Three modern dance students at the Cornish College in 1935 wearing similar knitted leotards are seen experimenting with the dynamics of stretch and tension through the interplay of shared weight relayed along an adjoining ribbon (Figure 2.1). The elasticity of their rehearsal costumes is a subtle accompaniment to the angular movement and body-fashioning associated with Graham's evolving choreographic vocabulary: a commanding

Fabrications. Rachel Fensham, Oxford University Press. © Oxford University Press 2026. DOI: 10.1093/9780197699638.003.0003

FIGURE 2.1 Imogen Cunningham, *Dance 3, Cornish School*, 1935. © 2025 Imogen Cunningham Trust, https://www.ImogenCunningham.com.

stillness, a deepening connection to the ground, a fluid balancing of weight, the use of breath, planted feet, and expressive hands.

With a focus on the trope of resistant fabric, this chapter explores two silhouettes of female dress—the column and the full-length circle skirt. One might think of these forms as operating on two planes, the vertical line of the spine and the horizontal base in the triangular shape of an extended skirt. When either the vertical axis or the horizontal balance is tilted, in body or fabric, new tensions are created in relation to gravity.[1] To analyze the dynamics of such interlocking shapes in modern dance, the chapter examines the legacy of Martha Graham's personal involvement in costume-making, particularly her "love of wool jersey" (Herring 2023). Throughout Graham's career, as she pursued her aspirations and sculptural ideas for choreography, her dancers wore many garments fabricated of knitted wool that explored dramatic and physical tensions, most notably in the bias-cut skirt.

In keeping with the weave of this book's argument, this chapter historicizes the collaborative aspects of Graham's enterprise in making modern dance sculptural. From the late 1920s, she was aided and influenced by a cosmopolitan circle of friends and associates—photographers, sculptors, dancers, designers, and dressmakers—whose modernist aesthetics involved formalist approaches to light, structure, geometry, and materials. Many of them were émigré artists or dual American citizens, whose ambiguous relations to nationhood were sorely tested by the Depression and the approaching war.

The chapter focuses on Graham's choreography in the 1920s and 1930s. It aims to elucidate how knitted wool jersey skirts became a partner to choreography, bringing weight, feminism, and emotional content into the aesthetics and politics of movement in modern dance. The chapter ends before Graham's major dance-dramas in the 1940s, because by then her formal interaction with costume design was mitigated by the professionalization of scale and structure in her choreography.

Few of Graham's original early costumes survive, because the company's studio in Bethune Street, New York, was flooded in the aftermath of Hurricane Sandy in 2012.[2] For archival sources, the chapter has mostly relied on the secondary evidence of replica garments as well as photographs, memoirs, reviews, film, and limited rehearsal experience of her 1936 work *Chronicle*.[3] The Graham Company is, however, still a professional company remounting works from her repertoire. In collaboration with contemporary designers, they commission costumes for new dances and produce duplicate sets of the classic works for rehearsal and study. There are also reconstructed "original" costumes supervised by costume design consultants such as Russell Vogler, Jeffrey Wirsing, and Karen Young (Conover 1993). The costume store is maintained by Joyce Herring, director of Martha Graham Resources and a former Graham principal dancer.

Now housed on an upper floor, the room is an archive of the present as much as of the historical Graham. The fabrication of replacement costumes responds to contemporary tastes, as well as the current availability of textiles. Wool jersey may be replaced with cotton jersey; colors change with new dyeing techniques and in response to the effects of modern lighting. The later years of Graham's company were also shaped by designers such as Calvin Klein and Roy Halston Frowick, known professionally as Halston, who sought to emulate (or, some say, undermine) the resistant energy that the earlier costumes had provided to the dancer. These processes have portentously transformed the tubular dress and woolen skirt, a complex artifact of colonial American womanhood, from a resistant uniform into a conservative mode of dress.

"Made in Allegheny" and Wool Stockings

Martha Graham was born in the Pennsylvania city of Allegheny in 1894, a doctor's daughter from a Presbyterian family with a will to express an inner self (Figure 2.2). Allegheny was an industrial city, and goods "made in Allegheny" were distributed by railway around the nation. Wool textiles were among its primary exports; it housed the last US "wool pulling factory."[4] Like many other regional cities, it was home to a significant immigrant population, including a large group of German craft workers who had

FIGURE 2.2 Imogen Cunningham, *Martha Graham*, 1931. © 2025 Imogen Cunningham Trust, https://www.ImogenCunningham.com.

migrated in the eighteenth century. Frequently referred to as "Deutschtown," it was connected by rail and road with the similarly named Germantown on the northern edge of Philadelphia. Allegheny was absorbed into Pittsburgh in 1907.

While fine silk stockings had been produced in France and England for centuries, the mills of colonial Pennsylvania produced more robust household goods, most famously the stockings worn by soldiers during the American Revolutionary War.[5] Sturdy woolen stockings were also a staple of working people's attire in America, as cultural historian Emily Whitted observes:

> Knit fabric encased the legs and feet of almost all early Americans, acting as an additional membrane between skin, shoe, and the outside world. . . . Stockings outlined the shapes of calves, softening the legs under uniform fabric, and effectively masked all manner of sores, calluses, bunions, and other colonial foot woes. (2020: xxii)[6]

The flexibility of these stockings depended on the properties of the woolen fibers, which naturally contain elastane, and the garments' mode of manufacture, which required a

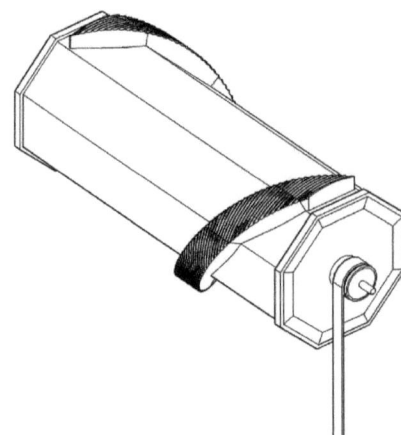

FIGURE 2.3 Diagram of cylindrical stocking machine for interlocking, showing the mechanical differences of Germantown frames from English frames. Courtesy of Emily Whitted. Image: James Kelleher.

cylindrical formation of interlocking stitches. In hand knitting, the circular shape was maintained by using four or more needles, or two needles linked by wire, but this technique was difficult to adapt to machines built on flat wooden frames.

The solution was to install mechanical stocking frames (Figure 2.3). Whitted describes how these worked: at the base was a wooden cylinder holding rows of threads, which were rotated by a spiral mechanism that mobilized interlocking needles, ensuring that the stockings retained their stretch properties. Whitted also observes that the machine-worker's body would lean into the frame, so the maker's rhythmic spiral actions would be preserved in the mobility of the fabric as it encased a customer's leg or torso (2020: 37–38). As an animal-based fabric, wool was one of the most common fibers for clothing and sheep farming was a large part of the American economy into the early twentieth century (Thanhauser 2022: 226). As the United States industrialized, wool, like silk, was however subject to technological innovation, as well as the expanding industrial-scale efforts of human labor.

Graham's lifelong interest in textiles may have been influenced by the long history of wool manufacturing in her hometown. During her middle-class childhood, the family dressmaker would have used the fabrics supplied by Allegheny's stores. Nevertheless, when Graham chose a fabric for experimental use in the studio, she selected a cheap frame-knitted "tubing of white wool," a stocking stitch fabric made for men's singlets, that was only available in dull white or cream. This stretch material not only made the first leotards for Graham's students but was the fabric she repurposed in the knitted tubular costume of *Lamentation* (1930), her most famous work, and the other solo choreographies of her "woolen period."[7]

Fabric as Choreographic Medium: *Lamentation* (1930)

When Martha was fourteen years old, the family moved to the "clean air" of California because her sister suffered from asthma. There, Graham experienced dance for the first time, witnessing a performance by Ruth St. Denis. A few years later, she joined the Denishawn company. In Chapter 1, we saw young Graham wearing a short, girlish tunic as part of a Denishawn tableau in a California garden in 1922. The following year, she moved to New York, where she undertook further dance training, secured some commercial contracts, and was exposed to artists from various cultural backgrounds who viewed performance as a way of expressing powerful and often political ideas (Jowitt 2024: 63–75).

Graham performed her first solo in 1926 (Figure 2.4). She was still wearing long and short tunics, and the name of the solo, *Tanagra*, was redolent of the neoclassical nostalgia for ancient costumes, not unlike other dancers captivated by what Ann Cooper Albright has termed, "the Tanagra effect" (2010: 60). Graham's draped costume however was stripped of its more literal representations of Grecian cultural tropes. Photographed by the Japanese-American photographer Soichi Sunami, Graham is wearing a braided wig and lifting her tunic stiffly, suspending the drape to cascade toward the floor. Rather than fluid motion, the fabric responded to the staggered movement of the gesture, and her immobility and downcast gaze suggest an architecture more than a figurative allusion.

Sunami portrayed Graham and the dancer–choreographer Helen Tamiris after a subsequent concert wearing a range of simple costumes as if they were three-dimensional objects.[8] In *Revolt* (1927), Graham wore a short, dark tunic slit at the sides, her arms

FIGURE 2.4 Graham in her premiere solo, *Tanagra*, 1926. Photograph by Soichi Sunami. Courtesy of Library of Congress. © Soichi Sunami.

rigidly extended as if carved in stone. In these images, the costume drapery featured as a formal statement as much as a moving expression. In launching her independent career, she appeared to shrug off the veils associated with Denishawn, demanding that the garment resist her pressure. Rather than using flow, she recognized the power of weight in a fabric.

As the opening anecdote from Dorothy Bird indicates, Graham was confident experimenting with textiles, manipulating them on the body to give form to her choreography. Graham's own "Notebooks" confirm this determined attitude towards dress and female subjectivity: "She seems to shed her large outer cape or dress as a cocoon—she emerges as tho' the inner nature was revealed" (Ross 1973: 104).

We can see a preliminary picture of Graham's manipulation of her "cocoon" in the three-minute choreography of *Lamentation* filmed at Bennington College in 1943.[9] Graham inserted herself into a tube of fabric wearing a boat-necked leotard with bare feet visible. The thick jersey completely covered her body. Her hands gripped an upper rim, while her knees pressed hard and wide against the sides to secure the lower edge of the material. For every move she made there was resistance, with both a pull and tug against her skin. The textile embraced her body, while at the same time she controlled it from within. In the choreography, her hands plunged into her pelvic core and rotated around it; by her own account, the "pelvic thrust" had sexual connotations for her hidden genitalia (Bannerman 2010: 31). The dancing has a deep, passionate life force that contradicts the mask of her stricken face. In this abstract costume that confines the body comes a revelation of as-yet-unfulfilled desire. Thus, an exertion emerges from the tactile sensation of synchronous and asynchronous causes mixed with localized effects and events.

Joyce Herring, who was coached in the dance by Martha and has performed it many times, recalls that she started to feel angry when doing this physically demanding piece. She asked Graham, "Is there are a place for anger?" and Graham replied, "Absolutely yes!" (Herring 2023). The torsions of body and affect range from the containment of pain to being tilted sideways, to being hollowed out, to gathering up and shutting down, and the elastic tubular garment follows these emotional highs and lows (Figure 2.5). Herring recalls performing this role: "She stands up in the end, she stands up this way and turns this way, and then all the way up, leaning forward. Finally, she stands up like a monolith, like a tower filled with grief, before it collapses and goes inside itself again. . . . The grief is a complicated emotion, the feeling of emptiness, the feeling that you've lost a part of yourself" (Herring 2023).

The materiality of this costume raises important questions about the authenticity of structure, weight, and color. It consists of a tubular length of wool jersey about 7 feet long cut from a 25-inch bolt width; it has no seams or hems. The dancer must squeeze into the costume so that the fabric is distributed evenly down her full length. It was marked only with a small string at the rear center so the dancer could pull it on symmetrically. The weight of the weave was always double knit, making it heavy and resistant to being stretched; the dancer had to work hard inside the taut material. The original color of the fabric is even harder to determine. The unstable Technicolor used in the 1943 film

FIGURE 2.5 Joyce Herring in *Lamentation*, 1930. Photograph by Martha Swope. Courtesy of Martha Graham Resources.

renders the costume in two tones, somewhere between maroon and purple-black.[10] More recent versions overseen by Graham were variously blue, lilac, and mauve, and some are made of lighter, cotton fabric and have seams.

According to Herring, if the color is too dark, the shadows are invisible under stage lighting, while if the blue is too soft, the depth of grief is diminished. Her preference is for a dark lavender. The specific tone of the original was probably produced by an indigo dye composed of three parts blue to one part violet; this dye would oxidize with light, giving it an iridescent duality. According to Victoria Finlay, *porphúra*, the Greek word for mauve or purple, has "a double connotation of movement and of change," reflecting in different tones depending on the light (2002: 414).

The organic antecedents of purple lay in a rare shellfish harvested along the Tyrian peninsula. The dye was costly, and as a result the color became associated with royalty and the sacred (Finlay 2002: 392). Restrictions on its use changed after 1856, when the chemist William Henry Perkin created the first aniline dye from a residue of coal tar (Garfield 2002). Both stable and cheap, this dye was widely adopted, and deep black–mauve tones became a favorite of the Victorian period, particularly associated with mourning (Finlay 2002: 394). Whether Graham's original costume was blue, purple, or

FIGURE 2.6 Variations of blue wool jersey for *Lamentation*, 1930. Photograph by Rachel Fensham. Courtesy of Martha Graham Resources.

maroon, the synthetic compound dye has lost its red tones under lights, eventually fading to blue.

Regardless of substance, the *Lamentation* costume has retained the multiple connotations of purple, both in the sensation of "movement and change" and the association with sacred iconography. Since the dancer pulls the fabric tightly around its neck opening, sometimes wearing it like the mantle of a weeping woman, sometimes as if it is a shroud, it is not difficult to identify the choreography of purple jersey, as many dance critics have done, with the grief of historical women such as Mary grieving for her son Jesus, or Mary Magdalene grieving for her lost Lord. Other narratives relate the choreography of *Lamentation* to the wives and mothers mourning America's civil war dead or experiencing the persistent grief of child mortality.[11] In one of her most famous quotes, Graham claimed universal meanings for the dance as a "witness" to the pain and "tragedy that obsesses the body" when suffering loss (Graham 1991: 117).

Rather than seeking a representational answer to the significance of *Lamentation*, new materialism, as the Introduction suggests, ponders the complex relationship between sensory experience and the politics of public articulation. In an essay on the seventeenth-century moral philosopher Thomas Hobbes, feminist theorist Samantha Frost writes about the illusion of autonomy in the face of social anxiety (2010: 159).[12] For resilience, she says, the imagination draws on the multitude of past experiences to navigate the unknown aspects of the future. Such a concept can be related to the political and moral causality which gives an individual a sense of purpose and control. The "passions" also play a role at a more basic level, as a corporeal process in which the sensations of the body are activated through "motion" (Frost 2010: 161). According to Hobbes, this movement is "vital to moral action," and every act betrays the complex of active and passive causes generated in and by the body. Causes, he writes, are not "one simple chain of concatenation, but an innumerable number of chains, joined together . . . and consequently the whole cause of an event, doth not always depend on one single chain, but on many together" (cited in Frost 2010: 161). Between my analysis of a stretching bodily form and the "innumerable number of chains, joined together" in the knitted fabrics that ground the aesthetic appeal of *Lamentation*, I propose an analogy of purpose. To identify causes, we need to unpick some of the chains Graham inhabits and connect *Lamentation* to other artists and art forms, as well as to dances that extend beyond this singular work.

Sculptural Materiality

While Graham's experimentation with fabric was integral to her choreography, her understanding of the formal attributes of costume design evolved from close associates and collaborations involving the new media of abstract expressionist sculpture and modernist black-and-white photography. To some extent, these relationships were circumstantial and proximate; the artists lived and worked within a few blocks of each other in mid-town New York, which at the time offered cheap rent for workshops, shopfronts, and studios.[13]

The artistic and intellectual affinities these neighbors shared were at the vanguard of international trends in modern aesthetics. As well as collaborating with composers and dancers, Graham embarked on a sustained partnership with the experimental sculptor Isamu Noguchi, who produced enigmatic set designs for her longer dramatic works. His influence, and through him other potentials for imagination, was causal before Graham's *Lamentation* achieved iconic status.

Noguchi's striking portrait of the *Magdalene* (1926) exemplifies the merging of cubist ideas with figuration inspired by the Romanian sculptor Constantin Brancusi's celebrated *Mlle Pogany* (1913). Initially carved from marble and later cast in bronze, Brancusi's bust has heavy eyelids and rests her hands on her left cheek, pulling the lines of an imagined sleeve toward the side of the head. The elongated nose and extended mouth distort the face, adding inner melancholy to her expression. Beneath the suspended head, it is possible to imagine the solitude of the absent body, while her seeming impassivity allows the spectator to read any number of sensations, moods, and concepts into its shadows. This enigmatic representation of a woman invites repeated consideration, as Alexandra Parigoris suggests, through the "permutation of curved forms, eyes taking over the oval of the face, neck subsumed by cascading hair" (Giménez and Gale 2004: 57).

Brancusi's exhibitions in New York and Chicago caused a sensation in the art world and inspired Noguchi to visit Paris.[14] In 1928, when he returned to New York, he shared studio space with Alexander Calder above Graham's dance studios in Carnegie Hall.[15]

On his studio wall, he had an image of Mlle Pogany; although he wanted to advance his own abstract sculpture, commissions for sculpting conventional heads and torsos paid his bills.

Chiseling into the surface, Noguchi's sculpted heads became increasingly angled and self-consciously marked by the hands and tools used to render the materials. Throughout 1929, while regularly visiting Graham's dance studio, he sculpted many of his artistic friends and associates, including Graham and Doris Humphrey (Grove 1989). The first bust of Graham has a flattened, textured face with downcast eyes; a second bust, more classical, tilts her profile slightly upward revealing the noble line of her forehead.[16] Graham vigorously rejected the somber portrait, saying, "I did not like it . . . he had seen too deeply" (Landau 2013: 13). With the qualities of a veiled face, the shaded eyes seem haunted by internal impressions of pain, and the incised lines tauten and unfold toward the ground.

The sequence of images in Figures 2.7 to 2.10 progress from the head of Brancusi through Noguchi's portraits of the Magdalene, and of Graham herself, to Graham's *Lamentation*. The sculptures show a seriality of figurative solutions for molding expressive contours in the facial portrait. Graham's choreographic work continues this sculptural enquiry by producing an emotive association with an inscrutable mask-like face by enclosing the body in a cylindrical costume.

FIGURE 2.7 Constantin Brancusi, *Mlle Pogany*, version I, 1913, after a marble of 1912. Image © The Museum of Modern Art, New York/ Scala, Florence, 2025. Artwork © Constantin Brancusi. ADAGP/ Copyright Agency, 2025.

FIGURE 2.8 Isamu Noguchi, *Magdalene*, 1924. Bronze. Photograph by Kevin Noble. © The Isamu Noguchi Foundation and Garden Museum, New York/Artists Rights Society [ARS]/ Copyright Agency.

FIGURE 2.9 Isamu Noguchi, *Martha Graham*, 1929. Bronze. © The Isamu Noguchi Foundation and Garden Museum, New York/ Artists Rights Society [ARS]/Copyright Agency.

FIGURE 2.10 Martha Graham in *Lamentation*, 1930. Photograph No. 11 by Herta Moselsio, c. 1939. Courtesy of the Library of Congress and Martha Graham Resources.

In January 1930, Graham performs *Lamentation*; presumably its creative process took place in 1929, contemporary with the making of the two portraits, although no credit is given to Noguchi for costumes. His sister Ailes Gilmour, however, was a dancer in Graham's first company and their mother Léonie Gilmour was the seamstress, so the entire family was intimately involved with Graham's early creations. Art historian Ellen Landau has documented how Noguchi's curiosity about corporeal form was piqued by watching Graham's dance classes, which exposed him to ideas about "the collapsed body, the body in tension" (2013: 15). Time in the dance studio preparing costumes on the body, or with Noguchi in the sculpture studio, must have played a part in the two artists' independent excavation of ambiguous emotional content in material forms. Their immediately subsequent works indicate that the sculptural potential of the hidden, yet expressive female body was an ongoing concern.

In 1931, at the height of an affair with the Chicago choreographer Ruth Page, Noguchi constructed two costume "sacks" for her; he used the silhouette of one of the sacks in his sculpture *Miss Expanding Universe* a metallic angel-like figurative work now on display in the Chicago Museum of Fine Art.[17] Fabric does not often feature in Noguchi's other work except in relation to set design; it seems likely Graham's *Lamentation* stimulated his continued interest in malleable materials animating the three-dimensional surface of a dancing body.

Page herself experimented with the sacks, using them in several short choreographic sketches (Olson 2020). But there are revealing differences between Graham's work and Page's, both in the materiality of the "sacks" and the resulting choreography. Preserved in the Chicago History Museum, Page's costume was made of wool jersey in a now-faded blue, with side seams and stitched neck openings that can be fastened with hooks and eyes (Pushor 2020). One has an elasticized waist and a closed seam at the base. Its butterfly shape delineates the abstract female body that appears in Noguchi's aluminum sculpture: the upper portion is molded by breasts and wing-like sleeves, while the lower half is an expanding triangle. It seems unlikely this outfit could be worn for dancing; indeed, photographs of Page wearing it show her recumbent on a studio floor or spinning like a kite.

The second dance sack pictured in Figure 2.11 is a rhomboid shape, with foot openings in the bottom corners. Its open shape allows the dancer to move within it, juggling its surface in different directions. Page used this sack in her choreography for *Expanding Universe* (1932), a dance which was abstract and somewhat comic. To expand her modern dance vocabulary into shape design in this period, Page became involved in experimentation with "sacks and sticks"; however, unlike Graham's *Lamentation*, the costume as prop was not harnessed to intense emotional content (Meglin 2022: 82–83).

At a material level, more notable differences between the sacks and Graham's tubular costume appear. The first is that Graham did not like seams and never wanted them to be visible. Visible at the necks of Page's "sacks" are the metal fasteners which resemble the closures used on costume bags.[18] Second, the Page costumes were cut with the warp

FIGURE 2.11 Isamu Noguchi, women's blue jersey wool costume designed for Ruth Page, 1932. Courtesy of Chicago History Museum. Artwork © The Isamu Noguchi Foundation and Garden Museum. ARS/Copyright Agency, 2024.

on the horizontal, presumably for durability, but this minimized their stretch. These material differences were perhaps insignificant for Noguchi's purposes, but they contrast with Graham's emphasis on sculpting with the fit and stretch qualities inherent to wool jersey.

The rhythmic sculptural qualities of Graham's choreography were noted by reviewers, who viewed her performances as "jagged with grotesqueries, distortions and lit with humour" (Kaufman 1930). This angularity attracted the photographer Barbara Morgan to document her work in the book *Martha Graham: 16 Dances in Photographs*. Morgan was another member of Graham's circle of artistic colleagues who experimented with the formal properties of materials, moving objects, and fractured three-dimensional surfaces. For Morgan, the abstract use of fabric and choreography lent itself to new concepts of photography and helped her to formulate a theory of "kinetic design," in which the camera captures the effects of light and shadow—"moving in opposition, by-passing, flowing together" (1953: 27).[19] Morgan explains this effect in her observation of Graham's *Lamentation*:

> In this picture, the oblique sweep of the thrust to the top must be countered. The head is counter, but I deliberately created this dark space in the lower left corner to do that. I also was intrigued here by the curve of the ankle, echoed in the upper knee. The curve of the ankle went with the curve of the knee which went with the curve of the head. (cited in Knappe 2008: 67)

The choreographic gestures on the photographic surface have their material echo in the spiral fabrics encasing Graham's body, as if dark and light are looped together by the cylinders of an interlocking machine. The twists in the fibers also stretch against the inner movements of the body. Alternating diagonal lines extend from pointed toe to knee, from knee to tightened grip, and from scapula to turned head. Graham was pleased with Morgan's book, her fourth close collaboration with a photographer. While she complained about Morgan's exactitude or the difficulty of caring for the costumes between shots, this understanding of what the camera could visibilize complemented Graham's knowledge of costumes. The folds of light and shadow echo the emotional landscape that Graham wished to portray, allowing its abstract form to reveal new content as the dancer works within the tubular garment.

The historical experience held in the *Lamentation* costume is thus magnified by each dancer who performs this role. The politics of choreography, as Frost puts it, will emerge from a "composite of sensory percepts and memories that arise and resound as the body ages, moves, and encounters and responds to the context of its action" (2010: 162). The body moving inside is not therefore an individual expression; it owes its motility to the social relations imprinted in a female dancer swathed in knitted jersey and seated on a bench in a bare studio. Indeed, as the costume ages, losing stretch, shades, and lines, the composition of the dance changes. Rather than viewing *Lamentation* as a singular portrait, a depiction of grief, or naming the genre a "tragedy," we can see that the materiality of this costume embodies multiple chains of signification. Indeed, the work of *Lamentation* reveals a vast arrangement of affective tensions for women that lie between desire and suffering.

Torsion in *Ekstasis* (1933)

In terms of fabrication, the material properties of knitted stretch tubular jersey transform the body from a recognizable person to an abstract composition. The taut fabric mostly covers the body except for the feet, hands, and face. Every movement or gesture then appears as lines and folds of tension twisted across a stylized shape.

In 1931, the West Coast photographer Imogen Cunningham met Graham and they "went to Martha Graham's mothers' farm, opened the barn doors, and with . . . the darkness of the inside barn behind Martha, took photos outside in the strong sunlight" (Partridge 2024). In a series of photographs, a relaxed Graham improvises with the elasticity of a woolen sweater and a loose skirt. These close-up portraits capture Graham alternatively plucking, furling, and folding the garments around her body (Figure 2.12). In Figure 2.13, she has turned the sweater upside down and folded its hem around her shoulders: the shell-like ribbing distorts across her naked torso while her arms reach delicately from within the cloth. The soft lighting, open profile, and caressing garment contrast sharply with the experience of *Lamentation* a year or two earlier. The portraits show Graham intimately involved with sculpting movement for dance from within the dialectics—soft and firm—of a woven, textured cylinder.

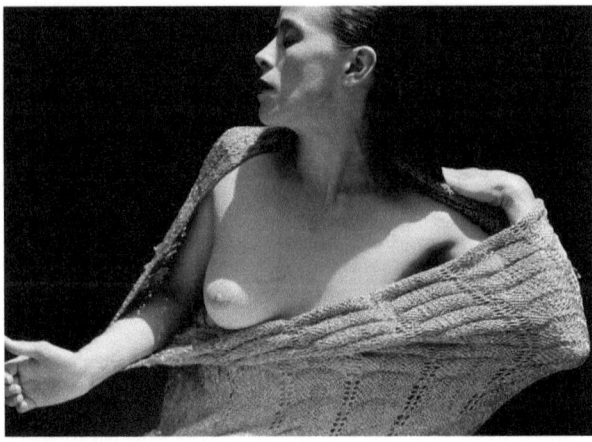

FIGURE 2.13 Imogen Cunningham, *Martha Graham 42*, 1931. © 2025 Imogen Cunningham Trust, https://www.ImogenCunningham.com.

FIGURE 2.12 Imogen Cunningham, *Martha Graham 54*, 1931. © 2025 Imogen Cunningham Trust, https://www.ImogenCunningham.com. quarter.

In her subsequent solos, *Satyric Festival Song* (1932) and *Ecstasies* (1933), Graham employed a woven-skin dress to different effect; the upper edges of the tube are rolled into a neck or collar, leaving the head generously exposed, and a row of piping appears under the bust. The costumes hug the body and no longer replicate the folds of drapery. Graham uses this costume, which keeps flesh largely hidden, to explore the beautification of female form. As in the Cunningham photographs, the body becomes a form of mesh, a network of sensory patterns played out on the surface.

In *Satyric Festival Song*, Graham is sheathed in thick stretch jersey, brightly colored and striped like a "kachina," the ancestral spirit of the Pueblo Indians.[20] Atypically, her long hair flies free.[21] Several Morgan photographs depict Graham improvising in this dress, bending from side to side like a disjointed doll, making the stripes slide along the ribcage as she shifts weight and shape through her feet. These pictures seem spontaneous, unguarded; they capture the cascade of her hair and the strange flowing mass of the totem pole releasing corporeal tensions. The program notes refer problematically to "mocking dances in Pueblo rituals," but her dancing of this costume seems non-representational and playful.

By way of contrast, the reconstructed *Ekstasis* costume is a cream monotone dress made from a single bouclé tube that clings to the torso and then hugs the legs from thigh to ankle.[22] In its full length, seen in Figure 2.14, the column of this dress supports an outstretched, off-centered body, while its knit structure (Figure 2.15) curves and folds

FIGURE 2.14 Wool tubular dress worn by Martha Graham in *Ekstasis*, 1933. Photograph by Hibbard Nash. Courtesy of Martha Graham Resources.

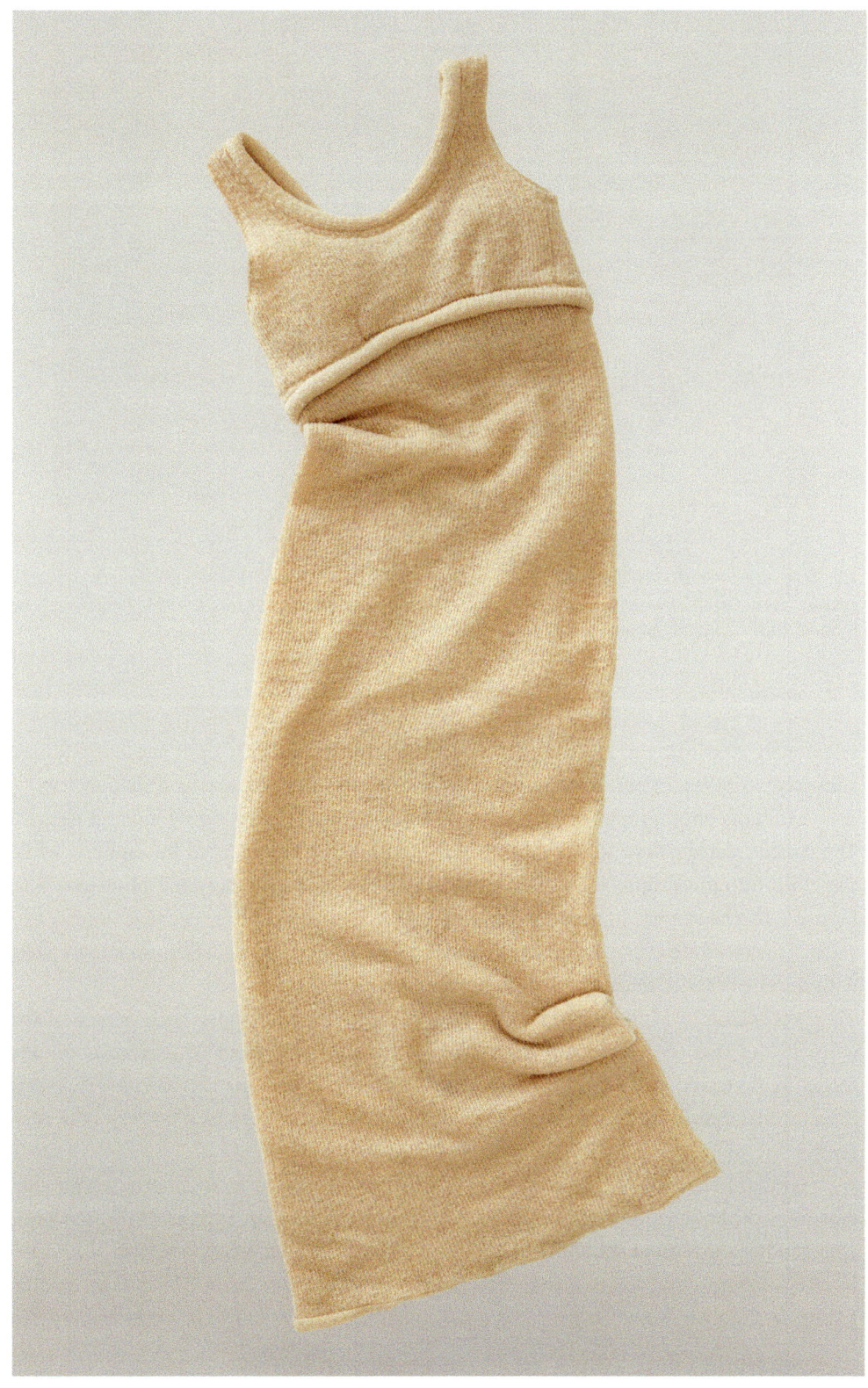

FIGURE 2.15 Detail of wool tubular dress worn by Martha Graham in *Ekstasis*, 1933. Photograph by Hibbard Nash. Courtesy of Martha Graham Resources.

sensuously. According to Herring, the costume was stretched very tight because Graham abhorred wrinkles; in performance, the soft texture also hugs breasts and shapely legs.

Morgan's photographs of *Ekstasis* treat Graham's body as monumental and elegant. The dancer reaches beyond the tubular form to embrace an enlarged kinesphere, while the close-fitting costume resists her expansive gestures. In the cropped photograph of Figure 2.16, the camera follows the ribbing pattern as vertical lines course sinuously upward. This costume exposes the feminine form, its looped construction forming a web, with minute holes of shadow breathing in and out as she moves.

According to Morgan, the "harsh lighting prominently displays the weave of the garment" so that "the bodies in their space" become "a series of convex and concave forms in rhythmic movement" (Knappe 2008: 68–69).[23] The distinct corporeality that inhabits this interlocked costume, with its oblique knotted curves, also becomes the choreographic subject.

Graham claimed this solo was critical to her formation as a choreographer: her discovery of the sensuous relationship between hips, shoulders, and pelvis in this dance changed her movement vocabulary (Figure 2.17). Watching a reconstruction of *Ekstasis* in 2017, the critic Martha Sherman described how the dancer PeiJu Chien-Pott "melted from the shoulder down in deep S-shapes, morphing from curve to crispness, angled

FIGURE 2.16 Martha Graham in *Ekstasis*, 1933. Photograph by Barbara Morgan. Courtesy of UCLA Library Special Collections and Martha Graham Resources.

lines and leg lifts" (Sherman 2017). The costume hugging the female body as the dancer reaches from grounded weight to open sky (Figure 2.18) displaces the energetic line of movement.

Activating these alternative embodiments, these tubular costumes do not depict "universal grief" or "ritualized worship." Rather, the materiality of American hosiery amplifies the dancing body as a "cycle of distortion." In an action that arises from thrusts of the pelvis combined with disequilibrium from leaning on one foot and the twisting of weight in the upper body, Graham's body rebels against a history of female containment. The form of the textile reveals a function, and the function reveals a form of off-centered verticality that becomes a signature property of the expressive female body in modernity. The use of tubular interlocking in a leotard and the creation of *Lamentation* are perhaps the purest traces of Graham's ongoing fascination with the sculptural qualities of knitted fabric to produce an abstract dancing body. Seen from within, Graham learns how the elasticity of fabric can enhance the expressive power of gestures for subsequent choreography.

FIGURE 2.17 Martha Graham in *Ekstasis*, 1933. Photograph by Soichi Sunami. Courtesy of Martha Graham Resources and New York Public Library. © Soichi Sunami.

FIGURE 2.18 PeiJu Chien-Pott in *Ekstasis*, 1933, reimagined by Virginie Mecene, 2017. Photograph by Brigid Pierce. Courtesy of Martha Graham Resources.

Fashion at the *Frontier* (1935)

In fashion history, Coco Chanel is credited with transforming wool jersey from a work-aday fabric used by fishermen to a fashion fabric featured in women's wear. Chanel used loose-fitting cuts of woolen fabric for skirts and jackets, draping the weighty organic weave around hips, shoulders, and sleeves. These outfits represented a dramatic change from the corseted and waisted garments of Edwardian fashion. Chanel's fashion system was championed by women who worked, spending their own money and eschewing the defining male gaze. The jersey knit garments gave women style while offering them the freedom to play sport, ride bicycles, and dance. The fabric was celebrated in dance in the costumes of *Le Train Bleu* (1924), which Chanel designed for Bronislava Nijinska's choreography with the Ballets Russes.

Another anecdote by Dorothy Bird leads us from Graham into fashion. Dancers in the early Graham Company would assemble in Graham's New York apartment to dye costumes, but the women were no longer making leotards; on this occasion, the model garment was an elegant silk Fortuny gown. In 1907, inspired by the Greek sculptures found by archaeologists at the oracle of Delphos, the designers Henriette Negrin and Mariano Fortuny began adapting the flowing qualities of the draped tunic for the French fashion industry, applying heat and pressure to silk to form hundreds of fine pleats that fell the length of the body. Their famous "Delphos" gown accentuated the wearer's height and allowed women of many shapes to appear elongated and columnar. Adorned with beaded necklines and delicate ribbons looped around the body, a Fortuny gown became a statement of both refinement and exoticism (Figure 2.19). Models wearing these gowns were

FIGURE 2.19 Marino Fortuny y Madrazo (designer), "Delphos," c. 1930. Image © The Museum of Modern Art, New York/Art Resource/Scala, Florence, 2025.

often posed like caryatids, and the gowns became extremely popular on both sides of the Atlantic, particularly in high-fashion artistic circles. Dancer Ruth St. Denis, Graham's teacher, was indeed one of the famous artists to promote this garment.

Graham also adopted fashionable style; Bird recalls her dress "camouflage" as simultaneously "hypnotic and overwhelming." The plan for one kitchen laboratory was to create Fortuny replicas for their next concert. Having bought "yards and yards of white cheesecloth," Graham supervised the dye vat: "We watched Martha, as one after the other, she mixed the different packages of terra-cotta, red, and sand color dyes in a huge cauldron on the stove." Eventually she declared, "This will have to do" (Gottlieb 2008: 737). The fabric was twisted to test for dye resistance, then removed from the "witch's brew," and put in a warm oven to dry. The result was not a series of elegant pleats but a wad of blotchy, stiff fabric. Nonetheless, Graham persisted; she used safety pins to demonstrate the desired form, then sent the dancers home with instructions to finish sewing their costumes there.

When the hapless Bird failed to return with a finished garment, Graham "went to work fiercely yanking the cheesecloth into shape on my body, pinning it here and there onto my leotard," Bird recalled. "She was hissing and cursing half under her breath. Anger was like fuel for her" (Gottlieb 2008: 738). It is clear from this anecdote that Graham herself closely supervised costume production, with assistance from her dancers. In a letter to dancer Evelyn Sabin in 1927, Graham writes, "I know what sewing means—especially to you and me."[24] During the first decade, Graham assumed full credits for "choreography and costume"; it was not until late 1939 that Edith Gilfonde was credited with the costumes for *Every Soul is a Circus* (1939) and *El Penitente* (1940) (Morgan 1980: 14–17).

These dates coincide with the arrival of men in the company; Erick Hawkins, Graham's romantic partner, joined in 1938 and Merce Cunningham in 1939.

Even in later years, Graham would visit the fabric industries and stores in Orchard Street on the Lower East Side to "find fabrics, scavenging, followed by working on the bodies" (Herring 2023). Over time, Graham and her collaborators evolved a detailed knowledge of costume fabrication that exceeded that of a regular dressmaker. The dance design process involved appreciation of the simple lines that accumulate from putting fabric on a body and watching it move. Seams were located in unusual places, perhaps held by a couple of darts, much like contemporary fashion techniques that examine how lengths of fabric drape when laid against a shoulder or placed on a hip.[25]

In Graham's own costume for *Primitive Mysteries* (1931), for example, squares of organza are used to produce floating sleeves and layered skirts that suggest the innocence and purity of a young girl. In both a romanticized and practical sense, Graham's early costumes document this devoted and creative design practice. Beyond the intimacy of the company making costumes together, a conscious artisanship unfolds in the material process of preparing a dance costume and caring for it. Handling fabric and its relationship to the body anticipates both its use and appearance. A "design" is not imposed by an external imagination; rather, designing is understood in embodied relationship to performance.

The inspiration of "fashion" and haute couture also enters dance from the intermingling of artists and intellectuals, and later from styles introduced by European political refugees. At the vanguard of New York's fashion avant-garde was the iconoclastic figure of Elizabeth Hawes, who had worked in Parisian ateliers during the 1920s, ironically making a living by producing caustic fashion journalism (Hawes 1938). Hawes returned to New York in 1928 and opened a dress shop in the mid-town West Side, only four blocks from Noguchi and Graham's studios. The shop attracted the wealthy and famous, and Hawes deployed the techniques of shaping dresses on the body pioneered by European designers such as Madeleine Vionnet, Coco Chanel, Christian Dior, and Elsa Schiaparelli.

In 1932, Noguchi made a bust of Hawes, which he followed with a 1937 surrealist maquette wearing a stylized dress. The maquette may have been used in Hawes's window display; both Noguchi and Calder helped to decorate her shop; Noguchi was also designing for Graham at this time.[26] The narrow waist and triangulated skirt of the maquette exhibit a sharp female motif, anticipating Dior's 1947 silhouette of tight bodice, mid-waist, and full skirt.

Having studied with the Paris couturier Vionnet, the innovator of bias drape, Hawes was notorious for spending a lot of time with clients, pinning and adjusting each dress to create "style rather than fashion" (Losey 2016). In the dress at Figure 2.20, this precise application produces a dramatic sense of fit, cut, and drape; with diagonal paneling on the bodice, the collar folds loosely, and an inset pleat widens the floor-length striped skirt.[27] The bias-cut skirt appealed to dancers and choreographers such as Graham because it

FIGURE 2.20 Elizabeth Hawes, evening dress in ivory, purple, and lavender striped silk brocade, c.1936. Courtesy of The Museum at FIT.

generated an expressive fluidity that was responsive to the hips. With the full-length circular skirt added to the costume repertoire of 1930s New York, Graham adopts this modern silhouette in the next phase of her choreography.

In Graham's solo for *Frontier* (1935), she wears a tailored dress with a cut-out bodice and boat-shaped neckline with a folded collar and contrasting cream mutton sleeves (Figure 2.21). In actuality, the rose-pink fabric of the skirt consists of bias-cut lengths of fabric joined at side and back seams, with the upper edges of a front panel drawn together in a diamond point between the breasts (Figure 2.22). The intricate construction of the gathered bodice avoids the waistline and sculpts a smooth space between bust and hips. The inserts create a wide hem that strokes the floor and falls in massed folds around her ankles in a style very similar to the Hawes dress.

The great volume of the skirt provides space for one of Graham's signature dance motifs—the lengthened leg outstretched to the back or side. This metaphorical opening of the gate is often, but not always accompanied by a tilted torso or an upraised opposing arm to complete the extension. The ballet equivalent of this pose would be the arabesque, but a barefoot dancer in a full skirt needs an accompanying action to hurl the weight of fabric into the air. The fabric then commands a powerful dynamic that the tutu and tights-clad ballerina cannot match. Visible force is required for the massive volume of wool jersey to catch the air on the upward kick and resist gravity. In this gesture, the garment

FIGURE 2.21 Dress with sleeves worn by Martha Graham in *Frontier*, 1935. Photograph by Hibbard Nash. Courtesy of Martha Graham Resources.

FIGURE 2.22 Detail of dress with sleeves worn by Martha Graham in *Frontier*, 1935. Photograph by Hibbard Nash. Courtesy of Martha Graham Resources.

FIGURE 2.23 Martha Graham in *Frontier,* 1935. Photographer unknown. Courtesy of the Music Division, Library of Congress, Washington, DC, and Martha Graham Resources.

wobbles, crafting its own unique pattern of turbulence—unpredictable and thrilling—as the skirt falls. The costume shows itself to be no inert matter but a substance whose fibers react in resistance and response to the dancer's musculature.

Another photograph by Morgan (Figure 2.23) shows how Graham made the energies imbued in the fabric ripple upward against gravity from the thrust of an extended arabesque. Morgan herself was deeply attuned to the dynamics of the skirt. She wrote:

> At 1/500 second shutter speed of the camera, the Frontier costume billows; at 1/1000 second it would have lashed out, destroying that gentle buoyance. . . . In a centrifugal whirl, the body center is moving more slowly than the fingertips and the costume at the periphery. (1980: 151)

Morgan timed her photograph to catch the moment when the sense of motion between center and circumference was "frozen . . . or increased by blurring" (1980: 151). The arching of the back body and leg had caused the fabric to fan open. The dancing skirt and its crinkled hem thus rendered the choreographic mood visible in that moment when Graham counterposed the direction of bodily energy with movement in space at the "frontier." Against the vast but empty horizon of Noguchi's set, the costume fills the stage with florid excitement: "I'm here! And I'm travelling!"

Circular Form: *Celebration* (1934)

For the modern dancers of Chapter 1, the experience of dance was elevated beyond raw sexuality to the spiritual realm. A similar narrative was arguably reinforced by the mythic symbolism of Graham's later religious works, such as *El Penitente* (1940), her representation of the Shakers in *Appalachian Spring* (1944), and her 1991 autobiography *Blood Memory*. In the late 1920s and early 1930s, however, Graham's work aligned modern dance with more secular ideas. As this chapter has proposed, she was inspired by how modern art, photography, and sculpture changed the perception of the female body. She also sought a distinctively modern form of women's fashionability—sophisticated, eccentric, but unadorned. In the next phase of her costume invention, she challenged the conditions of possibility for a stylized narrative choreography in which the role of the skirt became central.

For Roland Barthes, the vestimentary code of a skirt is assigned by its "shape (wrap-around-, hoop-, short-)"; it varies in length and is subject to modifications in fabric, style, and expectation (1990: 110). Historical variations stimulated by fashion can hobble leg movement—the tube—or liberate it—the circular skirt.

The Graham archives include a revealing instruction sheet on "How to Make a Graham Rehearsal Skirt 101." The process involved cutting a length of folded fabric into a quarter circle across the full width of the fold, with a small quarter-circle cut into the top corner. When opened, the selvedge of the resulting semicircle became the front center line, and the two open edges were seamed together. The skirt front lay down the weft, while the sides and back were cut on the bias so that the warp and weft pulled against each other under the force of gravity. The garment was pinned to see how it draped, and it would then flow or swing off an individually shaped female figure.

Cutting against the grain, the fabric of fashionable dress, as exemplified by Halston designs in the 1970s, became "very stretchy" but could "drape more closely, and softly, around body contours" (Gross and Rottman 1999: 113). These careful cutting and layering actions are easily adapted to dancers of various shapes, particularly if the textile has a fair degree of stretch and weight. In terms of repetition of a costume type, the full-length bias-cut circular skirt began to determine the look, the vocabulary, and the feeling of choreography, not only for Graham but for other modern dancers.

For decades, a full skirt was a staple of the costume and rehearsal wardrobe for Graham dancers, who had to learn to manage the heavy skirt, even when it extended almost to the floor (Herring 2023). A skirt had several other valuable qualities: it allowed the dancer freedom of movement but could be animated to produce thrilling effects; it was modest, as neither legs nor thighs were fully exposed; and it emphasized the elegant tapering of the waist and the hollowing of the back and pelvic basin when the wearer was seated. Furthermore, it was not decorative or layered, but modern and perhaps somewhat masculine.

Choreographically, this austere silhouette recalls the uses of the skirt in folk dancing. According to Graham, a woman wearing this garment was "like a gypsy dancer" (Ross 1973: 104). With its volume and elegance, sexuality and severity, the woolen skirt becomes a uniform that manifests a new kind of dance subjectivity, one that will speak through Graham's nonconformist choreography.

Many photographs of Graham's choreography capture the movement of the skirt. In *Deep Song* (1937), a work created in response to the Spanish Civil War, the soloist wears a lily-shaped skirt with black-and-white panels that unfold like an accordion. Set to percussive music, the dancer dashes between floor and uprising, every tormented gesture amplified by the stark contrasts of the skirt. In *Imperial Gesture* (1936), Graham hoists her skirt with two hands and stretches it against her face; the skirt falls in deep ripples like a curtain or tent, revealing an interior darkness. Choreographically, the skirt facilitates the wide-legged stance Graham instilled in her dancers, but it also contains a bowl of erotic space or female power in the fall of cloth between open legs.

In *Celebration* (1934) and *American Provincials* (1934), the ensemble of female dancers wore prairie-style dresses with overskirts that flowed generously around their legs and tightly fitted bodices (later sometimes substituted with leotards). The dress pattern for *Celebration* was strikingly asymmetrical; the contemporary version of this costume has the potent contrasting colors of maroon and apple green (Figure 2.24). Splitting the skirt down the center adds to the sculptural dynamics: the scooped half-circles move adjacent to one another, and as the dancer turns, the two colors revolve.

FIGURE 2.24 Trio of multi-paneled short-sleeve dresses worn by Martha Graham Dance Company for *Celebration*, 1937. Photograph by Hibbard Nash. Courtesy of Martha Graham Resources.

FIGURE 2.25 Members of the Martha Graham Dance Company in *Celebration*, 1937. Photograph by Barbara Morgan. Courtesy of UCLA Library Special Collections and Martha Graham Resources.

Black-and-white images of this costume cannot do justice to its striking contrasts, but Morgan's photos give a sense of its impact. In *Celebration* (1934), three dancers leap almost vertically, their skirts frothing gently around them (Figure 2.25). Morgan writes: "muscular effort . . . had been spent and momentary relaxation conveys triumph rather than strain" (1980: 151).

The group effect is enchanting—the flicking of skirts, the boldness of a jump picking up the hem, the twisting and contracting of the torso, immediately echoed by an equivalent twitch in the opposite direction from the fabric. The weight of the skirt here produces its own force. Across these works, the skirt performs as a partner to the choreography, particularly in the work of the dancing chorus.

The Skirts of *Chronicle* (1936)

The Notebooks of Martha Graham, curated by Nancy Wilson Ross in 1973, provide notable insight into the "moveable scenery" of costume in Graham's dramatic imagination. Not surprisingly, they include numerous references to skirts. In Graham's choreographic thinking, the skirt often stands in for all women. Many of her works exploit the gendered but depersonalized costume for dramatic effect: so "the moving skirts of the women's dresses" (68), and a "crowd of skirts" become metaphors (71). Other circular garments— "a cape, a coat, a cloak"—work in similar ways, depending on how the object functions in performance. The voluminous hemmed skirt in *Imperial Gesture* (1936) becomes a tent of hidden darkness over which Graham's head peers (Ross 1973: 249). In other words, a garment exists as the synecdoche of repressed contents. Writing of one section in *Cave of the Heart* (1946), Graham asks: "What is happening under cloak to Yuriko, to me, to Erick, to May?" (Ross 1973: 60). Indeed, what is happening choreographically under the skirt or under the cloak?

The labor of the skirt is dialectical, complex, and contradictory. On the one hand, it carries Graham's personal wish fulfillment as a woman and lover. She imagines her-self wearing "a large, skirted dress which at times becomes a great sail or a curtain" re-ceiving gifts from men which "makes me what he dreams—a wreath, a veil, a fan, a whip, a dagger. Each man dreams & says I Salute my love" (Ross 1973: 116). On the other hand, the skirt represents an instrumental power that may annihilate the subjectivity of the individual dancer. In unrealized choreography for a motion picture project based on Nathaniel Hawthorne's *The Scarlet Letter* (1975), Graham imagines the skirt transforming not only the soloist but also the chorus. The skirts of the chorus "resolve into the wings of great birds—creatures half women—half birds—like the Harpies." They dance with the soloist girl-child, "sweeping her off her feet with their dresses," then "thrust her back-wards falling, falling into the arms of the Demon" (Ross 1973: 71). The women's skirts suture the dialectical costume to its other, the blowing skirt to the masculine eros. The voluminous skirt may offer escape at times of crisis, but it may also collapse into capture.

If the skirt depicts a certain solidarity between women, Graham's own costumes were often similar in style to those of the chorus but strikingly different in hem length or color. She stands with and for the other women but is outside their lived reality. An excep-tion, however, was her deep engagement with the movement of the chorus in *Chronicle* (1936), an extended work that canvassed questions of collective action. How does a com-munity of bodies move? Do they move in solidarity or opposition? And how are they led into action? These questions became central to the work of many choreographers who aligned dance with left-wing politics during the Great Depression of the 1930s and the emergence of fascism in Europe.

As a result of the stock market crash in 1929 and the company failures that followed, many Americans lost their jobs, were evicted from their homes, and struggled to feed their families. By the winter of 1932, approximately a third of all Americans were living in poverty, and one in four workers was unemployed. It was a particularly difficult time for women, many of whom had only just entered the workforce. New York was especially hard hit by the recession. In 1936, approximately 1.5 million people in the city were de-pendent on some form of public relief.

Morgan, who was photographing Graham at this time, felt the whole city was de-spondent. She wrote: "Day after day men out of work shuffled listlessly through Madison

Square. In the west, I had witnessed dire poverty . . . [but] not the claustrophobic, spiritual poverty of the city breadlines in a machine world" (cited in Knappe 2008: 29). Many New York artists started to examine the discriminatory effects of capitalism on ordinary people's lives. Hawes, for instance, became active in union politics and scornful of the "rich bitches" she had serviced in her fashion atelier (1943: 18). Dance artists forged new alliances with trade unions and choreographed works that championed "mass action" for a better deal on the factory floor (Franko 2002: 26–27).

After almost a decade of acclaim as America's foremost modern dance artist, Graham herself began to branch out in new directions. She established strong attachments with the growing community of artists arriving in New York to escape Nazism in Hitler's Germany. Refugee artists such as Hanya Holm began teaching German *Ausdruckstanz* (expressionist dance) in New York, and the ever-inventive Graham incorporated its percussive tonalities and dynamic shapes into her choreography. Graham was also supportive of Jewish dancers such as Anna Sokolow, who joined her company.[28] In 1936, she took a public stand against the Nazi regime after she and her company were invited to perform at the Berlin Olympics as representatives of the United States. In forthright terms, Graham refused to participate and also pointed out that some Jewish members of her company would not be welcome in Germany (Franko 2012: 14). Understanding the effects of fascism on the arts, in Spain and Germany, also changed what Graham wanted to express choreographically in the United States (Franko 2012: 17).

Though Graham's personal inclinations were toward individual emotional narratives rather than collective representation, her choreography for *Chronicle* (1936) appears as a critical work of "group dance." It had a tripartite structure, moving from an episode titled "Before Catastrophe" to a second "After Catastrophe" and a third "Prelude to Action." This structure was prescient in that it drew attention to Hitler's increasing influence. The final section was called "Unity—Pledge to the Future." In performance, all the dancers wore very thick woolen skirts. They harnessed Graham's principles of core contraction and release of powerful pelvic energies to compound the effect of dark forces pressing down on the stage.

The black costumes for "Steps in the Street (Devastation—Exile)" are simple in style: a squared neckline contrasts with the gently curved waist, while an overlapping front pleat adds extra volume but also swings open (Figure 2.26). Sweat patches, distorted sleeves, and the huddling together of these dresses replicate the ambivalence and anxiety of women who must dance in the face of war. It began with the dancers walking backward with a stilted step, their feet barely visible beneath their black skirts.[29] One dancer took center stage wearing a waisted skirt dress. She sent out an alarm, kicking her straight leg sideways so the skirt flapped rapidly like a flag. It was a call to action: other dancers side-hopped on stage, and the marching beat of the music quickened. Together, the dancers threw their arms at an angle in the air and bent their legs as they leapt across the stage. The bundled fabric of the skirt could be galloping horses or refugees on the run.

FIGURE 2.26 Black short-sleeve dress worn by Martha Graham Dance Company for *Steps in the Street*, 1936. Photograph by Hibbard Nash. Courtesy of Martha Graham Resources.

There was palpable tension as the soloist turned around, twisting her torso and knotting the skirt behind her. Returning from the other side, the marchers stepped forward and back, fists raised in a series of strident gestures. The black costumes enveloped their bodies, creating turbulence in the visible movement of the masses. Forward and back, the serried rows of dancers pressed their exposed hands down, across their heads, behind their necks, and then in front, where they grasped the space and pulled it toward them. In unison, they were contained, clustered into knots of intense affect. There was nothing to distract from the dark compositional forces that mapped the diagonals of the stage.

Between the downward thrusts, the counterpoint of the sideways open leg gesture appears repeatedly; it is visible in the 2014 production of "Sketches from Chronicle" in Figure 2.27. This action expands the black skirt to full volume so that the cavity between the legs and pointed toes extends a question—the skirt seems to be asking, "Where shall we go?" In the last minutes of this choreography, the dancers walk forward with their arms outstretched, as if sleepwalking toward the coming catastrophe, their bell-like skirts carrying forward momentum. The soloist walks in the opposite direction, then bends backward and flings her arms forward. For a moment, she rocks back and forth on her back leg, and her resistance calls back the other dancers, who initially seem compelled

FIGURE 2.27 Atsuko Tonohata, Jacqueline Elder, and Mariya Dashkina Maddux performing Martha Graham's *Steps in the Street* from "Sketches from Chronicle," 2014. Photograph by Costas. Courtesy of Martha Graham Resources. © Costas.

to follow her. Yet they again become somnambulant, swept up in an undertow and flurry of skirts.

The dance historian Mark Franko argues that the more radical group choreographies of the 1930s worked affectively, as much as representationally. Mass dance, he writes, "provides the sensation of intensely compressed experience characterizing momentous historical events" (2002: 27). In *Chronicle*, this affective power is realized in an unglamorous "political" choreography that epitomizes some of the ways in which the skirt empowers the female dancer with its enveloping folds. In the skirt, she is not alone in her movement journey, however bleak, because it accommodates the wide, expansive actions of her legs while not revealing the shape of her thighs, the thickness of her calves, or the length of her torso. Its copious generality as a shape, as a plain color, and as a modest textile seems kind to the dancer, even though it restricts movement. The choreographic authority of the skirt must be harnessed to the group effect, its rhythmic patterns, and political coherence. Moreover, as a dialectical costume, the skirt holds complex memories that can be both a resource and a limitation for many struggling women who are claiming space, refusing to be objectified in actions of protest, even when stripped of their humanity. Benjamin argues that the recollection and simultaneous rupture of the fragment animates the present; in this choreography, the remembrance of being held by one's gender in solidarity with others—in the jersey bias skirt—activates an immanent politics (1999: 210).

"A Crowd of Skirts": Pathos and Poetics

After the Second World War, with American triumphalism and paranoia resurgent, a certain melancholy and retrospection emerged in the aesthetics of artists such as Graham, Noguchi, Morgan, and Hawes. Having carved out cultural space through modernist abstraction against threats of ideological control from right and left, state and enemy, they looked to art to restore a lost innocence and create a time before the present. Robert Starrs argues that the "affective pull of a feminine figure" within artistic modernism paradoxically produces "the pathos of melancholy loss" (2011: 134). He argues that this feminine pathos also ignites the call of tradition in nationalist ideologies. In dance, when female dancers in skirts become universal symbols rather than individuals, we could say that the affective pull of the "feminine figure" in Graham's choreography risks losing the radical intent of American modern dance inside a more conservative cultural agenda.

Graham herself danced until 1970, when she was seventy-six; her full-skirted gowns wrapped up her aging body and protected it from scrutiny. By then, she had largely relinquished her hold over the design and manufacture of the company's costumes. Much of that responsibility was borne earlier by the Japanese-American dancer Yuriko Kikuchi, who was also a trained seamstress and undertook to fabricate many of the company's costumes after the war (Perron 2022). These garments mostly conformed to the existing mold of the tight-fitting bodice and full skirt, though they added ornamentation, such as symbolic jewelry, helmets, and gold trim, and used more contemporary synthetics.

The tubular garment and jersey drapery had a final flourish when Graham began collaborating with the fashion designer "Halston" who was renowned for creating fluid, feminine outfits for celebrities.[30] They shared a love of drapery and the bias cut, with much of Halston's fashion reputation built on the minimalism of the diagonal line.[31] In 1975, he was commissioned to design costumes for Graham's *Lucifer,* and he went on to create costumes for *Acts of Light* (1981), update *Clytemnestra* in 1984, and design costumes for *Night Chant* (1988). Many of these costumes, however, were not admired by the New York dance critics (Kisselgoff 1987; Acocella 2003). In 2003, the Los Angeles critic Lewis Segal (2003) called for a "redesigning of their [the Graham company] sets and costumes where needed" because they were "in thrall to a phantom."

As a contrast with Graham's more lurid late choreography, we can turn to the reconstruction of one of her earliest works, *Heretic* (1929). In the original, she wore a long, formal white dress and faced twelve women wearing black skirted garments stretched across their bellies—perhaps adherents of some exclusive religion. The choreography is stiff and stark; the dance revolves around the woman being repudiated and cast out (Figure 2.28).

In rehearsal for a reconstruction of *Heretic* in 1986. Graham, aged ninety, is wearing a purple draped priest-like robe and long black gloves to cover her arthritic hands (Stalpaert 2012). She grips the extended arms of Takako Asakawa, who is dancing Graham's younger "heretical" self in a pure white stretched gown, surrounded by attentive neophytes in leotards and black rehearsal skirts (Figure 2.29). The torsion in the

FIGURE 2.28 Martha Graham and members of the Martha Graham Dance Company in *Heretic*, 1929. Photograph by Soichi Sunami. Courtesy of Martha Graham Resources. © Soichi Sunami.

FIGURE 2.29 Martha Graham rehearsing Takako Asakawa and dancers in *Heretic*, 1986. Photograph by Martha Swope. Image © Billy Rose Theatre Division, The New York Public Library for the Performing Arts.

fabric and the spiral action moving through the costume into the body reactivate the dialectical image as both poignant and eerie. It holds the complexity of a dance career made of gestures and symbolism, embodied faces and covered bodies; the colors and costumes chiseled into memory. Fashioning the body inside a choreographic system, they represent a shorthand for women who are intensely self-critical and discordant.

In spite of new textiles and increasing theatricality, by the 1980s, Graham's dance aesthetics had become superseded by the minimalist and pedestrian costume choreography featured in the following chapters of this book. This excavation of the unique properties and principles of dance costume, pioneered on Graham's body in collaboration with fellow artists and dancers, documents however an acute moral attunement to actions made in contexts of great change.

Conclusion

In the epigraph to this chapter, Benjamin cites the minor philosopher F. Th. Fischer making a comic observation about bias-cut fabric exaggerating the belly. While the jersey wool tube and skirt in Graham's choreography were rarely used to comic effect, this remarkable way of using fabric, allowing the weave of wool to stretch diagonally on the female body, extended a potency to women in ways of moving that were distinctive, sculptural, and erotic.

In particular, the chapter recalls how a repertoire—of silhouette, fabric, figuration of the body, and stock gestures—reveals a passionate imagination of causes and effects, as well as memories of repression and loss. The knots in modern choreography articulate chains of action, as the feminist critic Frost proposes, involving time, work, and elaboration, harnessed to a trained movement system and yet resistant to external forces such as gravity. The causality of choreography lies as much in the materiality of the garment as in a dancer's cellular body. Indeed, the techniques of contraction and release identified with Graham require, or demand, energetic propulsion against the tensile strength of cloth and this force articulates the formal subjectivity of the gestural attitude. Through the choreography, historical and personal conflicts between religious fundamentalism, secular modernity, and a capacious and convulsive pelvic sexuality become expressed concretely as physical resilience. These material chains embodying abstract social relations also gave Graham, and the dancer in the cylinder or skirt, a means to keep reinventing her autonomy as an artist.

In dance history, the materiality of the jersey skirt does not belong to Graham alone. Jersey wool gave modern dance the robust weight it was seeking, its tensile resilience, and fabric volume. The form allows for an overt feminization of the body, with the drape adjusting to the shifting of hips and expanding the space to be animated. Many other choreographers have relied on these shaping effects of flowing skirts and clinging jersey, now worn also by men, to support their choreography.

The skirt fabricated for modern dance is not that of a pretty girl or folk dress. Its cultural significance for experimental design and choreographic invention was fitted to a formalism that overflowed from visual art and fashion in Europe and America, while remaining flexible and refined. The specific shape was enacted by the knitting machine of American wool manufacturers, and its solemn drape by the pragmatics of proto-feminist design, and this combination marked a change in how a dancer moves and what she represents. The bias-cut skirt and the jersey tube could encircle the dancer's body and reveal her curves without restricting her gestures. But such a movement was expressive only for a time, since the artistic production of the dancer's dress would be further transformed through industrial and political conditions, and the diasporic diversification of fashion.

Cotton Petticoats and Stripes
Katherine Dunham

Squares, o square in Paris, infinite showplace, where the modiste Madame
Lamort winds and binds the restless ways of the world, those endless
ribbons, to ever-new creations of bow, frill, flower, cockade, and fruit—
> R.M. Rilke, cited in Benjamin (1999: 63)

In a diaphanous white petticoat threaded with dark lace at bodice and hem, the African American choreographer and dancer Katherine Dunham performs a twist, flicking and flirting the skirt lifted front and back. Her pose carries a spiral of energy from her toes through her hips, expanding through her torso into her fingers. Her costume plays a defining role in the movement. The delicate white strapless dress, a petticoat made of sheer voile or cotton batiste, contrasts with her darker skin. An embossed ruffle adjoins a gathered skirt. Both hem and bodice are edged with *broderie anglaise* in embroidered and cutwork lace, while a black ribbon adds a contrasting decoration that is reminiscent of blouses from Martinique (Kabir 2015: 218). The movement of air catches the skirt from below and creates a turbulent surface around Dunham's body. A portion of the skirt cascades over her navel, as if the fine woven fabric breathes, revealing a glimpse of frilly lace knickers. At the arch of her neck rests a pearl necklace, and a striped and knotted headscarf casts a shadow on her face.[1] By way of contrast, her downcast gaze suggests a self-possession that makes this dance portrait (Figure 3.1) taken in London both seductive and commanding.[2]

Dunham is recognized as a leading artist of black diasporic "fusion" in modern dance, and the costumes for her dance company, mostly designed in partnership with her husband John Pratt, form a central aspect of their dance repertoire from the late 1930s into the 1950s. With multiple costume changes in one program, the dancers were "decked out in singular hats and dresses, daring to wear feathers, bright colors, soft fabrics" (Clark and Johnson 2005: 5). Dance critics praised the authenticity of Dunham's costumes, citing the ways in which the dancers represented Haitian, Brazilian, African,

Fabrications. Rachel Fensham, Oxford University Press. © Oxford University Press 2026. DOI: 10.1093/9780197699638.003.0004

FIGURE 3.1 Katherine Dunham in *L'Ag'Ya*, 1938. Photographer unconfirmed, possibly Baron Studios. Courtesy of the Missouri Historical Society, St. Louis.

or "primitive" cultures. And in global and national concert tours, "Dunham charmed and dazzled audiences with brilliantly staged, exquisitely costumed, energetic productions," according to the African American dance critic Zita Allen. In her words, "Picture a pretty woman with sparkling eyes and skin the color of café au lait gliding across the stage in a sea of ruffles disguised as a John Pratt costume" (Allen 2001). We may not use these terms today, but these descriptions of the costume repertoire focus attention on Dunham's significant contribution to the fashioning of American modern dance.

Her pioneering role as an African American choreographer has been the subject of much scholarly attention. Joyce Aschenbrenner's *Katherine Dunham: Dancing a Life* (2002) was a seminal biography and has been followed by Joanna Dee Das's politically nuanced *Katherine Dunham: Dance and the African Diaspora.*[3] For Das, Dunham's artistic ambitions always moved beyond representations of "the minstrelsy, vaudeville, or Cotton Club jazz that dominated black dance in the 1930s" (2017: 26). When she established a mixed-race company and school in Chicago and presented *Fantasie Nègre* in 1932, the dancers wore costumes that resembled the severe lines of the Graham wool jersey tunics discussed in Chapter 2.

This choreography aligned Dunham with her ballet teacher, Ruth Page, and interpretive modern dance, but Dunham soon embarked on creating more ambitious dance dramas that could both educate and entertain. Hannah Durkin (2019) argues that Dunham's artistic practice, in its range and examination of class and race, was politically unsettling for middle-class and mixed-race communities.[4] Like Das, Durkin stresses that Dunham's "exploration within the field of spectacle, voyeurism, and racialized hierarchies" produced "distortions that defy straightforward interpretations" (2019: 137). As this chapter shows, there are many productive, if complicated, embodiments arising from the design and manufacture of affective desire in dress, particularly for modern black dance.

Valerie Steele's pioneering book and exhibition on *Dance and Fashion* (2014) devoted much of its chapter on black dance to costumes from Dunham choreography, particularly her Caribbean works, such as the "woman with a cigar" character in *Tropics and Le Jazz Hot* (1940). Steele argues that the Dunham Company's fashionable attire "introduced American audiences to sartorial details—bright, contrasting prints, intricate headwraps, and deep ruffles and flounces"—that became developed as a "tropical vocabulary in American sportswear" (2014: 274). Travel articles and political speeches also promoted the value of the Caribbean to American "soft power" diplomacy. In 1935, Thomas Kernan, writing for American *Vogue* from his hotel balcony in Martinique, lyricized about the "expanse of starched and embroidered petticoat" worn by the "island women" (Steele 2014: 274). Steele astutely identifies the whiteness of Dunham's "cotton skirt and blouse ensemble" as nostalgic inspiration for the white dresses worn in Alvin Ailey's choreography for his seminal black dance work, *Revelations* (1960):

> The effect of this "woman in white" costume is soft and feminine, yet boldly dynamic, as the skirts can be whipped into a frenzy of movement, hiding or exposing the legs. The look is historic and ethnic, but the color and silhouette render the costume ubiquitously female, and, on African American dancers, effectively represents black womanhood. (Steele 2014: 278)

For Steele, the white cotton dress—with its lacy trims and dynamic movement—has accumulated "expressive and passionate meaning" in relation to modern black dance (2014: 280).

This chapter presents a more nuanced picture: it argues that the dialectical costume of the white petticoat represents only one component in a choreographic system whose significations are more complex than they might at first appear. The malleability, use, and visibility of cotton fabrics are extremely prominent in the Dunham-Pratt design and use of costumes, but the visual and material fabrication of the full suite of costumes is also highly inventive, expensively crafted, and historically charged. From hats to men's trousers, and from skirts to bandanas, their multi-layered fabrication greatly enriches the material culture of mid-twentieth-century dance and entertainment history. The chapter also examines how the volume, design, and variations in dress of the Katherine Dunham Company impacted the movement potential of the dancing and new meanings generated for the choreographic repertoire.

Since the 1980s, when Dunham began establishing her own archives, her legacy has been preserved in a range of locations and in diverse media, ranging from video recordings to databases.[5] The Dunham costume archive at the Missouri Historical Museum in St. Louis is a vast collection assembled by former company members with an inventory produced by costume conservators, although not all items are catalogued. It includes more than a thousand items from the Dunham repertoire, as well as numerous props and personal dresses. The Katherine Dunham Museum in East St. Louis houses a selection of original hats and fans, which the company appears to have copied with replacement headdresses, while Dunham's documentary archive, preserved at the Southern Illinois University in Carbondale (SIUC), includes folders containing costume and design sketches, reference materials, and production notes. There are also account books that record costume expenses as well as track the company's fluctuating commercial fortunes.

Navigating this extensive and dispersed collection has required me to piece together clues—a faded dress with a series of photographs, a sketch with a date in repertoire—to construct what costume historian Veronica Isaac (2017: 131) calls "the multiple narratives present within historic stage costume." Over its twenty-year existence, Dunham's touring company sometimes produced sketches and letters referring to works that were never realized; more commonly, it remade costumes to new specifications with a similar design or modified them to fit new dancers in a role. Changes were also made for contextual reasons, perhaps to ensure that the costumes were fashionable or acceptable to different audiences. Traced in the continuum of time, as Isaac explains, garments become "ghosts" of the stories and memories of earlier dancers (2017:118).

But the cotton petticoat is more than the ghost of Dunham's dancers. It becomes a synecdoche for the millions of intimate female garments that have been eroticized and stylized by dance, fashion, and popular culture. In addition, the white petticoat is both a sign and the material artifact of socio-economic conditions for the choreography of African Americans in mid-century America, from which a complex range of histories and memories can be interwoven.

The "constellation" of white petticoats represents only one of many dialectical costumes in Dunham's seminal work L'Ag'Ya. Following the structure of that ballet, this chapter will unpick the narratives that inform its costume vocabulary and examine the construction and repetition of motifs, patterns, and alternative modes of dancing black history in "primitive dances" such as Rites de Passage from L'Afrique and Barrelhouse and Honky Tonk Train from Dunham's Americana dance suite. The conceptual organization of layers and stripes then accumulates a new significance in the design and understanding of black modern dance representations. There is also a problematic side of Dunham's repertoire: while she locates the frames of desire imposed on black bodies, the choreography also risks eliciting racist tropes that are familiar, or acceptable, to a white audience. By way of contrast, her archive offers a rich knowledge of the material conditions utilized by Dunham-Pratt for contesting and reconfiguring those frames of desire by fashioning the stagecraft of modern dance dress in mid-century America.

L'Ag'Ya (1936) and John Pratt

L'Ag'Ya debuted in 1936 under the banner Ballet Fedré in Chicago and later toured to New York and was the first full-length ballet choreographed by Dunham. During two years of ethnographic fieldwork research in the Caribbean in 1935–1936, Dunham had been creatively inspired by her observations of extant dance practices. She had witnessed unique village festivals, noting details of rhythm, footwork, and costume in her diaries, and filmed the occasions with the assistance of the British cinematographer Fred Allsop.[6] On returning to Chicago, she began developing the narrative for a full-length dance drama with funding from the Federal Dance Project.[7] While crafting a new genre of dance storytelling and recalling the couple dances and traditional folk forms she had witnessed, Dunham also experimented with the "plastic aspect of the dance," which epitomized the interpretative approach of modern choreographic methods.[8]

L'Ag'Ya is based on a narrative in which two men, Alcide and Julot, compete for the favors of an attractive woman, performed by Dunham. Performed at full scale for just over thirty minutes, the choreography calls for nine men and nine women, as well as two "native" drummers and singers (Figure 3.2). It consists of five parts: Overture, Market Scene, Pas de Deux, Zombie Scene, and finally a Festival Scene. It combines ballet and modern dance, as well as traditional folk and social dance forms such as the Cuban habanera, Brazilian majumba, and Martinique's themzouk, beguine, and ag'ya. Das (2017: 61) describes its genre hybridity as the "hallmark of a diasporic aesthetic." In material terms, Dunham now had the resources and professional support previously restricted to white artists. From this season forward, the company's dramaturgical ambitions are marked by scale—"A very large wardrobe room is required with a great deal of hanging facilities as there are many costumes"—with multiple works and dancers in each show.[9]

Her production team included John Pratt, a graduate of the Chicago Art Institute who designed for several local choreographers, including Page and her dance school and company. Both Pratt and Dunham were active and influential in the dance and visual arts scene of bohemian Chicago.[10] The artistic young white man with powerful connections and access to resources soon formed an alliance with Dunham, who was in the final years of a brief, unhappy marriage. Their interracial relationship was unusual, but they must have both understood they could achieve more together than alone. Aschenbrenner argues that their "union of art, theater, dance and text . . . was the powerhouse that carried the Dunham company through world tours for thirty years" (2002: 117). Whatever the substance of their collaboration, Pratt changed the look and production values of

FIGURE 3.2 "Festival Scene" from *L'Ag'Ya*, 1938. Photograph by Edward Lewis Kennedy c. 1940s. Courtesy of Special Collections Research Center, Southern Illinois University Carbondale.

Dunham's choreography as together they met the forces of an expanding global entertainment industry.

In biographies and program notes, Pratt features as the company's costume designer. Reviewing the premiere of *L'Ag'Ya*, the Chicago *Tribune* remarks on "John Pratt's handsome tropical costumes," and elsewhere, stage manager John Brooks observes that Pratt "designed all of the costumes, most of the stage, most of the lighting" (Aschenbrenner 2002: 117, 191). Pratt also designed many of Dunham's own dresses, and they made an extremely elegant society couple. For a while, Pratt continued to make fashion sketches and design for other Chicago choreographers, but when the company expanded and embarked on extensive tours, his role as production supervisor and company administrator eclipsed his other work.[11] Dunham herself commissioned other designers, including John Carlis Jr., Vladimir Barjansky, Karl Priebe, and Vani, but Pratt's oversight of costume remained the determinant of the Company's practical and visual aesthetics.[12]

It is essential to assess Pratt's role to understand the gendered, racial, and economic implications of the costume choreography. According to Aschenbrenner, the *L'Ag'Ya* costumes included "authentic hats, designs, and materials [Dunham] had brought back from the Caribbean" (2002: 117), but Ananya Kabir argues that they also drew on historical sources (2015: 219). The archival record demonstrates their further imaginative elaboration by Pratt. He writes, "My interest is in designing dance cloth, dynamic cloth, cloth that moves, rather than in the pageantry of costumes. . . . I've always been more interested in dance design than in historical postures" (Missouri History Museum 2008). The costumes were always about creating viable movement on stage, extending the capacity of cloth to communicate through the dancing body. With high-quality design and construction, Dunham-Pratt's costumes also function as fashion statements in African American performance culture.

The creative pairing of Pratt and Dunham complicates relations between appropriation and authenticity, since all the costumes were assemblages, taken from varied material contexts and always consciously theatrical. At first, Pratt was not personally familiar with the Caribbean, and his initial designs for L'Ag'Ya seem to have been copied directly from ethnographic films made during Dunham's research trip: the women wore striped skirts and plain scoop-neck blouses, while the men dangled straw hats. After the production's transfer to New York, or perhaps when it was remounted for national touring by Sol Hurok in 1943, the costumes were enhanced using images from magazines, the news media, and fashion photography. The comparative iconography of costume illustrations in the archive adds new significance to the embodied transmission and ethnographic veracity of Dunham's repertoire.

Cotton Dresses and *Washerwomen* (1945, 1952)

Unlike the diaphanous petticoat with which this chapter opened, the cotton skirts that feature in L'Ag'Ya are heavy with gathers and ruffles. Similar skirts appear across Dunham's later works, *Cabin in the Sky* (1943), *Acaraje* (1940), and *Bahiana/Batucada* (1939). The opening scene of L'Ag'Ya is set in a marketplace in the Martinique village of Vauclin and romanticizes the subsistence economy; island life appears as an idyllic pastorale where men sell fish and women carry trays laden with cakes and fruit. The choreography combines delicate reverie with mimetic character dancing. Adding to this casual abundance, the nine female dancers wear skirts scattered with embroidered flowers and enlarged by petticoats with ruffles and lace (Figure 3.3), while the men have "ragged trousers" in striped cotton.[13]

Six surviving "ladies' dresses" and two pinafores from L'Ag'Ya reveal their robust construction. Fabricated from patterned seersucker cotton with a slight sheen that gives the impression of a softer, somewhat luminous surface, the skirts are shaped by dense gathering at the waist with cascading tiers attached to the heavy cotton trimmings, which consist of both eyelet and crocheted lace on each garment (Figure 3.4).[14] Variations in

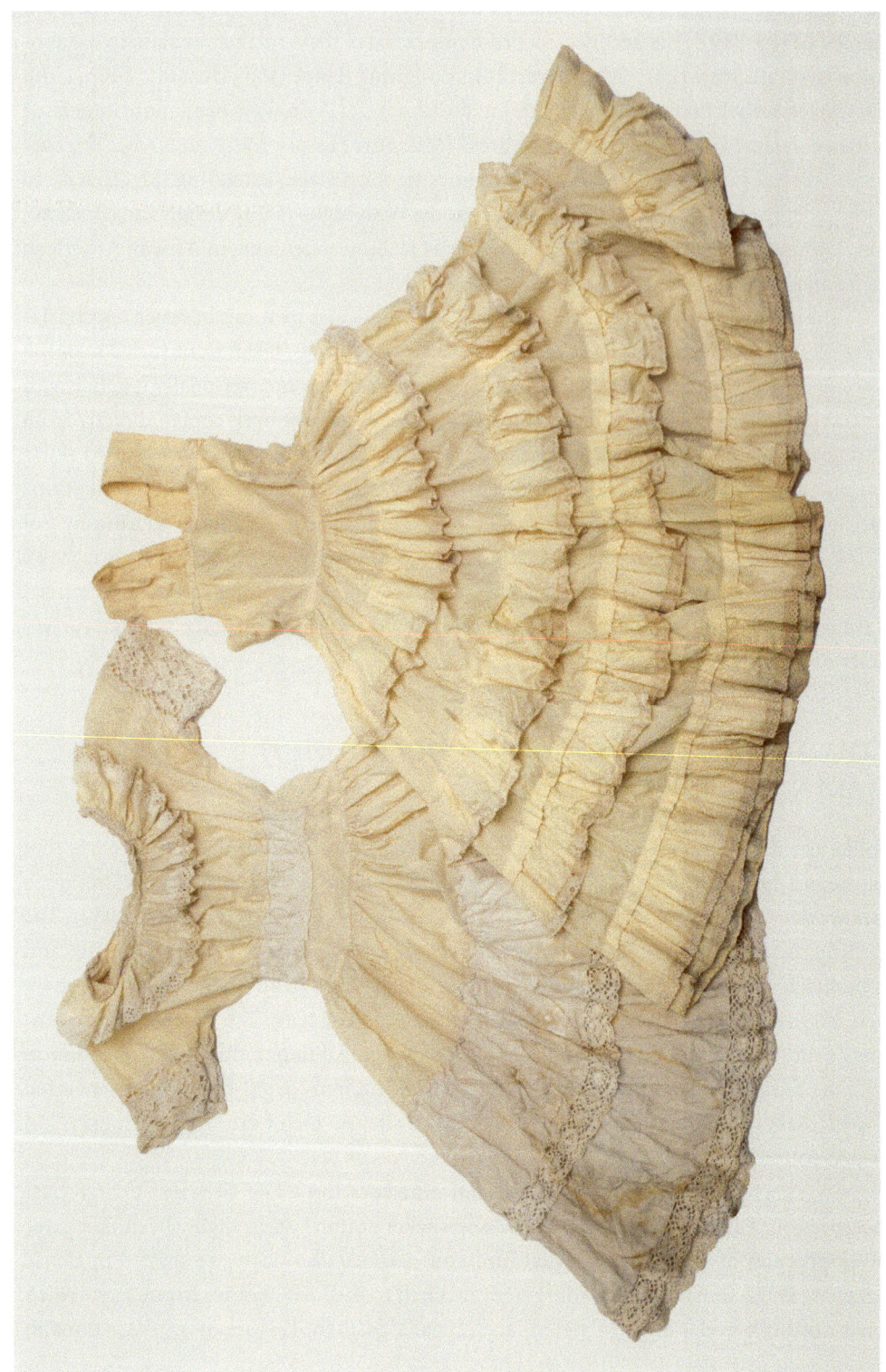

FIGURE 3.3 Cream cotton dresses, *L'Ag'Ya*, 1938. Photograph by Cary Horton. Courtesy of the Missouri Historical Society, St. Louis.

FIGURE 3.4 Skirt detail of cream cotton dress, *L'Ag'Ya*, 1938. Photograph by Cary Horton. Courtesy of the Missouri Historical Society, St. Louis.

FIGURE 3.5 Bodice detail of cream cotton dress, *L'Ag'Ya*, 1938. Photograph by Cary Horton. Courtesy of the Missouri Historical Society, St. Louis.

the neckline reflect changes in this costume between 1938 and 1954, and the color is now cream as the fabric has aged with washing (Figure 3.5). The bib-like lace front on the bodice accentuates a sense of virtuous maidenhood, especially paired with the petticoats' numerous layers of overstitched ruffles.[15] While suggesting the strict morality of a colonized Christian community, this costume also establishes a false sense of nostalgia for a past that was less troubled than the Caribbean present.

The use of seersucker in these costumes was not nostalgic but remarkably contemporary in the 1930s. Trade in this fabric originated with the East India Company and its etymology in Persian recalls the "milk and sugar" of its granular, puckered surface. Allowing for more air movement, this double-weave cotton became popular in

New Orleans in the early twentieth century to provide smart but comfortable suits for the humid climate. Pratt adapts this fabric into heavy workaday outfits for the market women, with full skirts that provide scope for vigorous circular movements while remaining gracious and modest.

These costumes also activate consciousness of the cotton industry's fraught history. Cotton is a semi-tropical plant with seed heads containing white, gauzy bolls attached to spiky cases, and numerous labor-intensive steps were required to turn the bolls into woven fabric. The bolls had to be plucked, separated from their cases, de-seeded, cleaned, fluffed, spun, and woven into textiles ranging from dense carpets to delicate muslins. This ancient fiber has been used in garments and household items for many thousands of years, with cotton's range extending from Peru to North Africa, India, and China. In the industrial era, the "lust for cotton" played a key role in the exploitation of the Global South, both on and offshore (Perry 2022: xviii).

In *Cotton: The Fabric That Made the Modern World* (2017), the cultural historian Giorgio Riello argues that cotton production has transformed global relations of labor, production, and consumption; furthermore, attempts to control the cotton trade have led to competition between nations, the establishment of market elites, and expanding patterns of commodity circulation.[16] The American historian Sven Beckert follows a similar theme in *The Empire of Cotton*, pointing out that the production of cotton was dependent on a "regime of violent supervision and virtually ceaseless exploitation" (2014: 91). Slavery was that system, and it was the backbreaking labor of millions of enslaved people that built the competitive economy of the textile industries in Britain and Europe.

In the eighteenth century, much cotton production was based in the Caribbean, especially in Haiti, then a French colony, where half a million Africans were subjected to a brutally repressive regime in the plantations. The island had the world's highest cotton yields and was a source of fabulous wealth for the slave owners until the late eighteenth century, when the resident black workers of Haiti mounted an uprising. Violence ran intermittently from 1791 until 1804, concluding only when the French withdrew and Haiti was proclaimed an independent republic. During the uprising, cotton growing in the Caribbean collapsed, and the cotton industry shifted its focus to the Southern United States.[17]

For almost sixty years, British manufacturers prospered from their close relations with the owners of American plantations, but this cozy arrangement collapsed in the 1860s. The outbreak of the American Civil War in 1861 disrupted the supply of raw cotton, leading to factory closures and unemployment in Britain's cotton towns. For many years, raw cotton remained difficult to obtain, and its price tripled when manufacturers could not locate a supply. European textile manufacturers soon began exploring new sources of raw cotton from Africa and the Middle East.

When slavery in the United States ended in 1865, the empire of cotton was forced to shift to paying for wage labor, but "the rhythm of work, and the pattern of plantation life" barely changed (Beckert 2014: 283). This remained the case for decades. Eartha Kitt, a singer, dancer, and activist who joined Dunham's company in the 1940s, recalled working on cotton fields as a girl, when the "sharp bulbs left her hands raw from the hours of trying to meet her quota."[18] Many African Americans sought to escape the chronic poverty of the plantations and the discrimination and violence that marked the Jim Crow era in the South. Between 1910 and 1970, in what became known as the Great Migration, some six million African workers moved to the industrial cities of the northern and western states.

Control of cotton production became a major point of international tension, particularly during the 1930s Depression, when the United States government offered agricultural subsidies on a sufficient scale to depress world prices, aiming to undercut other producer nations and restart American cotton production. With local cotton growing and manufacturing both reviving, fabric designers began experimenting with cheaper cotton textiles, such as seersucker and brushed cotton moleskin. A greater range of printed fabrics also infiltrated fashion, stage, and costume design. Techniques were developed to embellish cotton so it could substitute for more expensive fabrics, and the American clothing manufacturers became increasingly determined to displace their European counterparts in the fashion industry.

One inspiration for the market women's costumes, located in the Carbondale Design files, appears in a 1940s advertising sketch prepared by the Mexican artist Miguel Covarrubias for the Container Corporation of America. It depicts three black women in colorful full-length skirts with petticoat ruffles carrying a range of goods on their heads, not just foodstuffs but boxes and buckets intended for American consumers. This image shows how "chains of spatial connections" can appear in many guises: "starting with trade and empire, then turning inwards to the material self, before tracing connections between modern networks, energy use and people's habits" (Trentman 2017: 203). This chain of connections includes the Dunham-Pratt dance works, because cotton fabrics recall the global histories surrounding the transport of human labor, and the use of black labor to carry cargo.

The abundance of cotton in the Dunham repertoire exploits cumulative associations between slavery, plantations, the Southern states, and Northern industry, but the cotton petticoat in the dance also recognizes the efforts of working black women to survive. It seems significant that Dunham's personal history was shaped by a childhood spent in a laundry managed by her parents where she often assisted by folding the clothes. This background contrasts vividly with Martha Graham's middle-class exposure to wool manufacturing and fashion design, but it would have helped Dunham become attuned to differences between garments defined by class.

The continued trace of histories of female labor can be found in *Washerwomen*, first performed for a New York production called *Carib Song* in 1945 but filmed in 1952, a work that was explicit about the connections between black women and care for clothing.[19] "Even after migrating to the North, washing other people's clothes remained one of the only independent occupations open to Black Women," according to Helen

FIGURE 3.6 *Washerwomen,* 1956. Photograph by Richard Tucker. Courtesy of Special Collections Research Center, Southern Illinois University Carbondale. Image © The New York Public Library.

Bradley Foster (1997: 129).[20] Dunham's choreography transforms the productive effort of laundry work into movement effects fabricated by gathered skirts. (Figure 3.6).

The dancers enter carrying flat baskets on their heads filled with white cotton sheets. They are the women who do the laundry of the wealthy, and they wear flat scarves with mottled patterns to carry their loads. The stage is relatively bare, with only one wooden pedestal structure. A vocal dancer calls to the audience while the women gather and sort the sheets. One woman (Dunham) removes her jacket, exposing bare singlet arms, and begins a solo spinning in a pirouette, toes turned up and jiggling, until the others leave their baskets and join her. With tight-waisted scarves, relative to the loose flow of sheets, they let the shoulder straps fall down their arms and their jacket tails fling widely until they are tossed aside. The muscular energetic work of washing requires their arms to be free. With vigorous hip movements, they lean back through their buttocks, then lunge forward with the sheets in their hands. This action agitates the white cotton skirts, which resemble swirling suds.

The dancers kick up and from side to side, swinging their arms in contra-motion. They form pairs to grab each other's sheets, then twist them together, as if wringing out the water. They perform these gestures with great hilarity, smiling and laughing together: "Washing is such fun," they seem to say, as if giving the lie to the necessity of labor. Many theatrical entertainments and documentary films of that period represented workers as "happy" colonial subjects. During the duets, Dunham rushes through the ensemble, waving her sheet behind her like a flag, and takes center stage. The dancers form a tightly knit circle, revolving together, then falling rapidly to the floor and using their leonine arms to knead the sheets. In a final sequence with individual baskets on their heads, they whip from side to side in rhumba rhythm. Their hems lift as they sway, overtly enchanting the spectator, and the film ends abruptly with one woman's sheets cascading out of her bundle.

Choreographically, the white sheets fold around high and low diagonal planes, so that the flourishes appear baroque, an impression furthered by the ecstatic transformation of the dancers' faces and the sparkle of brilliant white lighting. The movement vocabulary echoes the rhythmic patterns of the drumming, while teetering semiotically between erotic titillation and the celebration of female labor. The frenzy of this ensemble is dependent on the effect of the massed costumes that animate the dancers on stage. While this is not a revolutionary dance depicting protests and strikes, which feature in other modern dance pieces, it generates an affective dynamic of collectivity and a kinesthesia of effort that inhabits each of the bodies and their expression.

The "Pettycoat" in a "pas de deux"

Under the heading "Costume requirements," a Dunham stage diary notes: "Kine should be asked to work on pettycoats. Archie suggests that no net be used but strong tulle against danger of rips."[21] The word "petticoat" comes from the French *petit* and describes a small garment worn under an outer dress or coat. In women's clothing, the petticoat evolves from a gown or nightshirt worn as an undergarment to more elaborate versions worn by wealthy women underneath the expensive, decorative fabrics of their external dress. By the mid-nineteenth century, this garment had itself become something to display in layers of fabric that support the shaping of a dress, visible below a crinoline or in the neck of a bustier. As markers of status, ornate petticoats became trimmed with lace, used finer fabrics, and were often pleated across the front. In poorer households, the petticoat was an important additional layer of warmth and practicality, often protecting the day-dress from wear and tear. If they could afford more than one or two items of clothing, women would wear a petticoat along with a dress and/or another coat. The sketch of Loulouse, Dunham's character in *L'Ag'Ya*, in Figure 3.7 depicts her in the simple form of a short cotton petticoat.

The silk tunics of Chapter 1 have similarities with petticoats as undergarments, but they differ in purpose. In Roland Barthes's cataloguing of costume genera, he considers the petticoat a distinct classification because it has symbolic iconicity and unique functionality: "Though invisible, the petticoat can contribute to meaning by altering the volume or the form of the skirt." He adds a footnote: "the fullness of the skirt is often moderate and soft or else imposing and stiffened by petticoats" (1990: 108). Petticoats became associated with dance in two ways: the shortened, corseted versions became the

FIGURE 3.7 John Pratt (attrib.), "Loulouse," *L'Ag'Ya,* 1938. Undated design sketch. Courtesy of Special Collections Research Center, Southern Illinois University Carbondale.

classical stiff ballet tutu, while frothy underskirts and black tights, often worn with no panties, became a mainstay of cabaret. Petticoats stiffened by the use of "strong tulle"; as even Walter Benjamin surmises, provide an "agreeable and salutary coolness which the limbs enjoy underneath" (1999: 63). Lifting such soft skirts for a peek could also excite the audience of a chorus line. Thus, the dance petticoat, far from assuring simple personal enjoyment, became indelibly associated with female desirability.

Both the *pas de deux* and the Charm Dance of *L'Ag'Ya* give Dunham visible roles that require dance virtuosity. The former is an elegant duet between Loulouse and her lover Alcide, while the latter is an intoxicating dance with the usurper Julot. For the *pas de deux*, Dunham wears a short, basic petticoat, recognizable from the sketch by the rectangular neckline and single row of lace on the bodice (Figure 3.8). The soft cotton appears domestic and locally made, and it lacks the full gathered skirts worn by mature women. Performing as an ingénue, she wears the fresh white dress as a kind of prize. Like the market women, she wears a headscarf, but without the burdens they carry, and she skips lightly as she flirts with her dance partner. Does she lighten her step to embody the formerly enslaved, and under what circumstances can a black woman in a petticoat enjoy an innocent coupling?

Dunham is free to dance on the concert stage in this semi-undressed state, but she was performing at a time when other black bodies were less free; although technically at liberty, African Americans living in the South during the 1930s would have had very few clothes. The abundant petticoats in the Dunham productions might be seen as a synecdoche for the abundance awaiting those who escaped plantation histories and joined the Great Migration.

FIGURE 3.8 Katherine Dunham with Vanoye Aikens in "Pas de Deux" from *L'Ag'Ya*, c. 1938. Photographer unknown. Courtesy of the Missouri Historical Society, St. Louis.

In the colonial period, mulatta women working as servants were represented in popular magazines and imperial lithographs wearing short pinafores, thus confirming the connection between the slip, often a hand-me-down from the white mistress, and their seduction by the master. In another work, *Los Indios* (1941), and a segment called Plantation Dances, Dunham-Pratt writes: "Field Hands costumes will be used," and "No shoes needed."[22] In a choreography photographed in 1950, the men working the fields wore loose cotton striped trousers trimmed with black cord to emphasize their holes and ragged hems (Figure 3.9).

Likewise, female workers on plantations often only possessed the clothes issued as rations by their owners, according to dress historian Betty Wood: a "short skirt of coarse linen," or a "petticoat" which left their "Upper body. . . bare," with perhaps "a handkerchief to cover the head," and a "shimmy of coarse yellow cotton was often all they had even through the winter" (1995: 58, 148).

Appropriation of European styles of "clothing, jewelry—rings, earrings, and distinctive hairstyles" allowed enslaved peoples to "assert their individuality to each other as well as to their owners and other whites" (Wood 1995: 61). This "self-adornment, and the financial outlay it entailed in local stores . . . was an integral aspect, a visual expression,

FIGURE 3.9 Striped seersucker trousers, *Los Indios*, 1950. Photograph by Cary Horton. Courtesy of the Missouri Historical Society.

of a continuing struggle to assert individuality, dignity, pride, and self-worth" (Wood 1995: 61). Fugitives often took control of their attire by adding minor adornments such as a "black or silver lace hat-band" or "red garters" (1995: 59).[23] And those who escaped took items of clothing from their masters in the service of a new life (Wood 1995: 61).

In the Dunham choreography, the field trousers and petticoats were appropriated into an entirely different yet synchronous visual and dress economy. In the Caribbean, the former enslaved were influenced by French culture and possessed greater autonomy, for which clothing was an essential status marker. European styles were relentlessly studied, copied, and adapted in moves that remind us of Homi Bhabha's notion of colonial mimicry. Dunham had keenly observed the significance of mimicry in Martinique and Haiti, where colonized peoples had learned to imitate the behavior of their former masters; for example, colonial genres of dancing such as the quadrille were very popular (Thomas 2004: 283). Moreover, items of clothing in the Caribbean participate in a wide range of economic transactions, including bartering clothes for food, trading them for labor, and gifting personal favors (within the bounds of decency).

There is a palpable and purposeful accretion of these multiple meanings into Dunham's choreography, even though the reality of the master's wardrobe was distant from her immediate experience. Unlike raw cotton fibers or the rough-textured garments of bondswomen, the matter of Dunham's cotton petticoat ripples in her coquettish dancing. Alcide teases her with his scarf, looping it around her waist and pulling her close in the *pas de deux*: she is his willing partner but not (yet) fully seduced. Their animated costume play is, however, only the first act of Dunham's encounter with the potent vitality of men from the Caribbean islands.

"Primitive Dances": *Rites de Passage* (1941)

A much-cited feature of Dunham's repertoire is her imaginative, partially researched, invention of choreographies from the African American diaspora. In addition to her personal knowledge of Caribbean dance forms, she learned dances from Brazil and Colombia from fellow dancers and explored their cultural significance through readings in symbolic anthropology. Fascinated by the effects of trance and other forms of collective transformation, Dunham incorporated many of these ritualized performance genres into her choreography. Her own writings on "primitive dance" outline "primitive patterns" and social systems that respect the "tradition" of these dances, and in her teaching she identified rhythmic structures that connected to the solar plexus as a source of movement (Das 2017: 45).[24] Furthermore, the so-called primitive dances in her repertoire were enlarged by heightened visual effects in her choreography.[25]

Her first move in this direction was the representation of the Zombies in *L'Ag'Ya*, which used threatening or fearful figures from Haitian "Vodou" culture.[26] Presumed to be dead spirits living in the jungle, these figures symbolize the counter-reality to a village world assimilated to colonial economic and social life.[27] In the dramatic choreography of this central scene, scary figures emerge from each side of the stage walking with stiff legs and arms, and splayed fingers and toes. The male dancers wear scalloped, wide-legged trousers edged with lighter-colored piping and loose open-sleeved jackets showing bare chests; according to the costume inventory, there are "stilts, 7 Black Straw Hats, 6 Black Kerchiefs, 8 Black Jersey Dresses, [and] 8 Black Jersey Men's Shirts." Pratt's design for the Zombie King (Figure 3.10) illustrates him as a hairy creature wearing a top hat and black jacket with tufts of raffia extruded from his neck, hat, and underskirts.

Although seemingly rudimentary, such costumes are the precursor to other representations of "primitive" dances that Dunham-Pratt created in works such as *Rites de Passage* (1941), *Melanesian Love Ritual Dance* (1942), *Primitive Mysteries* (1943), *and Raratonga* (1943). Some of these choreographies only appear in repertoire for short periods, while others are adapted and extended; together they play a central role in Dunham's conception of the erotic nature of courtship rituals, while also exploring notions of collective obligation in "primitive culture." For anthropologists such as Arnold van Gennep, the author of *Rites de Passage* (1909), key societal rituals surround an individual's acceptance into adulthood. For Dunham and subsequent black artists, the concept of rites of passage

FIGURE 3.10 John Pratt (attrib.), "Zombie King," *L'Ag'Ya,* 1938. Undated design sketch. Courtesy of Special Collections Research Center, Southern Illinois University Carbondale.

has provided important processes for imagining connections back to a shared African heritage—legitimizing African diasporic roots—or forward into a more inclusive society (Johnson and Oliver 2017; Burt 2001).

From the perspective of this book, however, the costumes also instigate considerations about the extent to which "costuming the primitive" depends on talismanic tropes—"Cretan–Etruscan–Egyptian"—or specific material properties.[28] Pratt's visual research for many Dunham costumes transmitted general concepts, as well as adding specific ornamental details to their representations of alterity, or the "tribal," in dance.

The design folders in the archive include a series of postcards called "L'Afrique qui Disparait" produced by the Polish photographer Casimir Zagourski. These images echoed the mid-century assimilationist theory that "tribal and traditional cultures" were "disappearing" and that Europeans should document them as a matter of right or necessity (Geary 2002). They depict "African men and women" at ritual dances (unspecified), a circle of men wearing fringed skirts, a "girl dancer of the Congo region" wearing a close-fitted beaded and braided headdress, and a woman from Lusambo with a bound torso and knotted skirt. On the verso of the last image, Pratt has inscribed "a midwife—a witch-doctor (female) her dress may inspire you for one or other act!"[29]

One cannot but be struck by the inventiveness of the garments created by Pratt-Dunham in *Rites de Passage*, visible in Figures 3.11 to 3.13, the careful detailing, and the singular use of cord, which has been coiled, twisted, looped, and knotted. They establish a vocabulary linked to the uses of twine in basketry or fishing—they are coarse, robust, and decidedly sensuous, with an array of potential effects. Together, the attributes of rope accrue power because the same raw material becomes adapted for different purposes.

FIGURE 3.11 Brown and red cord masks, *Rites de Passage,* 1941. Photograph by Cary Horton. Courtesy of the Missouri Historical Society, St. Louis.

FIGURE 3.12 Brown and green cord headdresses, *Rites de Passage,* 1941. Photograph by Cary Horton. Courtesy of the Missouri Historical Society, St. Louis.

FIGURE 3.13 Mask for Witch Doctor costume, *Rites de Passage,* 1941. Photograph by Cary Horton. Courtesy of the Missouri Historical Society, St. Louis.

Further costumes for *Rites de Passage* are listed as "6 Rope Skirts, 6 Rope Bras, 7 Rope Bottoms—Brown, 1 Black Rope Bottom . . . and 4 Piece Death Costume (Witch), Extra Trimming, 1 Black Tailcoat (Witch Doctor)." The men wear the densely braided green and black rope loincloths with long rope fringing. The women wear rope bras and shorts (Figure 3.14) with braided black wigs shaped into cones, while both men and women have rope arm and ankle bracelets constructed from coiled cording wound back and forth and stitched onto robust calico undergarments, then edged with olive green or red braid. Hours of work went into making these costumes and fitting them to different bodies. The use of rope has a double connotation: the hanging rope braids suggest both trailing vines in the jungle and key parts of the body covered in matted hair.

Another Zagourski photograph depicting a man in a tall, feathered cap and long sarong with ankle bracelets is copied into the Witch Doctor costume, which consisted of red shaggy rope covered with clanging cowbells and tokens. In this role, the Dunham dancer Talley Beatty wears ribbed cord leggings and leaps in the air with a forward pedal kick, making the looped ropes fly up and between his legs in different directions, amplifying the aerodynamics of his jump. His exposed torso is also like a series of ropes

FIGURE 3.14 Green cord brassiere and drawers, *Rites de Passage*, 1941. Photograph by Cary Horton. Courtesy of the Missouri Historical Society, St. Louis.

rippling in the action. Dancing in front of a concert stage, the contrast between Beatty in the ropes and the suited white men in the orchestra could not be greater.

The choreography in *Rites de Passage* includes a "fertility" ritual in which young women perform a sexual initiation; in Figure 3.15, dancers in the rope bikinis and headdresses prepare the scene with gestures invoking the unsettlement of maidenhood about to occur on the stage. In this photograph, taken a decade after the dance's creation, the gaze of watchers in the wings intensifies the gap between staged enactment and ritual presence that was so important to Dunham. Later, a vivid net cape with red satin rings scattered across its surface is thrown over the young maiden to suggest the blood of puberty. This red cloth was possibly inspired by the symbolism of Serge Diaghilev's *The Rite of Spring* for the Ballets Russes. In the "funeral ritual," the dancers form lines to bear a young man above their heads, as well as squatting to barter or exchange hand gestures. The rope costumes expose the dancers' muscularity while the black wigs and face masks anonymize their visages; simultaneously human and mythic being.

By way of contrast to the ensemble costumes for *Rites de Passage*, Dunham wears a gorgeous silk chiffon dress dyed in subtle hues of gray, pale red, and cream, decorated with light cord piping across the draped panels of a relatively narrow skirt (Figure 3.16).

FIGURE 3.15 Two dancers in front of stage performing "Fertility" from *Rites de Passage,* 1941. Unknown photographer, photographed in Singapore, c. 1957. Courtesy of the Missouri Historical Society, St. Louis.

FIGURE 3.16 Detail of dress for Queen costume, *Rites de Passage*, 1941. Photograph by Cary Horton. Courtesy of the Missouri Historical Society, St. Louis.

With side slits to let it move, its wavy lines animate the body. The waistband and collar, which alternate red, black, and cream bindings, are reminiscent of the elongated necks and long earrings of the Nuba people from central Sudan. Dunham's headdress is an elaborate rope wig consisting of a cylindrical coil of braids threaded by red pipe cleaners that dangle braided plastic tendrils. It is a regal crown, a theatrical imitation of braiding, an ornamentation signaling Africanist presence in her choreography.[30]

With heavy eye makeup elongating her eyes and darkening her lips, Dunham attempts to pray to ward off her fear that she is expected to procreate with her dead husband's brother. Beside her stands the Warrior Chief, wearing his tall-feathered headdress, a bold necklace, and rope loincloth. Dunham's attractive costume works both to shield her as a dancer and to ensure her dramatic vulnerability as a character to his symbolic power.

Given the more somber and threatening scenes in *Rites de Passage*, the duet of "mutual attraction" that underpins the fertility ritual has an intense structural dynamic. The male dancer hooks his body around the female dancer by raising his shoulders and extending his arms; as much as she is attracted, she is also nervous. Dunham believed her dancers needed to understand the sexual significance of the choreography as both an individual and communal rite. When reconstructing the work in 1970, Dunham was adamant that Doris Bennett should have "the burning sort of African heat in her, she is . . . a girl who is being really aroused . . . [he is] drawing her into womanhood . . . sort of evangelized into the feeling . . . which should be so magnetic . . . with this slight pulsation in their stomach."[31] The slim costumes, the exposed bodies, and the powerful combinations of red, black, and dull green in the tapestry of rope were enhancements ensuring that representation of the primitive was strange and otherworldly, as much as lived and felt by her dancers, even if knowledge of the rites was more important to Dunham at a personal and professional level.

In the creative invention of these costumes, rope, masks, feathers, armbands, and anklets assemble the material signs of the "primitive" as properties that are frequently reworked into modern dance choreography. They also participate in a wider infusion of African aesthetics into clothing history; French fashion magazines of the 1930s, for instance, promoted Africanist styles, the adornment of bracelets, and exotic fabrics with "primitive" textile motifs (Rovine 2015: 96).[32] In Dunham's work, the costumes were delocalized; they were never accurate representations of specific cultures or communities. Rather, the aim was to assist the spectators to see "traditions" as if in a "past," yet potent world. In a most complicated and problematic way, these modernist constructions transposed French colonialist ideas of the "primitive" to the concert stage through fabulous outfits.

The Stripes of Haiti

When Dunham arrived in Haiti to complete her fieldwork, the country had recently been through a period of internal political turmoil, and its economic and political conditions were dominated by the requirements of American foreign policy.[33] During the 1930s, the United States relied on cheap labor from Haiti to prop up its cotton and sugar industries, while also looking to the Haitian government to provide a political buffer against socialism in the Caribbean.[34] Dunham tried to navigate the politics in both directions; she had an affair with a leading Haitian opposition politician, who supported her research, while also cultivating connections with the ruling elite (Das 2017: 48).[35] Both in urban society and in the villages, she encountered many debates about Haiti's economic and political sovereignty as a modernizing island culture. She also became exposed to influential Caribbean writers and intellectuals, including Jean-Paul Mars, a Haitian anthropologist and politician, who was one of the first to explore how Africanist histories were defined by slavery, and the Martinique poet Aimé Césaire, who later evolved the philosophy of Négritude, a pan-Africanist critique of the oppressions inflicted by colonialism. The vehemence of these critical perspectives became apparent to Dunham as she spent her time absorbing and documenting the local cultural festivals and spiritual rituals.[36] Complex mixtures of attachment and distance, revelation and confusion, are not uncommon in anthropological research, but as an artist, Dunham wanted to transform her experience into choreography. This insight meant that the ethnographic process of sifting reality from impression would unfold in public view. Not surprisingly, a messy, incomplete picture emerges on stage, typified by the various colored stripes that appear in the costumes.

In the program notes describing the Festival Scene that precedes the fight, *l'ag'ya*, at the climax of the performance, the confusion of references is explicit. The scene begins with the "graciousness of a 19th century mazourka of the islands, followed by a struggle of a woman possessed by sex." For this dance, the "costumes are elaborate and elegant imitating those from the court of Louis XIV. The Women walk around fanning themselves."[37] Space, time, and style are hybrid.

The Festival women wear cropped jackets and skirts with multi-layered panniers, both in clashing stripes, while the Festival men wear flounced white shirts and shortened trousers (Figure 3.17). The costume inventory lists extensive items: "20 Fans, 5 Frames for Female Hats, 14 Ladies Jackets—Stripe, 14 Shirts—Stripe, 13 Pairs White Pantaloons, 12 Petticoats—White with Pink Trim, 14 Festival Pants, 14 Festival Shirts." In the archive, sets of candy-striped headdresses and jackets appear in three color combinations—red, pink, and yellow with white, perhaps also black and white—folded and stitched on the diagonal. On stage, the women's darker jackets, pinched in at the waist, make a dramatic contrast to the tiered skirts and lacy bodices, and when in movement, the conical hats bob around and tilt at awkward angles as the women lean into one another and their male partners.

FIGURE 3.17 Minnie Ellis with male dancer in ruffled shirt in *L'Ag'Ya*, 1938. Photographer unknown. Courtesy of the Missouri Historical Society, St. Louis.

For the French, Haiti was the "pearl of the Antilles," so the documentary archive includes extensive visual references to this Empire. These include colored lithographs from the Comédie-Française, depicting actors in silk dresses with lace bodices, wearing elaborate bustles and tiered headdresses, or carrying feathered fans (Figure 3.18).

Another potent design reference can be found in two postcards with illustrations of an African man and woman dressed in distinctive costumes, the first seated on a rock and the second in profile. First produced in 1794, during the Haitian Revolution, these lithographs were widely circulated to mark Haiti's racial egalitarianism with the French citizen. The male figure wears a loose white blouse with a red collar sash, red and yellow striped "sans-culottes" (workingmen's trousers, which were associated with revolutionaries), and a peaked headdress. The woman wears pearl drop earrings, a necklace, and a ribbon bearing the insignia of a level indicating their equal status. Her Phrygian cap and under-blouse are white with red stripes, and her collared dress is yellow with burgundy stripes (Figure 3.19). With the inscriptions "Moi libre"—me free—and "Moi aussi"—me too!—these engravings espouse the "free" society fought for by the charismatic Toussaint Louverture during Haiti's extended uprising. This complex representation of the stripes

FIGURE 3.18 Two women, Modes de Paris. Courtesy of Special Collections Research Center, Southern Illinois University Carbondale.

FIGURE 3.19 Moi Libre Aussi, Postcard, Société des Ais de L'abbe Gregoire. Courtesy of Special Collections Research Center, Southern Illinois University Carbondale.

worn by the liberated black citizen informed multiple design and color motifs for the dances in Dunham's repertoire.

What else might stripes on a costume bring to the performance? In his study of African and Afro-American art and philosophy, Robert Farris Thompson explains that striped broadloom fabrics, known as "kente," were a legacy of weaving practices from West Africa that were maintained by plantation workers and their communities in French and British colonies.[38] Strips of differing widths in "high affect colors" placed side by side are like the melodic lines on a musical stave, and Thompson suggests such patterns produce "willful, percussively contrastive, bold arrangements" (1983: 209).

In a cloth, there is more to clashing colors than sheer delight, because specific colors represent unique gods—"red and white honors Shango; a rainbow-like gathering of strips in many delicate hues honors Oshumare, Yoruba serpent-rainbow of the sky" (Thompson 1983: 214). An interruption by a non-striped or otherwise patterned fabric pauses the flow and can ward off evil spirits; the remedy is to procure "a shirt made of strips of red, white, and blue" (Thompson 1983: 221–222). These Mande cloth patterns of Ghana and the Ivory Coast have been adapted by modern technologies and European influences; although Thomson argues that these "rhythmic cloths" retain the effects of syncopation and "aesthetic intensity," even in a preference for striped cotton (1983: 209).

In Dunham's choreography, there is repeated use of "rhythmic cloths," in headdresses, in men's trousers, in striped fabric tied around the waist or used as bandanas, waved as props, or thrown in the air (Figure 3.20).[39] The syncopation of eighteen dancers dancing with these *L'Ag'Ya* striped costumes becomes kaleidoscopic. The festive

FIGURE 3.20 Striped scarves, *L'Ag'Ya,* 1938. Photograph by Cary Horton. Courtesy of the Missouri Historical Society, St. Louis.

atmosphere expressed in cotton candy stripes generates a "serpent-rainbow" carnival of color and commotion, along with the affective memory of powerful survival practices.

In another study of African American clothing, Helen Bradley Foster traced the head-wrap back to the seventeenth century in West Africa, from where it was brought to the Caribbean by enslaved women (1997: 282). In *L'Ag'Ya,* the freed subject's headdress becomes the towering striped hat of the female dancer, whose shapes and colors function as symbolic and kinetic communicative devices. In photographs, these costumes appear minimalist black and white, but the archival materials expose dynamic color contrasts between men's fiesta pants and women's headscarves, or between jackets and fans, so that the vibrant, garish, and strikingly bold ripples of choreographic power re-emerge.

Elaborate adornments, such as the conical headdresses, also exact a price from the dancer since they restrict movement in arresting ways. If stripes elongate and punctuate kinetic energy, the turning and whirling of the head works in counterpoint. Revolutionary and elegant at the same time, these striped costumes in *L'Ag'Ya* both mimic and assemble the multiple traditions of a divided Haiti in the process of weaving this hybrid stylization for the American concert stage. Stripes, or "strips" as they are also named in the Dunham costume archives, become not just an incidental textile motif but one that conveys the legacy of black histories, as well as adding dramatic intensity to performance.

"Americana" (1940–1953)

From the late 1930s, as her company toured more extensively, Dunham became aware that she could not continue creating dances derived from the folklore of other countries, and she choreographed a range of works that drew on popular African American dance forms such as "ragtime, blues, cakewalk, spiritual, and gospel."[40] In her dance programs, these dances usually formed the third section of a show under the generic title "Americana." Many of them were sourced with the assistance of brilliant black musicians and composers such as Noble Sissle, Eubie Blake, and Tom Fletcher.[41]

The choreography for *Barrelhouse* (1939) includes two dancers while a "second girl" sits on a bar stool alone, behind a bead curtain, wearing a green dress; it is "Saturday night in Jacksonville" in the 1920s.[42] Dunham dances with Vanoye Aikens, her long-time dance partner, and the couple groove together, performing what Durkin calls Dunham's "iconic celebration of mature female sexuality," in a competitive dance that involves unmistakable flirting (2019: 180). In photographs of Dunham dancing *Barrelhouse* over many years, she can be seen in a tight-fitting dress, her weight down low, her hips shimmying, her fishnet stockings taut with matching slingback peep-toe shoes. The shiny dress has split side seams to allow her twisting motions, and the dance requires a degree of acting to convey the melancholy desperation of the late-night liaison.

Production notes record the *Barrelhouse* dress as "satin royal blue" with "black horizontal bands of black beads [*sic*] fringes, royal blue cloche, royal blue sling pumps, royal blue net stockings." Dunham herself recalls the movement of the beads assisting with the animation of the shimmy:

> The steady half rotation, the first movement of the "twist," being toe ending in a second movement, weight dropped to the heel, the strength of the "twist" would cause these circles of black jet beads to whirl halfway round, then stop with a jolt when shifting weight.[43]

A dress in the archive is easily identified with its boat neck and black bead fringing, layered down arms and bodice; accompanied by a velvet beret studded with black animal prints and a dashing fish-tail (Figure 3.21). This fabulous dress is now in shades of pink and orange (Figure 3.22), fading as a result of the many occasions on which it was worn, and the beret is blotchy and brown. The only evidence that this costume was once blue lies under the neck facing, where there are the remains of a purplish tinge.

In the earliest photographs of Barrelhouse, Aikens wore a college-style boater hat, black check pants, and an oversized jacket, stylized in the zoot suit look popular among African American youth at the time, but it does not appear in later images. One wonders if the "zoot suit riots" of 1943 discredited the original outfit, particularly for white audiences?[44] Nonetheless, the archive retains a handsome black-and-white houndstooth suit with a velvet collar and matching jacket (Figure 3.24), but given its heavy wool fabrication, it must have

FIGURE 3.21 Dress and hat worn by Katherine Dunham, *Barrelhouse,* 1938. Photograph by Cary Horton. Courtesy of the Missouri Historical Society, St. Louis.

FIGURE 3.22 Detail of dress worn by Katherine Dunham, *Barrelhouse,* 1938. Photograph by Cary Horton. Courtesy of the Missouri Historical Society, St. Louis.

FIGURE 3.23 Detail of houndstooth suit from *Barrelhouse*, 1938. Photograph by Cary Horton. Courtesy of the Missouri Historical Society, St. Louis.

been replaced by the lighter jacket in performance. The original jacket with its black velvet collar shows no sign of wear, whereas the trousers have elasticized straps, a testament to the necessity for them to stay up during the energetic dancing (Figure 3.23). There is a new calico lining, and Velcro has replaced the original fly-fastening.

In these outfits, Dunham and Aikens are quite the pair to catch the eye on a dance floor (Figure 3.25).[45] Having abandoned the petticoats, Dunham's tight-fitting dress invites a different range of movement, the shimmy and corkscrew of the torso predating "the twist" of the 1960s.

They resemble a contemporaneous painting by Archibald Motley, *Nightlife* (1943), which depicts a bar in Bronzeville, a central neighborhood for Chicago's African American communities during and after the war. African American artists and writers would congregate in this district, and Dunham opened one of her several dance studios there after success on the white side of town eluded her. Motley's vivid painting is an image of black modernity, with well-dressed men and women relaxing together, intimate in conversation, drinking and dancing (Figure 3.26). A woman at the bar is wearing a

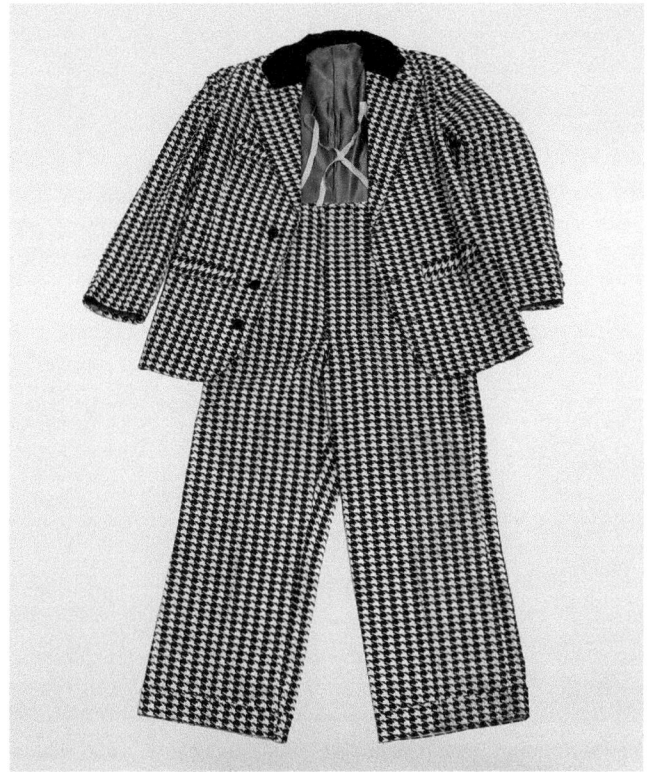

FIGURE 3.24 Houndstooth suit, *Barrelhouse,* 1938. Photograph by Cary Horton. Courtesy of the Missouri Historical Society, St. Louis.

tilted red beret shaped like the one from the archive, and a couple jiving in the foreground could be Dunham and Aikens.

Given the popularity of *Barrelhouse* in the repertoire, there is much evidence of wear, change, and modifications in the costumes as the dancers aged and the *mise en scene* needed updating. Images from the 1940s show Dunham in a black and pink plaid pencil skirt dress with her partner in gingham trousers—and a generally more comic style of moving. By the 1950s, there are other careful modifications—the beret is replaced by a blue felt cloche, and Dunham replaces the fringe dress with a similar but less fitted outfit, in which rows of black net substitute for the fringing. The net effect lacks surface playfulness. Aikens's outfit adapts to mirror a college preppy style with "pale blue v-neck sweater, gray striped trousers, gray and black cap, black shoes."[46]

This preppy look from the late 1950s and early 1960s has been radically revalued as "black Ivy" by Jason Jules, who argues that black men appropriated the style of a conservative white majority to engender their own sense of respectability and control (2021). Rather than regard the wearing of button-down shirts, loafers, pleated trousers, and soft-shoulder three-button jackets as co-option by white aesthetics, Jules argues it

FIGURE 3.25 Katherine Dunham and Vanoye Aikens in *Barrelhouse*, 1938. Photograph by Maurice Seymour c. 1941. Courtesy of the Katherine Dunham House Museum.

FIGURE 3.26 Archibald J. Motley Jr., *Nightlife*, 1943. Image © The Art Institute of Chicago/Art Resource/Scala, Florence, 2025. Artwork © John Archibald Motley Jr./Copyright Agency, 2025.

was an intentional choice to reframe their appearance as African Americans struggled for civil rights or toured as international musicians. The "black Ivy" look in Dunham's choreography—whether in flannel trousers or pin-striped suits—transferred from musical stages to dance as her dancers sought to transmit contemporary and local values about how the black male body might appear. The addition of the wool cap to Aikens's costume is another variation on this theme.

The later dancing style is still cheeky but less low-down, more a two-step forward and back, and the dancers are less in sync; they watch each other carefully. The *mise en scene* signifies the ironies of American culture, a Coca-Cola sign and bead curtain that masks the sweat and deterioration of the blue satin frock. What cannot be contained as they jive is the vitality in this dress with the "black horizontal bands" of beading and its flicking fringes. Like all flapper dresses, it swiveled and sparkled, anticipating the choreographic excitement for when the dancer finds her man.

When Dunham tours Europe, according to Durkin, her "interpretation of African American vernacular dance styles" and her choice of costumes for her suite of African American dances, *Jazz in Five Movements*, drew on her lived experience of "Midwestern black neighborhoods" (2019: 47). The authentication of a distinctive fashion and stylization of the black body belongs to this Southside Chicago community. An expanding company wardrobe also riffs on the shiny surfaces of new fabrics, such as cheaper satins, stretch materials, printed cottons decorated by many types of ribbons, feathers, beads, buttons, and other dangling adornments.

Other costumes associated with *Americana* include checked outfits for *Honky Tonk Train* (1938), which are a medley of clashing plaids—"Boy Black Taffeta Plaid Shirts—7 Girls Dresses Taffeta Plaid—4." In this vivacious choreography, the women's flared skirts were adorned with black and gold ribbons while the men wore tunic-style tops with wide collars and open sleeves. Each garment had an elaborate construction of diagonal panels, providing strong contrasting lines of black and orange or red and blue.[47] The fabric in these garments is remarkable, a high-quality satin strengthened with expensive black cotton lining, and every dress had to be assembled between the torso and sleeve, or bodice and skirt, for each dancer, which suggests a skilled seamstress was at work (Figure 3.27). The diamond design produces a greater fullness in the skirts but also gives dynamic patterning to the comic mayhem generated by the swing tunes (Figure 3.28). The visual effect of these strong color contrasts was relaxed but energizing—clashing lines across force fields—for a patchwork of bodies jiving in competition for attention, yes, but tolerant of difference.

The sequences in "Americana" were rapid, with costume changes providing an overt indication of a new musical rhythm or mood. For the men, the pants were often interchangeable between works—tan, peasant, yellow cotton, brown corduroy, as well as striped trousers.[48] The women wore more distinctive garments that were evocative but fragile. Five "pink satin" dresses for the female dancers of *Cakewalk* had narrow stitched pleats on drop-waists, that are now sweat-stained. In *Floyd's Guitar Blues* (1946), the lead

FIGURE 3.27 Dress and shirt with silk plaid patchwork, *Honky Tonk Train,* 1941. Photograph by Cary Horton. Courtesy of the Missouri Historical Society, St. Louis.

FIGURE 3.28 Detail of dress with silk plaid patchwork, *Honky Tonk Train,* 1941. Photograph by Cary Horton. Courtesy of the Missouri Historical Society, St. Louis.

FIGURE 3.29 Detail of red satin dress from *Cakewalk*, c. 1940s. Photograph by Cary Horton. Courtesy of the Missouri Historical Society, St. Louis.

dancer wore an olive-green off-the-shoulder "elastic tight-fitting dress" with covered buttons and a pleated flapper skirt with a headdress of "vulture feathers." In this choreography, Dunham "wiggles her legs together, shakes head, bouncing up and down—then scratches left foot on right leg" before starting to "sing the blues" with her partner nattily dressed in green.[49] Sadly, the sleek and shiny "black ciré silk" dress for *Tango* (1951) is absent from the archive, but the "black bugle beads" that adorned its front were found on the bodice of a red satin cocktail dress attributed to *Cakewalk* (Figure 3.29).

Striptease in a "Sea of Ruffles"

When the emergent bourgeoisie began attending balls and theater in Paris during the 1890s, the *arrivistes* were scorned by the noble class, who sought to protect their sense of distinction by tightening the dress codes:

> Eight flounces will be envied by rival dresses, with only four, five or six flounces. To have eight declares: I do things more lavishly than you; I am elegant to the

eighth degree; I have more than your two quarterings of nobility; I value myself and am worth two flounces more than you. (Wollen 2003: 137)

Too many flounces on a dress was regarded as an ostentatious sign of wealth and status in the modern public sphere. In the chapter introduction, I referred to "the sea of ruffles" attributed to Dunham's choreography, which could translate as postcolonial ostentation. Flounces appear frequently in clothes worn by both genders as a sign of layering effects and meanings that can be attributed to costume.

In Pratt's confection of the larger dance numbers of *L'Ag'Ya*. Alcide and the other male dancers wore ruffled collarless shirts, not unlike the ornately draped curtains, known as "Italians." In the design sketch in Figure 3.30, Alcide's dance costume includes a striped triangle kerchief at the waist, knickerbocker trousers that sculpt his thighs, and long black stockings to the knees (Figure 3.31). This silhouette of a stage gallant extends from the *danseur noble* to the male fashion icon.

The resulting shirt, made of apricot and peach silk, has three rows of tiny, ribbed pleats on each side of the buttoned front. There is a lace seersucker trimming, and the puff sleeves have rows of ruffles.[50] With the tight gathering of threads, these ruffles give volume, bounce, and flamboyance to the shirt. It is difficult to imagine the original colors of this garment with its small moth-holes and discoloration. The yellow knitting yarn stitched along the ruffles is a later addition, now feathered, and probably deployed to brighten up the fading contours.

Let us then consider the history of flounces. A flounce is an additional length of fabric attached by gathering, or perhaps fine pleating, to an existing piece of material. The

FIGURE 3.30 John Pratt (attrib.), "Alcide," *L'Ag'Ya,* 1938. Undated design sketch. Courtesy of Special Collections Research Center, Southern Illinois University Carbondale.

FIGURE 3.31 Pink silk shirt with ruffles, *L'Ag'Ya,* 1938. Photograph by Cary Horton. Courtesy of the Missouri Historical Society, St. Louis.

excess volume gives the flounce a mischievous turn on the edge of a more formal shape on a skirt or shirt sleeve. The flounce was a notable fashion statement for women during the Napoleonic period, as the grumpy French matron above suggests, but it was also much favored by gentlemen who wanted to impress their hosts by exposing their elegant shirts. As men's fashions in Europe became more streamlined for urban society, this display component of male attire became associated with propriety, exuberance, and wealth.

The ruffle was not only a historical reference but a contemporary fashion statement in the 1930s. As men's clothing moved away from stiff shirts toward softer fabrics and turn-down collars, the informal, "radical" look in high society became a decorative shirt-front. Men's dinner shirts with rows of ruffles extending down and across the front could convey class without a jacket, particularly, as one advertisement suggested, on "warm summer nights." This shirt style influenced white colonial fashions in the Caribbean and may have been worn by Pratt himself, either in Chicago or on a journey south. It was particularly popular with Caribbean musicians entertaining white audiences (Figure 3.32). The ruffled shirt also makes a retro-appearance for James Bond in *His Majesty's Secret Service*, set in a hot and sticky Portugal in 1969.

Such historical conditions establish the value that the white petticoat and ruffled shirt have in Dunham's repertoire since these commodity forms also measure the excess and abstract labor costs required to produce and maintain them. As we indicated in the introduction, Marx's theory of value depends on the social relations of production in "which an object of utility attains the possibility of becoming an exchange value" (1990: 182). Human labor power, even in the abstract, still requires concrete, embodied labor to make a shirt or compose a piece of music that becomes translated into a commodity, even in the sensuous form of the ruffled shirt.

FIGURE 3.32 White bolero jacket with yellow ruffles, *L'Ag'Ya,* 1938. Photograph by Cary Horton. Courtesy of the Missouri Historical Society, St. Louis.

Receipts in the archives indicate the continuous requirements of money in exchange for items of clothing that required replacement or reproduction.[51] To reflect on these petticoats and shirts as commodities that attain exchange value for the Dunham company is to recognize the labor of the seamstresses and tailors producing these costumes. The French journal *Querelle*, illustrating a Dunham tour, pictures a dark-haired woman, possibly their wardrobe mistress, Beryl Bethune, bent over a sewing machine, repairing costumes. She is surrounded by rows and rows of white fabric ruffles.[52] Like the character Rapunzel in children's books, her labor is enchained to the weaving of straw into gold—the transformation of sheets into ruffled dresses to be worn on dancing bodies. The exchange value exceeds the value of the object because the production of value is a dance fantasy, the redemption of the princess.

Benjamin highlights the Utopian dimension of fashion in the *Arcades Project*, as Peter Wollen suggests, by extending the Marxist abstraction of labor as

> utopian potential to the commodity itself and therefore the bourgeois dreamworld. The fashion object is defined by the processes and abstractions of commodity, but it is also concrete and sensuous. It is this sensuousness that mediates the relation of systemic, abstract exchangeability to the individual. (Rosen 2003: 13)

In this sense, the fabrication of tropical fantasy in *L'Ag'Ya* abstracts black plantation or domestic labor and replaces that labor with an excess of style, a dreamworld of skirts and ruffles, stripes and hats.

After the Festival Scene with its mélange of costumes representing pre- and post-colonial politics, the villain Julot returns from the forest carrying a magic charm from the Zombies, and Loulouse surrenders to its power. She performs "a love dance of ancient Africa,"[53] as a slow, sensuous striptease. Surrounded by other dancers and musicians in their ruffled shirts, Julot wears a garish, bright-colored shirt with patterned trousers and encircles her with enticing gestures.[54] As she dances, Dunham's multi-layered petticoats,

FIGURE 3.33 Katherine Dunham in "Striptease," *L'Ag'Ya,* 1938. Photograph by Roger Wood in London, September 1948. Courtesy of Special Collections Research Center, Southern Illinois University Carbondale. Image: Royal Opera House/ArenaPAL.

fitted beneath a striped blouson jacket, require lifting and removing. With exertion, the heavy embossed skirts are held aloft and dropped like cascading turrets, until eventually she is only wearing a gauzy underskirt and knickers (Figure 3.33). A pink-edged net petticoat in the archive is linked to this dance, but it differs from the iconic costume that opened this chapter. By the late 1940s and early 1950s, the sheer fabric of the striptease petticoat has become sexy lingerie, and the simpler cotton undergarments of the earlier dances has disappeared.

Whether nervous or entranced, the petticoat "girl" in *L'Ag'Ya* carries the dance pulse into the solar plexus and shimmers, waving her skirts, inviting the gaze.[55] "When Loulouse is stripped to her last pettycoat, Julot has already encircled her surrendering body . . . Alcide breaks through the stronghold of the two villagers . . . challenging his rival to the Ag'Ya and the famed fighting dance begins."

The erotic charge of this choreography is explicit in the staging of seduction and in the use of the skirts, and the layering of petticoats to manage the staging of desire. The "magic potion" removes intention from Loulouse, making it evident that Dunham is acting, not living the part. Akin to competitive dances such as *capoeira*, the *L'Ag'Ya* is an improvised battle dance regulated and enjoyed by men. Dunham always expected the precision and excitement of a "lethal battle" between her male dancers; the two rivals fight to the death, with the hero Alcide succumbing as a tragic finale to the ballet.

Conclusion

In this chapter's epigraph, Benjamin cites the poet Rilke observing a woman whose creative efforts at fashion are expended on twisting "those endless ribbons, to ever-new creations of bow, frill, flower, cockade, and fruit." Of all the dance artists in this book, Dunham's archive and repertoire offer the most extensive display of costume excess and ornamentation. It is truly a cornucopia of styles, fabrics, and theatrical design.

This chapter touches only briefly on the sensuous delights of the material objects that comprise the costumes—the silks, cottons, plaids, laces, ribbons, buttons, ropes, beads, tucks, frills, and nets. It also celebrates the creative relationship between Pratt and Dunham, extending over the course of the company's independent performing career, from its emergence during the Federal Theater Project to Hollywood, and from the vaudeville circuit to Paris and international tours, that gave unparalleled aesthetic consistency to the world-making of its choreography.

Pratt's work introduced sophisticated strands of fashion and historical dress research into a dance vocabulary that could only be assembled with intimate proximity to the making of choreography. Even when his work introduces problematic elements—unexpected appropriations and affectations—the quality of design and detailed fabrication of costumes was always a priority, and resources were harnessed to ensure that the company looked stylish. Given the scale of the company, varying between fourteen and twenty artists, determining there were consistent dress codes across the repertoire was a demanding undertaking.[56] This commitment to dressing well—"your hat is not the same shape as the others have. Please get it checked!"—determined the quality of performance.[57] Specific styles of dress—whether straw hat, rope bikini, or zoot suit—assisted the characterization of a dance sequence, particularly given rapid changes in genre and location, and influenced the variability of movement in the choreography itself. Hats tipping toward one another, whirling skirts, ragged trousers stamping, became distinctive components of the dance repertoire, often moving at an extreme pace (Figure 3.34).

Such transformation of materials, practices, and cultural values shaped interracial entertainments such as Dunham's in the United States before civil rights. With both Pratt and Dunham fabricating the visual and embodied effects of "large numbers of costumes," there is a process of *metissage*, a mixing of elements, from French imperial culture into cultures that were virtually unknown, such as those of Africa. This appropriation involved the theft of images and ideas from multiple sources, as well as the purchase of creative labor from artisans and manufacturers. Even costumes that dress historians might identify as "Caribbean" were the product of hybrid exchanges between European culture, enslaved persons, and newly freed communities adapting to climates and trading relationships in the Americas. Dunham's costume repertoire, therefore, documents a pan-American dress aesthetic that links the American South with a new form and stylization of black modernity.

This book attends to how genres of costume repeat in dance and in choreography. Fragments of the petticoat continue in the more static net of the ballet tutu, but in *L'Ag'Ya*, the cotton petticoat animates the energetic flow and labor of Dunham's dancers. Its density and its layering commanded effort and released the performers to enjoy the garment's embodied weight. *En masse*, the colored lines cross, flow, lifting like a light wave through

FIGURE 3.34 Katherine Dunham and her company in *L'Ag'Ya*, 1938, captured in what appears to be multiple exposures. Photographer unknown. Courtesy of the Missouri Historical Society, St. Louis.

historical space and time. The petticoat has been the costume of the enslaved girl and the working black woman, the underskirt of the prostitute, and the fabric supporting the bourgeois woman's crinoline. Made of cotton, its manufacture carries the material trace of economies that have been linked to slavery and empire. Do these multiple inversions and appropriations of the cotton petticoat, stripes, and flounces in and beyond Dunham's archive signify accommodation or subversion? Probably both, because the creative production of, and demands for, costume styles belonging to African American modern dance are not yet exhausted.

The Spandex Unitard

Merce Cunningham

The costume of the cyclist, as an early and unconscious prefiguration of sportswear, corresponds to the dream prototypes that, a little before or a little later, are at work in the factory or the automobile.
 Benjamin (1999: 62)

In the opening of *Suite for Five* (1952), Carolyn Brown, in lemon yellow leotard and tights, has a long, exquisite solo with extended balances, followed by a slow walk around a rectangle; she is both sunbeam and daffodil, stamen and hovering bee, the yellow giving light. A final duet with the choreographer Merce Cunningham is "an anguished sequence that ends with him holding his hand plaintively out to the audience (Figure 4.1);" center stage; and he wears a blue polo shirt and tights—her tonal opposite—that soaks in the yellow radiance and afterglow (Riley II 1998: 249).

Color was always a significant aspect of the choreographic transmission of affect in his works, and in this costume, Cunningham figures as a "blue boy," not unlike Gainsborough's famous painting of the same name.[1] The young man of that portrait is an aristocratic subject self-conscious about the impression of his comportment—hand on hip, buttoned waistcoat, and neat breeches in Prussian blue—but, as with Cunningham, dignified in repose.

The color blue has a long history in visual art, particularly cobalt blue in its association with the cloak of the Virgin Mary in Christian paintings. This deep blue pigment was traditionally sourced from lapis lazuli, a rare stone mined in parts of the Urals (Finlay 2002: 318).[2] Many other shades of blue exist, not least the indigo of blue jeans and the porcelain blue of a summer sky—both colors favored by Cunningham and his collaborator John Cage; Cunningham's gray-blue eyes were often partnered by a cornflower blue shirt, and his choice of casual dress and rehearsal clothing frequently included a similar polo shirt with cotton jersey trousers or tracksuit pants pulled up tight around the crotch

Fabrications. Rachel Fensham, Oxford University Press. © Oxford University Press 2026. DOI: 10.1093/9780197699638.003.0005

FIGURE 4.1 Carolyn Brown and Merce Cunningham in *Suite for Five,* 1956. Photograph by John Ross. Courtesy of the Merce Cunningham Trust and the Jerome Robbins Dance Division, The New York Public Library.

by a waist cord. In this close-fitting but comfortable version of a "dance uniform," he always appeared self-consciously at ease (Figure 4.2).

This chapter focuses on the elasticized dance combination of leotard and tights, or unitard, which became the ubiquitous dance silhouette for the second half of the twentieth century. The unitard stretches elasticized fabric from the neck through the pelvis and legs to the ankle, sometimes with a back opening, sometimes with none. Leotards and leggings are not the same outfit since they distinguish the waist and leg joints, but they are companions to this chapter. Both costumes create an overall look for the torso, arms, and legs, while leaving the feet, hands, and head free of clothing. They also partially obscure the contours of the waist, and when made of spandex, they are highly responsive to the body surface. The wearer of this smooth, fitted garment feels the physical sensations on the skin just as a viewer perceives the visual image of the dancer's body in outline.

The history of the unitard overlaps with the textile economy of synthetics, and the combination of leotard and tights has mirrored production technologies that were changing garment construction in the United States during the second half of the twentieth century. Innovations in the petrochemical industry, for instance, gave increasing strength to the "stretch" of the fabrics from which this ensemble for dancing would emerge. As a

FIGURE 4.2 Imogen Cunningham, *Merce Cunningham, Dancer 6*, 1957. © 2025 Imogen Cunningham Trust, https://www.ImogenCunningham.com.

result, synthetics, both as materials and as colored dyes, became integral to the appearance of modern dance.

In addition to the silhouette, the chapter focuses on how color acts in choreography, such as the Cunningham-Brown duet described above. Color in the visual arts is a field of immense complexity, shaped by understandings of perception and informed by artists such as Josef Albers, who used theory to discipline the experimental study of color. Designers for dance are sensitive not only to the properties of a fabric but also to the interactions of different colors in an ensemble. An emphasis on color was reinforced when color film came into general use to record dance. In addition to its narrative functions, abstract dance became a medium for experimentation with the tonal dynamics of costumes that could be kinetic, spatial, and affective. With the unitard, as dancer Jennifer Goggans says, "Color is the costume"; it animates and defines the silhouette for the spectator (2023). As a partner to choreography, color can also introduce variation, intensity, contrast, and mood.

This chapter examines the role of the leotard-tights silhouette with a concentration on works by the choreographer Merce Cunningham and the uses of color in his choreographic repertoire. For sixty years, Cunningham remained committed to the abstraction of movement and to a range of collaborations that include composers, visual artists, designers, and dancers. From the founding of the Merce Cunningham Dance Company (MCDC) in 1953, we can trace the various ways in which a selection of Cunningham designers—Remy Charlip, Robert Rauschenberg, Mark Lancaster, Suzanne Gallo, and Marsha Skinner—explored, modified, and contested the potential of the "basic Cunningham stage uniform" to engage with art, identities, and concepts from their own milieux.

Fortunately, Cunningham's archive has been well curated by archivists such as the late David Vaughan. Former company members produce his works under license, and the Merce Cunningham Trust curates and circulates key legacy projects. Most costumes are housed at Minneapolis's Walker Art Center, which was associated with the Cunningham company from the 1970s. They have been carefully catalogued, documented, and stored: as art objects, however, they are no longer viewed only as costumes but seen as artifacts of avant-garde art. The Walker has displayed Cunningham items in key exhibitions and published catalogues such as *Merce Cunningham: Common Time* (2017). Its archives hold many relevant resources, including design drawings, fabric samples, photographs, correspondence, and production notes. This collection includes costume multiples and variations that are critical to understanding the company's evolution and exploring how designers met the challenges of working "independently" but in partnership with the aesthetics and demands of a busy dance company.

To focus on the unitard is not to discount other costumes in Cunningham's repertoire, which include practice clothes, Rauschenberg's comical and disruptive experiments, and the fashion designer Rei Kawakubo's striped and padded "Bump" costumes for *Scenario* (1997) (English 2011: 72). There was also an occasional lapse into more conventional gendered costumes, such as the "full-skirted, bare-shouldered nylon jersey dresses" of *Banjo* (1953) or the halter-neck printed summer frocks in *Views on Stage* (2004) (Brown 2007: 73). This chapter, however, concentrates on how the specific properties of the unitard became identified with the shape and movement vocabulary of abstract contemporary dance. And, as the examples progress, it offers insights into tensions between the organic and the inorganic, nature and technologies, as materialities at work in dance costumes.

Cunningham and *Antic Meet* (1958)

In her memoir *Chance and Circumstance,* Carolyn Brown, who spent twenty years dancing in Cunningham's company, argues that he was never interested in costume; he "preferred the body unadorned," she says, except for that "troublesome area—the female derrière" (2007: 568, 147). The unisex uniform of tights and leotards suited Cunningham's demand for a design landscape that did not interfere with his choreography by elaborating racial or gendered otherness. Brown suggests that his insistence on a standard costume

FIGURE 4.3 Detail of wool sweater from Robert Rauschenberg, costumes for *Antic Meet,* 1958. Photograph by Cameron Wittig. Walker Art Center. Artwork © Robert Rauschenberg Foundation. VAGA at ARS/Copyright Agency, 2025.

FIGURE 4.4 Wool sweater from Robert Rauschenberg, costumes for *Antic Meet,* 1958. Photograph by Cameron Wittig. Walker Art Center. Artwork © Robert Rauschenberg Foundation. VAGA at ARS/Copyright Agency, 2025.

restricted the creativity of his design collaborators (2007: 147). But costume evidence in the archives belies this claim; it suggests that Cunningham was intensely aware of what he himself wore and how it moved, and that he cared about how the visual aesthetics of costume contributed to his choreography.

For instance, Cunningham might change his own clothes during a performance as if to resist the limitations of a single costume within a larger ensemble; he also

FIGURE 4.5 The Merce Cunningham Dance Company in "Bacchus and Cohorts," *Antic Meet,* 1958. Photograph by Anna Finke, 2011. Courtesy of the Merce Cunningham Trust and the Jerome Robbins Dance Division, The New York Public Library.

used costumes as props and extensions of other imaginative reckonings.[3] Writing on his solo for *Rebus* (1975), Mike Steele describes how Cunningham, "first in pajamas and finally in a red leotard, generates the momentum for the rest of the troupe as he dances . . . Cunningham is like a medieval jester—mad, clever, tragic at once" (Steele 1975). This fire-red leotard symbolizing his frequent role as a clown or trickster is held in the Walker archives. In other cases, Cunningham intervened creatively in the costume vocabulary for his dancers.[4] Confronted with an Andy Warhol installation of shiny, inflated cushions for *Rainforest* (1968) and a request for naked bodies, the artist Jasper Johns selected flesh-pink unitards as a substitute, and Cunningham suggested he "roughen them up a bit 'as if the skin were torn'" (Brown 2007: 500–501). Well before punk fashion, these ripped and knotted costumes created a surreal contrast between the flying, flailing movements of the dancers and the shiny reflective surface of the pillows bouncing on stage (Barnes 1968).

Even more poignant were Cunningham's contributions to the costumes for *Antic Meet* (1958), which included a "bizarre sweater with four sleeves and no opening for the head" (Figures 4.3 and 4.4) (Brown 2007: 214). The whole company contributed knitted triangles while touring together in their bus, and Cunningham devised a comedic sketch in this costume that channeled Martha Graham, entangled in many cylinders of knitted fabric. Dancing with four "swans" encumbered by heavy swathes of parachute fabric in dresses designed by Rauschenberg, Cunningham wriggles and wrestles with an inner animal self (Figure 4.5). The harlequinesque triangles and loose knitted texture of his costume add animated color to the floppy, crazed movement of the dance.

This book will not examine the details of Cunningham's personal involvements with costume, which would lead to the individual and idiosyncratic. My purpose here is to explore the typical, the repetitions, and variations that create the "uniform" for many contemporary dancers on multiple occasions. I will, however, briefly return to Cunningham's own costume sensibility in the conclusion to the chapter.

Color Theory: Remy Charlip and *Minutiae* (1954)

The most endearing costumes in the Cunningham collection are those made for *Minutiae* (1954) by the dancer-choreographer Remy Charlip (1929–2012).[5] First performed on December 8, 1954, at the Brooklyn Academy of Music, *Minutiae* consolidated the artistic alliance between Cunningham, the composer Cage, the visual artist Rauschenberg, and a cast of dancers who had participated in the Black Mountain College summer program the previous year: Marianne Preger-Simon, Jo Anne Melsher, Remy Charlip, Carol Brown, Viola Farber, and Anita Dencks (Harris 1987: 234). Rauschenberg's set was a freestanding trio of screens covered in brightly colored fabric, mostly in hot pinks, reds, and yellows.[6] Brown describes Charlip's costumes as "a complicated collage of rich, vibrant colors," and the Merce Cunningham Trust records them with "bright sections of dyed color in reds, pinks, oranges, yellows, blues, purples" (Brown 2007: 115).[7]

The archival garments are notable as material objects for three reasons. The first is that all the leotards are made of thick, knitted cotton, while the men's tunic tops are in a coarse-grained textured weave. Robust fabrics were required to endure the hard work of performance—including "scrunching along the floor on my behind" (Brown 2007: 113).[8] The second feature is that the seams are hand-stitched, so the rolled edges around the neck and legs are uneven at key points and would have curled and rolled as the dancers moved. These non-stretch garments have retained individual wrinkles and bumps, particularly at the knees, elbows, and waist, although conservators have tried to iron out creases. The third and most notable variation is that each item has been hand-dyed in two- or three-color bands and dipped in such a way that the colors blur into one another, either in graduated tonal contrasts or vivid shifts.

The dyeing process may have been a group project, but Brown describes "Remy" as having "his own kind of visual alchemy," sensitive to the particularities of each dancer (2007: 73). For instance, one pair of costumes goes from bottle green to olive to apple green in the leotard, with slate blue at one cuff and lemon yellow on the leg of the tights (Figure 4.6). Another set goes from vivid apricot through lemon yellow to muddy ochre. When colored water seeped into cotton fabric, the softness of one hue illuminated another, creating varying degrees of subtle intensity on the dancers' bodies, an effect achieved by a cautious attempt to apply color theory to costume.

Color theory was taught by the Bauhaus artist Josef Albers, whose teachings at Black Mountain College stimulated Charlip, Rauschenberg, and many other artists and designers.[9] For Albers, the experimental dynamic of art emerges from serious study of the structures and properties of primary elements as opposed to a process of composition that seeks to express content from within the subject. Committed to an abstraction that eliminated the imitation of "nature, stories, or sentiments," Albers's teachings on color and form were fundamental to what he called the "dynamic possession" of learning through experience and action (Harris 1987: 13).

Another fundamental tenet inherited from the Bauhaus was the artist's responsibility to participate in the technologies and industries of modernity; craft workshops at Black Mountain included every kind of material, from wood and textiles to plastics and

FIGURE 4.6 Dyed leotard and tights from Remy Charlip, costumes for *Minutiae,* 1954. Photograph by Cameron Wittig. Walker Art Center.

metals. Albers himself taught drawing and a color class in which students "studied systematically the tonal possibility of colors, their relativity, their interaction and influence on each other, cold and warmth, light intensity, color intensity, physical and spatial effects" (Harris 1987: 20). Albers's experimentation with *The Interaction of Color*, the title of his book on color theory, establishes the systematic elaboration of color in costume design for Cunningham and his collaborators. Moreover, the play of color in costume and lighting becomes central to the distinctiveness of Cunningham's choreographic field.

Many of Albers's exercises involve placing colored papers adjacent to each other and asking, "Which is the lighter and/or darker?" Rather than a hard edge, contrast emerges at "vanishing boundaries" (2006: 62), as when the blue of the sky merges with the gray tones of a cloud. Albers writes, "we do not see where clouds end and where sky begins" (2006: 63). For him, the "provocative color effect" that occurs at the boundaries is the "most delicate" form of intensity, and best achieved by allowing water to penetrate and distribute color particles in a surface material (2006: 63).[10]

Recognizing how costume materials evolve with the science of fibers and dyes, Charlip's experiments focus on the balance between boundaries diffused by diverse colors. Like the water droplets that create rainbows, the effect on textured cotton fabric differs from paper, since a color that seeps into another must navigate the uneven surface. A coarse cotton adds an inconsistent texture, producing a shading of colors at a soft, irregular edge. The materiality of textile therefore visibilizes the process of color absorption in the garment. In choreography, the costume worn on the body is not wet, and yet it retains the movement quality of the dye as if a liquid emanates from within. In combination, they give the dancers piebald, irregular skin markings (Figure 4.7).

FIGURE 4.7 Remy Charlip and Merce Cunningham in *Minutiae,* 1954. Photograph by Louis A. Stevenson, Jr. Courtesy of the Merce Cunningham Trust and the Jerome Robbins Dance Division, The New York Public Library.

Charlip's costumes are the first example in Cunningham's repertoire of an artist re-working the leotard, making it a surface from which choreography comes into play. The colors are organic shadings that contrast as the dancers lift and rotate around each other. The color blocks add to the choreographer's bodily shaping and design aesthetics; a set of green legs resonates with a pale yellow torso, or a dancer's blue cuffs may be lifted across the banding of a muddy tan in an upper chest.[11]

According to Albers, there are some "true mixtures," although most often one ad-ditive is dominant. The Minutiae colors perform as mixtures (2006: 106). In Brown's costume (Figure 4.8), the pelvic area is a deep peach color, somewhat vulgar like a baboon's bottom, one leg is saturated in a dominant fireman's red, and the torso emerges as rose pink deepening to indigo and purple on the sleeve. The process of adding or subtracting color affects our perception of light and shade because contrasts emerge between "mixture in direct color—which is light—and its opposite, mixture in reflected color—produced by pigment" (Albers 2006: 112). Color stains activate the process of oxidation through exposure to air, which further complicates the perception of color density.

FIGURE 4.8 Dyed leotard and tights belonging to Carolyn Brown from Remy Charlip, costumes for *Minutiae*, 1954. Photograph by Cameron Wittig. Walker Art Center.

For Albers, these differences in the appearance of one color over another lead to two conclusions: that the dyes "present" degrees of reflected light and that they "represent" the illusion of changes in surface or tone. In the case of Charlip's costumes, darker pigments move the dancer's costume toward the shadows of recessive space, while the lighter colors allow external light sources to move over the surface. Notably in the choreography, and against Rauschenberg's set, the lighter body parts become distinct Figure 4.9. Color differences across the chest or legs produce noticeably recessive or reflective surfaces. The illusion produced by the tonal variation reflects an invisible change, a displacement in movement. For instance, a rib cage seems to float upward, while darker legs might deepen a lunge, or in the case of the female trio, hone our attention toward the vulnerable groin.

These effects of light and dark color also produce the experience of spatial depth, as Albers writes:

> Colors appear connected predominantly in space. Therefore, as constellations they can be seen in any direction and at any speed. And as they remain we can return to them repeatedly and in many ways. (2006: 39)

Cunningham often cited Albert Einstein's remark, "There are no fixed points in space," to characterize his experimentation with choreographic space, time, and bodily orientation.[12]

FIGURE 4.9 Karen Kanner, Carolyn Brown, and Viola Farber in *Minutiae,* 1954. Photograph by John G. Ross, 1957. Courtesy of the Merce Cunningham Trust and the Jerome Robbins Dance Division, The New York Public Library.

This idea resonates with Albers's notion of color as a constellation that "can be seen in any direction and at any speed." The boundaries between light and dark in the dynamics of the colored costume—the pigment and its reflection—add to the minimalist kinetic and spatial variations of the choreography implied by the title of *Minutiae*.

While Rauschenberg's set for *Minutiae* has been acclaimed, Charlip's costumes for the company deserve a seminal place in Cunningham's choreographic history.[13] They were the precursor to Rauschenberg's own experiments with spotted color in the costumes for *Summerspace* (1958) and Jasper Johns spray-painted costumes for *Canfield* (1969). The fabrication of these subtly patterned unitards establishes an ongoing challenge for designers to make a minimalist costume both distinctive and aesthetically coherent. The uniform of leotard and leggings can be abstracted and differentiated by color rather than shape alone. For later artists, the costume surface will also function as a screen in order to communicate dramatic narrative and affective intensities in the choreography.

Charlip's costumes were among the last to be made of elasticized cotton, and they were handmade by a company dancer. Whatever value is placed on the local and intimate, a costume wrought by the designer-maker has rough-hewn possibilities. Garments made by artists closely associated with the Cunningham company reveal the imperfections of their fabrication as well as the skill of the artist.[14] In this dual sense, such costumes reveal a submerged history of communal craft in the leotard choreography of the Cunningham company.

Fiber K and the Unitard: *Suite for Five* (1956)

To appreciate the utility of the "unitard silhouette" in dance, we need to detour around the history of synthetic fabric production. In order to frame the role of new materials in choreography, it is essential to understand the rapid transformation of the American clothing industry in the 1940s and 1950s. This section will introduce the military–industrial complex that developed spandex and discuss the material's expansionist dynamics and resilient properties. In this complex assemblage of technologies, the modern dancer becomes an exemplary subject within a competitive economy of textile manufacturing, design, and consumption behaviors.

In her study of synthetic textiles, *Nylon: The Story of a Fashion Revolution*, Susannah Handley describes how a chemist working for the DuPont manufacturing company invented "Fiber K" in 1958. Unlike other petroleum-based products such as polyester, the new fiber possessed "exceptional qualities of stretch and recovery; stretching up to five times its original length" (Handley 1999: 146). Given the generic name of elastane, more commonly known as spandex, the fiber was branded and trademarked by DuPont as Lycra®. While lighter and more sheer than rubber-based stretch materials, spandex could be depended on for "containment." The fabric could be used in girdles, bras, and sportswear to restrain loose muscle or fat, with the wearer still feeling comfortable. Its mesh surface absorbed dye smoothly, and the fabric withstood robust washing and wearing. To understand this fabric's relationship with the moving body is to marvel at the potentials unleashed by the chemistry of synthetics.

The history of these synthetic fibers is driven by the compulsion to replace fibers made by plants and animals—cotton, linen, jute, wool, and silk—with fibers made by technology, even if they are derived from products extracted from the earth.[15] After decades of experimentation with spinning, DuPont could extrude long fibers from the by-products of cellulose (for rayon), coal (for nylon), and oil (for polyester). Chemists then divided the molecules within a chain by adding or subtracting other elements. The substance that creates spandex is a polymer consisting of at least 85 per cent long-chain polyurethane, produced by reacting polyester with a diisocyanate. The flow of matter is manipulated by piercing the substance with holes (adding space) or realigning its components.

Focused on chemical production, DuPont and its British competitor Courtaulds were two extremely powerful companies; they were the first duopoly, and they provided a compelling story of postwar capitalist expansion into the domestic sphere. On the US side, DuPont began as a manufacturer of explosives and farm chemicals, and then grew and diversified dramatically during the world wars. The company can be viewed as an industrial "war-machine," to use Deleuze and Guattari's analytical term: it was a technological outfit that waged a form of war, but also created the conditions of that war (1987: 416–19).[16] The materiality of spandex provides one illustration of how the military–industrial complex operated, with its tentacles of growth forever mutating.

Keen to build a positive image after World War II, DuPont developed advertising to promote its products, notably its vinyl house paints. Its move into textiles was helped by United States government policy, which sought to prevent Japanese manufacturers from reasserting their prewar dominance in the silk industry (see Chapter 1), and to replace American cotton with a reliable supply of synthetic fibers (Handley 1999: 35). Tariffs were once again used to protect local manufacturers from import competition (Thanhauser 2022: 185–8). As a result, DuPont and other US chemical companies became horizontally integrated with textile manufacturing, exerting monopoly control of product design, production, sales, and advertising, and assertively expanding their markets through intensive investment in product development. Handley describes it as a "three-part drama" involving the "research chemist, the fiber/textile manufacturer, and the consumer" (1999: 28). In 1965 alone, US synthetics manufacturers spent $136 million on research aimed at developing new fibers from petroleum derivatives and other products targeted at increasingly affluent middle-class Americans (Thanhauser 2022: 189). Given the industry's rapacious "frontier mentality" and the imperatives of geopolitics in that Cold War era, Handley suggests it is "impossible to imagine synthetic textiles being invented anywhere other than in America" (1999: 51).

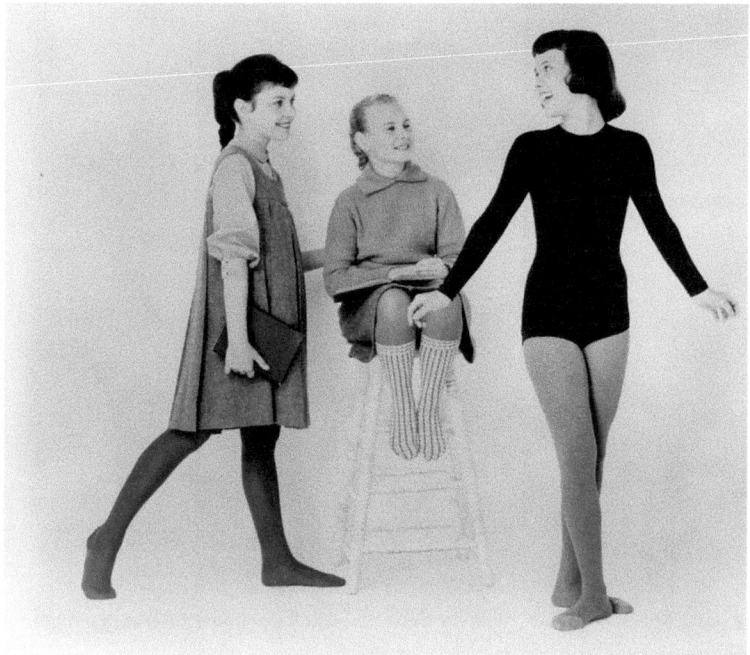

FIGURE 4.10 Three young girls wearing different styles of nylon tights made by Trimfit, Bluebird, and Danskin, E.I. du Pont Nemours & Company, 1958. Courtesy of the Hagley Museum and Library.

Sales campaigns for these "innovative fibers" used tantalizing messages to suggest they would offer a life of ease for the housewife, drip-dry travel for the salesman, and cheap luxury for the office worker (O'Connor 2014: 84). A DuPont advertisement from 1958 in Figure 4.10 shows that the passion for nylon stockings had extended to the choice of knit tights for schoolchildren and leggings for young dancers.

After spandex was launched in 1959, a boom in demand for "tights, in infinite colors and patterns, made great fortunes for all the synthetic-fiber manufacturers" (Handley 1999: 93). Capezio, formerly a shoe manufacturing company but specializing in dance by the late 1940s (as referenced in Chapter 1), opened a New York store and established two manufacturing plants to produce "a full line of body wear, including skirts, leotards, dance pants, and tights."[17] Capezio enjoyed an expanded market for its brand thanks to the rapid extension of dance education in high schools, local communities, specialist institutions, commercial entertainment, as well as ballet and modern dance companies. DuPont's promotion of synthetics became incorporated into dance advertising with the hook: "Capezio adds Lycra® to give you freedom in motion" (c. 1964).[18] Like Shawn's Men Dancers, the Cunningham company was another trial partner for Capezio in the expansion of new designs and technologies, and Figure 4.11 shows their label on tights from Charlip's *Minutiae* costume. Added to the material properties of spandex was an accumulation of ideological values—resilience, stretch, and now freedom.

FIGURE 4.11 Detail of dyed tights showing Capezio label from Remy Charlip, costumes for *Minutiae,* 1954. Photograph by Cameron Wittig. Walker Art Center.

By the early 1960s, this techno-optimism about textile variants had overtaken fashion magazines, trade displays, and popular promotions such as beauty pageants. In 1964, DuPont inaugurated a Stretch Corps of "120 men and women who traveled around the country to promote" spandex (Thanhauser 2022, 190). Handley argues that spandex's "second skin qualities" not only matched the sleek aesthetics of the fitness economy but also brought an illusion of "near nakedness" to fashion and to dance (1999: 149–150).

A dialectical image of this "synthetic utopia" can be found in the aforementioned, *Suite for Five,* the first Cunningham work costumed by Rauschenberg. Brown describes them as "simple in the extreme. . . . To the 'tank-top' leotards for the women, Bob's only addition was some thread tied around the straps to narrow them and secure them to the bra straps underneath. (No bra-less boobs in those days!) The men wore custom-made long-sleeved shirts" (2007: 148). These single-colored leotards are prototype elastanes, marginally stretchy, with conspicuous seams and rubberized waistbands (Figure 4.12).

Suite for Five was a choreography that gave "no room for distraction," accompanied by Cage sparsely plucking taut piano strings, the entire work generated an aesthetic of tension. Its sharp contrasts between stillness and motion involved rapid extensions and the holding of poses that, according to dancer Cedric Andrieux, required the "extremely difficult, yet pure, shifting of weight."[19] The colors were absolutes, with red omitted as too "aggressive," according to Brown: "blue for Merce, yellow for me . . . and the three secondary colors—purple, orange, and green—for Marianne, Viola, and Remy" (Brown 2007: 148). Of note, according to the writer Nancy Dalva, is that roles bore the names of

FIGURE 4.12 *Suite for Five,* 1956. Photograph by Louis A. Stevenson, Jr., 1956. Courtesy of the Merce Cunningham Trust and the Jerome Robbins Dance Division, The New York Public Library.

the dancers who created them across Cunningham's repertoire (2024). A costume worn by a new dancer executing the Merce or Marianne role would be remade, taking into account the resilience of new materials and its necessary fit to body shape (Finke 2024).

Brown describes *Suite for Five* as the "most purely classical work of Merce's entire oeuvre up until 1971" and identifies its choreographic attributes: "Formal. Refined. Simple. Unequivocal. Elegant. Reposeful. Understated. Clear" (2007: 148). In the 2005 reconstruction of *Suite for Five*, DuPont's Fiber K in the shiny, bold-colored unitard becomes the container—and symbol of an "understated elegance"—for asserting the twentieth-century classicism of this dancing costume. In the next sections of this chapter, we will see how different designers manipulated these 'utopian' properties of the spandex unitard to extend the vocabulary of costume design for the Cunningham company.

Pop Art: Mark Lancaster, *Neighbors* (1991) and *Roaratorio* (1986)

The British designer Mark Lancaster designed sets, costumes, and lighting for at least twenty works by Merce Cunningham Dance Company (MCDC) between 1973 and

1984, followed by individual works in 1988 and 1991. He recalls his first collaboration: "Sometimes I would find myself, visiting New York, spending a couple of days helping Jasper [Johns] to dye tights and leotards on his kitchen stove and sink" (Comenas 2004).[20] In 1973, Lancaster participated in a major Cunningham commission, *Un Jour ou Deux*, for the Paris Opera Ballet, which again involved dyeing costumes. Overcoming initial resistance, Lancaster said, "Merce won over almost all the dancers, and in the end, and after Jasper arrived, we re-dyed the costumes for the third time, all night in the bowels of the Opera" (Comenas 2004). These recollections give further focus to the "kitchen" labor of using color dyes to produce the integrated dance silhouette.

The mid-1970s also mark a turning point in the role of costumes in Cunningham's repertoire. The company appeared in a television series, *Great Performances: Dance in America*, giving it mass exposure to the home audience of middle America (Kinberg 1977).[21] Appearing on television required MCDC choreographies to be made in a three-dimensional space that could translate to the small screen, and one way to effect representation on this scale was to work more boldly with color in the costumes and set.[22]

Between 1972 and 1975, other changes were afoot, as can be seen from the wardrobe requirements of production coordinator Suzanne Weil. In 1972, the company only needed "space for each dancer's dressing room case (10″ × 30″ × 24″) and costume duffle bag," but the 1975 instructions were more elaborate: "The Company will need a wardrobe convenient to the dressing rooms, equipped with an ironing board and iron; access to washing and drying machines; and someone to assist the Company stage manager with costume maintenance."[23] The shift in scale, volume, and responsibility for the costumes includes assigning a wardrobe mistress (paid $56 in 1972) to support the company "artist-in-residence," Mark Lancaster.

After his apprenticeship to Johns, Lancaster officially became resident designer in 1975. Many of Cunningham's originating artists and collaborators had moved on with individual careers, and company dancers were younger, more technically trained, and less involved with the creative process (Noland 2019: 140–141). With increased touring, and professional budgets, the company became more of an industry than a "community," even if Cage and Cunningham remained at its center.

One of Lancaster's first assignments was to produce Cunningham's episode for the television special, and the small maquette at Figure 4.13 shows his experimentation with color and shape for *Video Triangle* (1976). Solid rectangles of cardboard—red, green, and blue—form a background for three sets of paper-doll cut-outs from the same card, and a fourth contrasting pair. These overlapping segments of the human pictogram replicate Josef Albers's studies in color relativity.[24] Using three bold colors, which dance duet is most visible? How do they work together? And how does color help the spectator see the dancer as an individual or within the whole?

Sliding the sheets of cardboard over one another creates four dance duet combinations, with each combination different in contrast, color density, or energetic relation.

FIGURE 4.13 Mark Lancaster, Collage study for *Video Triangle,* 1976. Walker Art Center.

This heightened employment of shape and color design is indicative of Lancaster's decade, in which the sleek and smooth unitard defines the Cunningham dancer, but its distinctive component parts are marked by subtle, ever-changing color contrasts.

In addition to the advantages of stretch and strength in spandex, exposure to "sweating ointment, body oils or detergents" did not change the color. Petroleum-based fabrics begin as a gray–white substance that easily absorbs dyes and evenly disperses them. The dyestuffs, however, are "fantastically toxic," as Sofi Thanhauser points out. Aniline dyes rely on "chromium, lead, cadmium, sulphur, nitrates, chlorine compounds, arsenic, mercury, nickel, and cobalt, formaldehyde-based dye fixing agents, [and] chlorinated stain removers" (2022: 191). Chemical stabilizers were then added to synthetic fabrics to prevent light and heat degradation or color loss from exposure to chlorine or other atmospheric contaminants.[25] The dye industry, led by companies such as Rit (United States), Tintex (Australia), and Dylon (UK), could now capitalize on commercial interest in new, bolder colors for clothing, screen-printing, and acrylic paints, such as can be seen in the jersey fabric samples for CRWDSPCR at Figure 4.14.

FIGURE 4.14 Mark Lancaster, color samples for cotton lycra mix fabric for *CRWDSPCR,* 1993. Courtesy of Walker Art Center Archives.

Instructions in the MCDC design files include lists of various dyes, divided into categories—acetate-nylon, alcohol-water, cold process, water fast, fast, cold water for natural fibers. There are also color and price charts and receipts for bulk purchases, including the solvents and fixatives. The costume workshop at this time is also a chemical industry.

Lancaster's design for *Trails* (1982) delights in Russian Constructivist colors: the male dancers wear gray tights with red long-sleeve tops, the women wear red or gray unitards, with natural or gray tights silhouetted against a set of red and black panels. In the bottom right-hand corner, Lancaster's handwritten notes trace the dancers' names in a spiral around the edge of a page—"Alan and Megan, Cathy-Robert-Lise . . . Lise-Joseph, long duet, Chris*Grey?, maybe grey leotards for Alan and Chris . . . Louise, END." In the top right-hand corner, he lists the company brands for his color scheme—Tintex RED RED, RIT Scarlet Dividend, and Tintex Gray—and the names resemble jockeys and horses called on a track. Located against the RED RED backdrop, the dye combinations provide unique markers for each dancer, complementing the choreography of overlapping duets.

In her review of the *Trails* premiere, the dance critic Anna Kisselgoff applauded its modulation of set, costumes, and lighting, which "literally glowed," giving the work a "striking . . .theatricality" (Kisselgoff 1982).[26] This reception of the vivid design transformed Cunningham's work from "trekking and trudging" on trails, as per the title, into a semaphoric drama.

Detailed color calculations feature in Lancaster's notebook for *Fractions* (1978), where shadings in color pencils assemble a draft matrix of leotards and leggings. His own mini-choreographic template, seen in Figure 4.15, pegs sample stretch fabric variations that mold each dancer's body: yellow–olive green—Lisa; pink–burgundy—Meg; powder blue–burnt yellow—Ellen; orange–brown—Chris; charcoal–light gray—Graham. . Designed by Charles Atlas, the set integrated four screens on which the dancers appeared

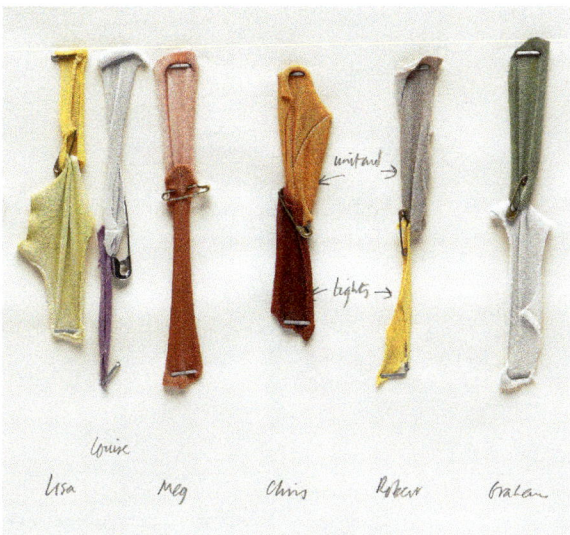

FIGURE 4.15 Detail of Mark Lancaster, costume color and fabric studies for *Fractions,* 1977. Walker Art Center.

simultaneously with their live performance in projected black-and-white footage. With the constant navigation of the screens, the complex patterning of trios and duets required rapid interchange, and the eight dancers could be identified by their pastel hues, resulting in a fractal effect for the choreography.

Skillful with pattern dynamics, Lancaster manages the Cunningham costume by segmenting the body with color changes at the leg joint or waist, or by splitting the color of the tights. Using solid blocks accumulates bodily contrasts internal to the geometry of the unitard.

In the ensemble for *CRWDSPCR* (1988), a rainbow of colors, including the bright hues of Figure 4.14 and earthier tones of Figure 4.16, was patched across the body, dividing upper and lower legs, the top of a torso from its middle, and giving some dancers armbands. The color breaks seen in Figure 4.17 between thigh and legs in the women's leotards sharpened the linearity of joints, while the waisted leggings for men structured the alternating rotations of pelvis and torso.

This zoning of the body is reminiscent of the wooden mannikins used by artists to practice proportions and coordinate gestures in their paintings. Choreographically, as the dancers fill the stage, rotate with arms raised, or tilt from side to side, the oblong segments of color appear like colored flags in a complex form of semaphore (Figure 4.18).

Beyond the concert stage, aerobics and disco-wear epitomized the sleek, "healthy" body in the 1980s, and changed the social dynamics of the unitard (Handley 1999: 146). Jane Fonda's *Workout* video (1982) launched an era of waisted leotards and fluorescent leggings across the United States (Figure 4.19); as Kaori O'Connor argues, spandex clothing

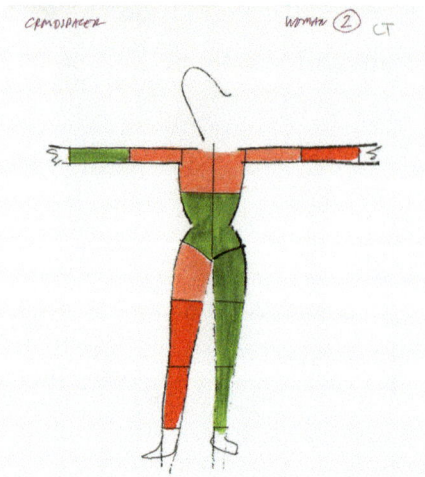

FIGURE 4.16 Mark Lancaster, costume sketch for *CRWDSPCR*, 1993. Courtesy of the Merce Cunningham Trust and the Jermone Robbins Dance Division, The New York Public Library.

FIGURE 4.17 Orange and gray multi-paneled long-sleeve leotard and footless leggings from Mark Lancaster, costumes for *CRWDSPCR*, 1993. Photograph by Cameron Wittig. Walker Art Center.

FIGURE 4.18 The Merce Cunningham Dance Company in a rehearsal of *CRWDSPCR*, 1993 from the Elliot Caplan film, *CRWDSPCR*. Courtesy of the Merce Cunningham Trust and the Jerome Robbins Dance Division, The New York Public Library.

FIGURE 4.19 Disco bodywear from DuPont Company Textile Fibers product information, 1978-08. Courtesy of Hagley Museum and Library.

FIGURE 4.20 Journalist and TV presenter Barbara Dickmann (front) performs aerobic exercises in a studio, March 1983. Photo: Picture Alliance/DPA/Bridgeman Images.

became "the signifying garments of young boomer women" (2014: 82). Supermarkets and local gyms promoted synthetic dance costumes as the commodity required for a sculptured body, and "the physical evidence of exertions made in the gym and aerobics studio" expressed social status (Figure 4.20) (Handley 1999: 148). On the dye front, manufacturers introduced Day-Glo colors that simulated the pop-art revolution for the athleisure industry (Barton 2009).

Lancaster's sketches indicate his fascination with the artistic potential of both these features of fitted stretch fabrics for *Five Stone Wind* (1988). The tights are pale gray and shell-pink, while the leotards traverse the color spectrum from crimson to deep green and navy, interspersed with tertiary colors (Figure 4.21). In part two of the performance, he offsets the unitards with short rah-rah skirts (the bouncy miniskirts worn in cheerleading) and bell-shaped trousers in black and white.[27] Cunningham himself appears dressed in a cobalt outfit split down the middle, with one half plain and the other cross-hatched. His costume matches the dense blue and violet scrim, and it graphically merges with the background, while the other dancers are exposed as the playground figures.

In Lancaster's designs, the color variations sometimes sharply contrast, at other times they diffuse the impact of one dancer's costume against another. The dance critic Robert Greskovic credits Lancaster with maintaining the sense that Cunningham's dancers "are more colored figures than clothed ones" (in Celant 1999: 258). The choice of color palette does not restrict the representation of dance to abstraction, and quite deliberately, it may remind a spectator of a context that exceeds the dance itself. A tension between colors is also connotation, as well as a formal element that is intrinsic to the materialist conception

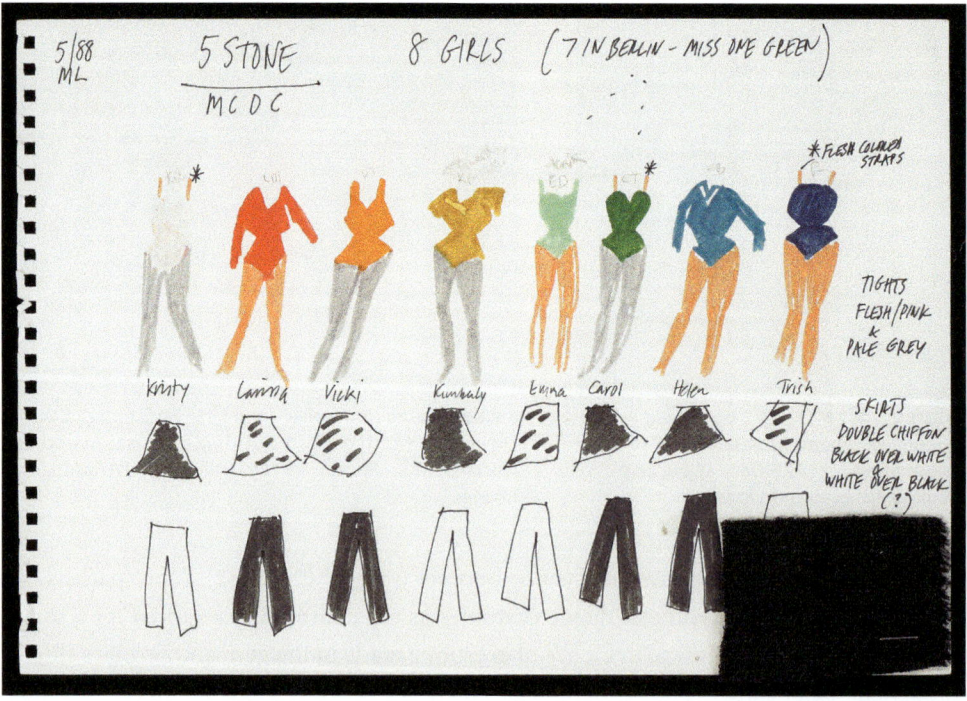

FIGURE 4.21 Mark Lancaster, study of women's costumes for *Five Stone Wind*, 1988. Walker Art Center.

FIGURE 4.22 Pierre Cardin striped jersey leotards and wool panel skirts from the winter haute couture collection, 1968. Photograph by Yoshi Takata. Courtesy of Gestion Pierre Cardin. © Pierre Pelegry.

of choreography. Pattern and color, diffraction and energetic shifts, will stimulate the affective contents of memory, narrative, and cognitive dissonance.

One can identify other cultural leitmotifs in the costume designs, including an obsession with space travel, dating back to the Cold War in the 1960s. Astronauts' costumes—brightly colored NASA overalls and space helmets—spread into popular culture through the influence of films and television shows such as *Star Wars* and *Doctor Who*, in which the protagonists wore tight-fitting suits in lurid colors with black trims. Shiny PVC plastics and silver polymer coatings for clothing also entered fashion. In 1965, the designer Ungaro went on a silver binge: silver wigs, silver-soled boots, silver buttons, collars, and mesh stockings. As Handley puts it, Ungaro's clothes "were always sprinkled with Space Age lunacy" (1999: 88). Using the new artificial fabrics to create bold geometric designs, a Pierre Cardin catwalk launch in 1968 featured outfits for "moon maidens and cosmonauts" (Figure 4.22).

Nostalgia for this space fantasy persisted into the 1980s and 1990s. In designs for *Neighbors* (1991), Lancaster created a space nostalgia moment. The dancers wore miniskirted flip dresses over unitards, and the outfits were divided vertically, with one side in silver or gold lurex, an expensive, shiny fabric made from synthetic film with a metallic layer vaporized onto its surface. The parallel panels to the lurex are in saccharine tones—dusty pink, ice-cream pink, pale orange, and lilac—and the outfits have contrasting short collars made from stretch materials. These playful outfits in Figures 4.23 and 4.24 are part harlequin, part cheer squad, and part figure-skating dress.

FIGURE 4.23 Metallic and pastel short dress and metallic and pastel leotard and tights from Mark Lancaster, costumes for *Neighbors*, 1991. Photograph by Cameron Wittig. Walker Art Center.

FIGURE 4.24 Detail of metallic and pastel short dress from Mark Lancaster, costumes for *Neighbors*, 1991. Photograph by Cameron Wittig. Walker Art Center.

The significance of color in the Cunningham costumes was augmented by the prominence of gay designers in the fashion industry during the 1980s. A related factor was the impact of the AIDS pandemic on the artistic and gay community. In their costume fabrication, designers and dancers acknowledged the fluidity with which the company's visual aesthetics (Figure 4.25) and indeed the sexual identities of Cunningham dancers and designers interacted with the smooth life flows of New York's gay community.

Designers such as Perry Ellis (1940–1986) and Bill Robinson (1948–1993), with their own eponymous brands, were leading figures in the New York fashion world and are credited with introducing a more relaxed look to menswear. According to Bonnie English, "The svelte American image relied on non-restrictive comfort combined with casual elegance, impeccable grooming, and a healthy, streamlined physique" (2007: 68). Fitted but casual coordinates appeared in Ellis's range during the late 1970s and early 1980s. If they did not define a gay aesthetic, they emphasized the active body in everyday men's clothing (Trebay 2013). Robinson, on the other hand, was known for "arresting combinations of just-off colors," not unlike the palette Lancaster was using on the stage (Pace 1993).

FIGURE 4.25 Patricia Lent and Alan Good in *Neighbors,* 1991. Photograph by Johan Elbers. Courtesy of the Merce Cunningham Trust and the Jerome Robbins Dance Division, The New York Public Library.

Whether working in the dance sector or not, designers such as Ellis and Robinson were Lancaster's peers, and the downtown arts scene absorbed these new styles and performances of masculinity. Handley says that the "peacock male" displaced with gender dressing taboos during this era, and emerged wearing floral shirts and "pink and red slacks" (1999: 105). On and off stage, men wore variations on "classic" leisure attire, such as neat sweatshirts or loose trousers, a look readily adopted by gay men in the meeting places of large cities. The casual indirect glance at the length of a man's sleeves or the toned muscles of his chest was not too distant from other trends being mainstreamed from gym culture. Given the role of exercise in the boom economy, even ungainly legwarmers became popular dress items.

Lancaster incorporates many of these styles into Cunningham's choreography for *Roaratorio* (1983), a work inspired by Cage's long fascination with James Joyce's *Finnegan's Wake*. Purchasing off-the-shelf clothing, Lancaster displays a layered, casual look, with bright shirts underpinned by gray shorts and pink leggings, and singlets slung over sweatshirts. Legwarmers in bright colors—reds, grays, and greens, sometimes mismatched—highlight and segment the calves; they also simulate the laced boots of those performing the Irish jigs and reels that reverberate in Cage's music.

FIGURE 4.26 The Merce Cunningham Dance Company in *Roaratorio,* 1983. Photograph by Anna Finke, 2010. Courtesy of the Merce Cunningham Trust and the Jerome Robbins Dance Division, The New York Public Library.

Lancaster generously distributes "separates" among the men's costumes—a knotted sweatshirt in burgundy, a pair of track trousers in lime green, a polo shirt in pale lemon yellow. Across the whole are flashes of Irish green in a pair of leggings, a flared dress, or a loose sweater (Figure 4.26). Notably, the clothing is more modest than the unitard—the T-shirts are looser, shorts cover the pubic region, and track pants flow around the legs, enabling the dancers to execute the intricate footwork with ease. The overall effect is to multiply the hop-point-hop patterns woven into the Cunningham-Cage medley of Irish nostalgia. The casual visual aesthetic enhances this choreographic rambling, the couple-dancing, the square dances, the chorus lines, the waiting for a turn on the sidelines, and structured tomfoolery.

In this tribute to Joyce's Dublin, dance scholar Carrie Noland claims that *Roaratorio* produced "a stunning but chaotic complexity" of rhythmic expression for the ensemble (Noland 2019: 161). Its performance was uniquely joyous, perhaps Joycean, in a New York sense. *Roaratorio* appears to be an act of defiance for the artists involved, a celebration of life lived in fullness, in Joyce's own words—"flirtsome then and she's fluttersome yet"—being out and in community (1975: 28). If Cage and Cunningham focused on the underbelly of Irish poetic language, the "roar" of patchwork colors and costume adornments unleashed by Lancaster was also a tribute to the gay community in the United States facing the force of the AIDS epidemic.

In June 1981, the first medical reports of AIDS appeared, and by the end of that year, the United States had 337 reported individuals with severe immune deficiency; of these, 130 were dead.[28] In 1985, activists conceived the idea of an AIDS memorial quilt, which eventually became the world's largest collective textile work. For the MCDC repertoire, the celebration of color and men's pleasure in clothing and design forms part of the embodied and affective patchwork of this decade. The layered and casual elegance with which Lancaster visualized the stretch forms of the unitard on male and female bodies reflects the dramatic changes taking place in social attitudes, which were simultaneously embracing a "conspicuous leisure" culture while celebrating the relaxation of normative structures of gender and sexual relations. Lancaster's tactile relationship to the color spectrum and his respect for the distinctiveness of each dancer recall the chemistry and artistic potency of a design-informed choreography that was very much in style with its times.[29]

Suzanne Gallo, *Biped* (1999), and Oil

In the 1990s, Cunningham departed from the use of a single designer and tested a range of new possibilities. An important constant was his "wardrobe mistress," Suzanne Gallo. Gallo joined MCDC in 1982 but did not begin creating her own designs for that company until the 1990s, with works such as *Ground Level Overlay* (1995) and *Pond Way* (1998).[30]

During this period, Cunningham begins experimenting with computer-assisted choreography, and the unitard becomes more troublesome. Its power to serve as a unifying silhouette that hugs the body contours and extends the reach of limb movement was replicated by the software, which reduced the body to a stick-like figure that emphasized joint segmentation. Fortunately, Gallo's intimate knowledge of the dancers softens, almost imperceptibly, the interplay between technical proficiency and costume design, and she makes many adjustments to the outfits that various collaborators present to Cunningham.[31]

A dramatic shift in dance composition occurs when Cunningham begins his association with the architects of Life Forms, the body-mapping software program with which he constructs *Biped* (1999). Cunningham would select phrases on his computer, and then the dancers would assemble the strange and angular connections in the studio. According to Paul Kaiser, one of the computer artists on *Biped*, the installation was "conceived independently," upholding Cunningham's principle of autonomous creative processes. The choreography was "about technology," according to Cunningham, and would be like "flicking through channels on TV." "As his independent collaborators," Kaiser (1999: 2) responds, "we understood that we were free to follow up on these little hints or to ignore them altogether." The "visual décor" of "projections and virtual choreography" was relayed via a transparent scrim draped across the front stage.[32] The lighting, designed by Aaron Copp, unfolds across grid lines shot through with deep blue laser lights. A slow, brooding score gives the piece a feeling of otherworldliness.

FIGURE 4.27 Trio of spandex unitards from Suzanne Gallo, costumes for *BIPED*, 1999. Photograph by Cameron Wittig. Walker Art Center.

Almost as an afterthought, Kaiser (1999: 2) acknowledges the costume designer: "Suzanne Gallo created marvelous costumes with an iridescent metallic sheen so that the dancers would not be lost in this huge spectacle. Instead, they would shine in the light, both of the stage and of our projections." The male and female dancers wear truncated unitards, some shaped as short leggings, with a variety of necklines including singlet and halter tops, rolled collars, and scooped and cross-strapped backs (Figure 4.27). In these costumes undistinguished by gender, some female dancers have cropped hair, and there are men with longer locks.

The fabric is a technological marvel; its texture is formed from a stretch material that used foiled thread to create pixelated light cells.[33] Mimicking the optical units that make up the compound eyes of insects, allowing them to perceive light from many different directions and reflect different wavelengths, this hologram fiber consists of thousands of tiny independent photoreception units. When viewed from different angles, the unitards glow; they are also glossy, since they "reflect all wavelengths at once, creating a mirror-like effect" (Lynch 2022). The multiple light sources deflect attention from bodily boundaries but enhance the detection of fast torso movements.

In a material sense, these mesh garments resemble chain mail and are "scratchy" to wear (Goggans 2023). In performance, the "iridescent sheen" functions like a slick of oil on water, a disturbing black base that ripples alternately from yellowish, purple, or blue into a violent green. These associations add to the eeriness of the costumes, and their links to oil are not coincidental. In the decade before *Biped*, the world witnessed numerous catastrophic oil spills, including the Exxon Valdez disaster of 1989, in which 11 million gallons of crude oil were spilled into Prince William Sound in Alaska. Artists became increasingly aware that oil on water was a dangerous cocktail; the fashion designer Issey Miyake once asked his synthetic fiber manufacturers to "make me a fabric that looks like poison" (Handley 1999: 134). As the earlier discussion of synthetic fibers attests, when we wear spandex, we are already wearing an oil byproduct. In this dialectical costume, Gallo surfaces the chemical properties of this novel fabric—its shimmering liquid, its melting metal, and its oily iridescence—not as fantasy but as actuality. In the shadowy lighting, the fabric gleams, while the projected dance phrases play through the scrim; on the screens are skeletal figures—the jointed inscriptions of living bodies—but the embodied costumes function as the defensive exoskeletons.

In Kaiser's phrasing of Cunningham's choreography, the blue lighting that illuminates the stage emphasizes the dancers' veins, and these reflections execute the almost impossible moves (Figure 4.28). The dancers themselves occupy the stage like beetles inspecting broken terrain. A female duet turns together with bent interlocked arms, suddenly jumps from standing still, and executes arabesque motifs accompanied by more jumping. In a later sequence, the men wear pale gray organza over-garments, and the women wear kimono-style jackets decorated with delicate frog clasps and silver beading (Figure 4.29). These gauzy costumes blur the movements, one dancer performing a series of extended bourrées as if ready for lift-off, before the dancers depart into a shimmering of watery clouds.[34]

In the Cunningham oeuvre, Biped is celebrated for its technological innovation and collaboration with the software engineers, but its annals must include the technical innovation of the engineers and designers who fabricated Gallo's costumes. While the motion capture data reveals the digital projections and compositional sequences, the dancers' flesh on stage is exposed around the corners of the costume. When their bare arms and necks connect, the "life forms" of the dance emerge from the "poison" costumes as resistant. The costume choreography manifests that dangerous liminality between the human and non-human that always accompanies technological progress.

FIGURE 4.28 The Merce Cunningham Dance Company in *BIPED*, 1999. Photograph by Stephanie Berger, 2011. Courtesy of the Merce Cunningham Trust and the Jermone Robbins Dance Division. © Stephanie Berger 2024.

FIGURE 4.29 Pair of sheer kimono-style tops from Suzanne Gallo, costumes for *BIPED*, 1999. Photograph by Cameron Wittig. Walker Art Center.

The Nature of *Ocean* (1994): Marsha Skinner

In this final section, I return to an ever-present partner in Cunningham's choreography: his relationship to the natural world. In dance, the potential to evoke the strangeness and beauty of nature, with or without essentializing, is a constant. More than a century ago, the philosopher Alfred North Whitehead suggested that *The Concept of Nature* (1953) might be investigated across three different, but interconnected, questions: "What is the nature of the event? What is the event of nature? And what is the nature of perception?" The perception of nature locates the human subject in relation to animal, bird, fish, and insect species, plant life, and other organic matter.

Both Cage and Cunningham were fascinated by "nature" as a form of inspiration; Cage collected and studied fungi, while Cunningham spent hours illustrating birds, cats, and other creatures. Yet human perception also participates in the experience of nature on an ontogenetic plane, responding to the unique sensory changes that our bodies experience. This inner experience of "nature" impelled Cunningham to reflect on the extent to which "nature" emerges from complex technical instructions or from ordinary rhythms and actions. He has said his choreographic work requires understanding what is "different in duration . . . size [of bodies]. . . people . . . quality" (Dalva 2008). Such distinctions are perceptual, minimal, perhaps occasional. His own juxtapositions of chance procedures were part of his lifelong experimentation with the potential to experience and constitute the "event of nature" and to shape the "nature of the event." His preparation for the making of choreography thus involved thinking about the properties of "nature," whether through reading or observation. Such too was the "nature" of Cage's engagement with Joyce's writing, which motivated the last work by Cunningham to embody the couple's love affair with making art and living together.

Created two years after Cage's death, *Ocean* (1994) was a homage to a non-existent work about the ocean by Joyce.[35] Described as a "pure-dance work, without scenery," it was nonetheless set in a circular space, initially in a baroque amphitheater, the Cirque Royal in Brussels, and then in 2008, outdoors in a Minneapolis quarry.[36] Stringently structured to ninety minutes by a count-down clock visible to the audience, it was accompanied by a full orchestra performing a sound score curated by David Tudor and Andrew Culver. Operatic in scale, *Ocean* has a large ensemble dance cast. Reviewing the 2011 film version by Charles Atlas for the *New York Times*, Alastair Macaulay reflects that the event of "nature" in *Ocean* seems ambiguous:

> Its structures and images vary considerably: at times it's possible to feel shifting surfaces, immense depths, whales, albatrosses, wrecks, and mermaids, but the choreography also has many stillnesses, hard angles, and sequences that do not easily melt into any marine illusion. (Macaulay 2012)

Such variable images of "nature" and the "nature of the event" unfold via the "shifting surfaces" of the dancer's body encased in a diversity of sleek unitards.

These costumes were designed by the visual artist Marsha Skinner and implemented with the assistance of Gallo. Skinner herself is a watercolorist, a painter who lives in New Mexico, where she observes and paints the atmospheres of nature—sky, clouds, desert, and trees. Very few women artists appear among Cunningham's genuine collaborators; mostly, he and Cage chose male colleagues. Skinner (2023), therefore, makes an interesting choice; a female artist steeped in Eastern philosophy, she reached out to Cage for his Buddhist knowledge when she was trying "to integrate Chinese calligraphy and landscapes with dance." Intrigued by the fleeting qualities of movement, her painting techniques include throwing the I Ching to produce a delicate but random layering of brushstrokes on canvas or paper.

Having spent hundreds of hours sketching Cunningham dancers in New York, Skinner was invited to "collaborate." She designed evocative costumes for several seminal works—*Beach Birds* (1991), created for Cage's last piece of music; *Change of Address* (1992); the elegiac *Enter* (1992) after Cage's death; and *Ocean* (1994), the monumental tribute performance to Cage. Two curved strokes of black on white create the stylized image of a penguin or gull, and from that sketch (Figure I.3), *Beach Birds* adapts the white unitard with a solid black upper torso stretching down the arms to black mittens.[37] Skinner's distilled nature views the fluttering of a blackened wing as the becoming of a bird, and the resulting strange choreography by Cunningham was partly mimetic and very elegant.

Skinner's commissions were concurrent with Cunningham's grief over Cage's death, so she had little or no direct contact with him.[38] Nonetheless, Cage had chosen Skinner as designer for *Ocean*, so she and Cunningham were "freely side by side in our respective work. . . [he] recognized that I was as embedded in my [desert] landscape as he was in his ocean landscapes" (Skinner 2023). With Gallo's support, MCDC returned to the solid tonal unitards—in "sea colors, from violet to the darkest ink"—that animate so much of Cunningham's career (Mackrell 2006).

For Gallo and Skinner, the color logics required sourcing fabrics that "would reflect and shine in all possible ways—short silk or extremely fine . . . stretch fabric like another layer of skin" (Skinner 2023). In tonal range, the blues, greens, and purples reflect the varying depths of the ocean, from the tinges of turquoise in a coral reef to the deepening blues of a murky sea to the final depths where little light can reach (Figure 4.30). A process of "trial and error" led Skinner to the poetics of Homer's "wine dark sea," which designer Anna Finke (2024) pinpoints as "deep, deep purple, to be precise, Pantone 2755 C." The sumptuous costumes are thus deeply responsive to the rhythmic nature of a watery environment.

If their hues infuse the ocean depths, repeated viewing of the *Ocean* choreography, carefully recorded by Atlas, evokes the numinous. Strange patterns emerge from the depths of a darkened arena: a male dancer wearing lilac slowly extends into fifth

FIGURE 4.30 Trio of long-sleeve unitards from Marsha Skinner, costumes for *Ocean*, 1994. Photograph by Cameron Wittig. Walker Art Center. Artwork © Marsha Skinner.

position, bending back and around through his torso, every sweep allowing the back to lean lower. Then, hopping around in a circle, he elevates his leg, twisting into a half arabesque and pointing bare feet. Ribs show through the neat costume, round neck, and bottom creased; each shape occupies a different elevation before mutating into another. There's the sound of a drone in Tudor's music. A buoyant duet holds still while a soloist continues with uplifted arms. Perhaps like waves, but it is hard to imagine them rolling to shore. Another man in turquoise is swirling and bends back, while a woman in orange sits on his torso, the musculature of her belly and the man's upper thigh wrinkling in tension. Their leotards are shiny surfaces on pliable bodies. A color-wave of female dancers enters—chrome yellow, saffron, and poppy red, through to ice blue and aquamarine.

In an amphitheater, the audience peers down on the work, but on a screen, the camera lens positions the viewer as if they are seeing into an aquarium tank. There's nothing to hold onto; long similar phrases are accompanied by an awkward, disturbing soundscape. It may be possible to construct a narrative—a form of descent in response to the calling of the Sirens—but the dance combinations clash and overlap and wash away certainty.

FIGURE 4.31 The Merce Cunningham Dance Company in *Ocean*, 1994, Photograph by Tony Dougherty, 2005. Courtesy of the Merce Cunningham Trust and the Jerome Robbins Dance Division, The New York Public Library.

Deep purple costumes are everywhere, like a pod of dolphins, with every leap, a curving back (Figure 4.31). Midway, the elongation and massing of the blue-purples shifts to a play of red elements. A female dancer appears in a gauzy mid-calf skirt. More women arrive in floating tunics that drape over the leotards. This diaphanous layering produces a moiré effect—rust over red and magenta over blue—with the squiggly lines ceaselessly altering the light that passes through them. These sheer costumes hold the wind and mute the spandex (Figure 4.32). One woman with shaved hair wears orange over green with blue leggings; she dances like a large frond of kelp.

For the last fifteen minutes, the choreography occupies the perimeter, with each dancer in continuous movement—swooping, scooping, bent arms, rocking, with one turn affecting the other in a circular configuration. Suddenly, a dancer in electric blue enters, and the dancers are propelled in new directions—more elevated.

The physical and psychic effects of the *Ocean* choreography recall Albers's concept of vibration, in which "changes in climate or temperature, in tempo or rhythm" from the juxtaposition of colors can provoke "changes of atmosphere or mood" (2006: 44). When the score becomes ominous—gulping sounds—the sixteen dancers fill the arena, colored arms raised, upward pressure through the toes, the shiny skins are exposed and taut, shaping the air, then ascending so fast there are almost collisions as they surface. The brilliant unitards bounce and glisten like light on water, while every shadow formed on the contours of the body produces a vibration—"an illusion for which we have no explanation," as Albers puts it (2006: 182).

FIGURE 4.32 Pair of silk chiffon knee-length dresses from Marsha Skinner, costumes for *Ocean*, 1994. Photograph by Cameron Wittig. Walker Art Center. Artwork © Marsha Skinner.

FIGURE 4.33 Holley Farmer and Jonah Bokaer in *Ocean,* 1994. Photograph by Tony Dougherty, 2005. Courtesy of the Merce Cunningham Trust and the Jerome Robbins Dance Division, The New York Public Library.

In *Ulysses,* Joyce wonders: "What in water did Bloom, waterlover, drawer of water, watercarrier, returning to the range, admire?" (2011: 783). What in water did Joyce and Cunningham admire, or did Skinner reveal? The artist-scholar Mårten Spångberg suggests that the ocean is "a container for all the possible and impossible actualizations of the world that did not and has not yet been actualized . . . agitations of space, pockets of time, pure synthesis of speed, direction and rhythm" (2009: 31). In this expanded vision of an event of nature, Skinner's design for *Ocean* is the dialectical costume for Cunningham's choreography (Figure 4.33). In color, texture, and subtle layering of reflected light, the audience perceives the event as a consciousness—the detailed, even obsessive, observance of a finite yet boundary-defying existence that ceases after 90 minutes. Skinner's agitations of space align with Gallo's persistent craft to actualize a transformation of materiality in the unitard. I hesitate to call this antithesis of form "feminine," but the costumes of *Beach Birds, Elegy,* and *Ocean* undo the neutral, proficient dancing body. Curves and shapes suggesting birds, fish, and waves surface as the flickering signs of multi-dimensional, biodiverse environments.

A materialist perspective, on the other hand, would demythologize *Ocean* as an event of nature aligned with the nature of "pure dance." In every wash, synthetic garments shed microfibers, and "our old friends polyester and nylon" float off in small, invisible filaments (Handley 1999: 140). Sea creatures and humans who eat fish consume these microplastics, and their concentration is growing in our bodies and in our oceans. Perhaps the critic Macaulay was correct in saying that we cannot "melt into marine illusion" in Cunningham's *Ocean* when the choreography is filled with particles, light filters, electronic sound effects, and stretchy spandex unitards. In his paean to the ocean's "restlessness," Joyce too observes its "noxiousness" (2011: 783–785).

The perception of nature—the duration, complexity, and intensity of abstract elements—comprises the choreographic score for *Ocean*. In the fashion assemblage of the unitard, modern understandings of color technologies, the allusion of fabric, and the effects of corporeal plasticity, embrace these watery depths. Given the progression and quality of still and sudden movements, the nature of the event fabricated by Cunningham, with its swirling motions, thus constitutes the immateriality of an ecological dance aesthetic. Faced with these contradictions, for the moment, as philosopher Whitehead writes: "We are stopping at the point where a boundless ocean of enquiries opens out for our questioning" (1953: 163).

Conclusion

In the epigraph to this chapter, Benjamin draws an analogy between the prototype for "sportswear" and the advent of fast-moving vehicles and industrial production. These juxtaposed images of modernity offer sleek proportions in the body, in transport, and in manufacturing, that accompany changes in the experience of motion.

The rise of the unitard, unifying a leotard and tights, that becomes the prototype for the contemporary dancer, is congruent with other shifts in perception, movement, and imagination in the second half of the twentieth century. Dance costumes also appeared in nightclubs, in gyms, and in fashion, celebrating textiles that elasticize the body. These stretch fabrics exposed the desirable silhouette of a healthy body, and their tactility gave the wearer a greater sense of intimacy with their flesh. For Cunningham, the closeness of costume to skin was foundational for dancing. He said, "Anybody moving can provide a revelatory experience, like watching a wild animal. Only I am concerned with the movement contained within the skin of a human, which gives an experience you cannot get in any other way" (in Fields 1970: 12).

The Walker Art Center retains the faded gray-blue duo-tard from *Suite for Five* that opened this chapter; the all-over woven wool top and knitted leggings bear the imprint of Cunningham's dancing body. The slim hips and extended legs, the stretched arms and

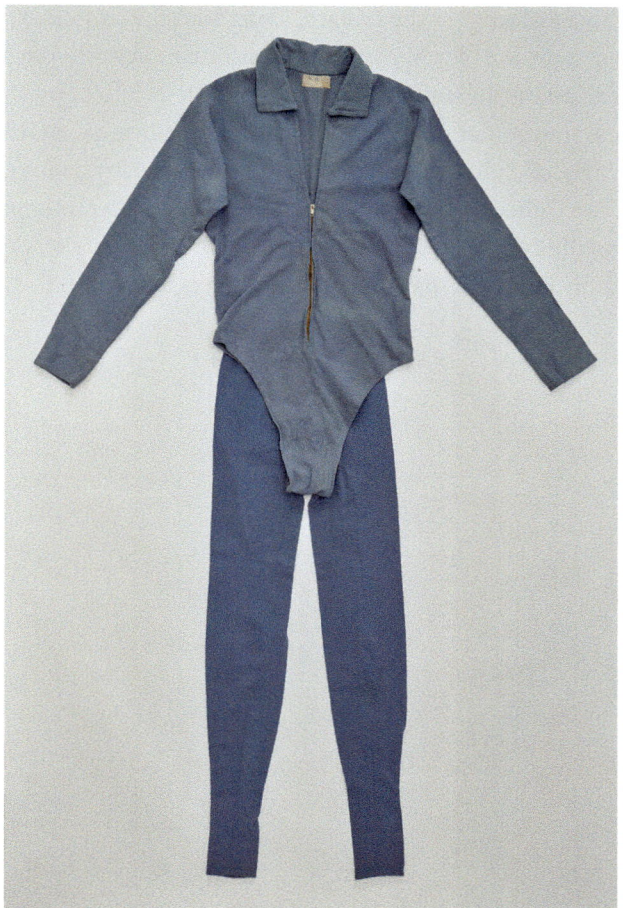

FIGURE 4.34 Wool leotard and wool tights worn by Merce Cunningham from Robert Rauschenberg costumes for *Suite for Five in Space and Time*, 1956. Photograph by Cameron Wittig. Walker Art Center. Artwork © Robert Rauschenberg Foundation. VAGA at ARS/Copyright Agency, 2025.

sleeve seams are gestured out of shape. This garment emanates a unique history, the aesthetics of a choreography encased in a second skin but free to move like a cloud adrift in a spring sky. Its blue color is recessive:

> "Blue is the invisible becoming visible," wrote the artist Yves Klein. "Blue has no dimensions." (cited in Wolff 2013: 2)

In the materiality of this singular blue costume, Cunningham sought the immanence of dance, thereby asserting the portrait of a dignified, yet melancholic, masculinity.

Beyond his unique presence, Cunningham appreciated the stretch qualities of the unitard as a uniform that exposed the visible self of his dancers. In the production of costumes for company dancers, his designers grappled with the material conditions of spandex and synthetic dyes when they adapted or embellished the unitard for individual dancers. From these dialectics of the unitard, along with the fabrication of the articulate surface, the costume projects the hypervisual transformation of choreography by pop art kinetics, theatrical luminosity, and the advance of screen technologies. It becomes, in this sense, the material transmitter of drastic changes in the "nowness" of dance modernity.

Across the field of dance for decades, the all-over stretchy dance garment makes a statement about the United States as a cultural and economic powerhouse. It sings of the blue boy who wore this uniform and created dances until he was a very old man, but also reveals how and why hundreds, nay millions, of dancers have worn this costume.

T-shirts and Loose Pants

Grand Union and Trisha Brown

In our predilection for the various shades of gray . . . running to black, we
find an unmistakable social reflection of our tendency to privilege the theory
of the formation of intellect above all else. Even the beautiful we can no
longer just enjoy; rather . . . we must first subject it to criticism with the
consequence . . . that our spiritual life becomes ever more cool and colorless.
    Theodor Lipps, cited in Benjamin (1999: 80)

In 1961, the artist Simone Forti presented two dance constructions, *Slant Board* and
Huddle, in Yoko Ono's studio in New York. Forti had been experimenting with how task-
specific instructions could concentrate the interactions between bodies and objects. In
Huddle, for instance, six or seven people tried to climb over each other while remaining
in close contact as a mass of bodies. The apparent simplicity of the improvisation contrasts with the complex considerations of weight, geometry, and movement awareness
required of the performers.[1] There is no pretending, no artifice, and no rehearsing of pre-
conceived choreographic ideas.

The performers wear loose clothing that does not affect the trajectories of their
bodies. In forming this mound of muscle and fabric, the interpersonal and the objective, the group choreography was making "space visible through movement" (de Langen
2022: 32). This enigmatic event was reactivated in 1982 for the Stedelijk Museum
(Figure 5.1), which situated this exploration in relation to the anti-figurative Zero artists
in Europe. As dance historian Marijn de Langen writes, many artists and performers of
the 1960s sought to "break through the idea of art as expression and went in search of
objectivity, playfulness, and abstraction" (2022: 29).

Performing similar conceptual dances in Rome at the Dance, Music, and Dynamite
Festival in June 1969, Forti again wore a plain white long-sleeved T-shirt over crumpled
cotton trousers; the same garments appear in subsequent New York performances of Solo
No. 1 at Sonnabend Gallery in 1974 (Janevski and Lax 2018: 40, 42, and 50). In these

Fabrications. Rachel Fensham, Oxford University Press. © Oxford University Press 2026. DOI: 10.1093/9780197699638.003.0006

FIGURE 5.1 Simone Forti, *Huddle*, 1982. Photographer unknown. Courtesy of Stedelijk Museum Amsterdam.

museum spaces, the seemingly practical dress maintains the neutrality of traditional mime and echoes the white cube aesthetics in which the dancers were being presented. In photographs, the costume draws attention because its basic whiteness differs from the audience's casual clothing—denim jeans, calico shirts, and gray to black T-shirts—and because the performers' bent postures and taut neck muscles contrast with the folded draping of the garment.

This chapter considers the combination of T-shirts and drawstring pants (sometimes jeans) worn by many generations of dancers who, as de Langen suggests, rejected the formal expressive attributes of modern dance. Within the first decades of postmodern dance, a particular silhouette and semantic unit, often made of calico, became a new uniform, one associated with ease of movement in dialectical relation to changes in everyday urban life.

In examining this phenomenon, this chapter draws on three strands of inquiry. The first is a reflection on the social economy of the 1960s and 1970s counterculture that gave rise to the minimalist and conceptual choreographies identified with postmodern dance. The focus will be on the choreographers Simone Forti, Steve Paxton, and Trisha Brown and their association with Grand Union, a collective that formed around Judson Church in Greenwich Village during this period. These artists evolved approaches to performance and artmaking based on principles or concepts that would test the limits of form, shifting the perception of the dancing body, the operations that shape an event, and the boundaries of the performance space. In doing so, they often worked with found objects, used task-specific instructions, and presented their works in non-theatrical venues.

They also chose not to make "costumes" a central part of their aesthetic, rejecting artifice and the constrictions of dress designed for dance. By turning to clothes that were mass produced, readily available, and cheap, they were also rejecting the conventions of gender and morality represented by their parents' generation. Instead, they turned toward Eastern martial arts practices to select garment silhouettes that gave more space to the surfaces between cloth and skin.

Brown, who went on to found her own company, became one of the primary exponents of a "cool and colorless" mode of dress, at once beautiful and intellectual while being deceptively ordinary. She worked with designers as collaborators, including Nancy Graves, Judith Shea, and Robert Rauschenberg, but she was also actively involved in costume choices for her choreography. In keeping with the book's focus on iconic forms, the chapter only briefly discusses the distinctive garments that evolved from these commissions, but it does consider how far Brown's personal preferences morphed into the silk tunics discussed in Chapter 1, as she pursued her interest in pure movement as a form of flight. The white costume and its resonance with visual forms of representation raise questions about whether the materiality of postmodern dance might be considered romantic, neoclassical, or even baroque.

Research on this period of costume history largely lacks an archive; few dancers kept the sweaty clothes they wore in those decades, and I have not found a museum that has collected them. T-shirts and pants have been replaced, always with slight variations— newer textiles, modified cuts, shorter sleeves, and different fastenings; all too often, the old ones have become waste. Photographs of original garments or their copies are rare, and only the secondary documentation proves that a certain style was repeated.

The second part of this chapter focuses on aspects of Brown's repertoire and confronts a different set of issues about the costume archive. The Trisha Brown Dance Company is still a performing company and maintains its own wardrobe, in which "original" costumes are still worn and kept to guide the fashioning of new ones. A selection of costumes associated with key early works, like Cunningham's costumes in Chapter 4, have been deposited at the Walker Art Center, particularly those with an artistic signature, such as that of Robert Rauschenberg. A small sample of these costumes is included in this chapter. The Tate Gallery in London has acquired a significant collection of materials screen-printed by Rauschenberg, including costumes associated with *Set and Reset* (1993), but these are not available for viewing or research.[2]

With or without the material remains, the chapter focuses on the distinctive unit of analysis provided by the cut, color, and texture of the assemblage of loose cotton trousers with T-shirts, and the assumed democracy of found clothing. As with other costumes in the book, for an outfit to become a "uniform" representing a distinctive choreographic style depends on its enduring value across choreographies that extend beyond Brown into the present day.

Found Clothing: *Floor of the Forest* (1969–1970)

In 1969, Trisha Brown created a work called *Floor of the Forest* in which dancers climbed into and around items of clothing woven across a suspended grid of ropes. A few years later, Brown described the construction to Anne Livet:

> Sleeves were woven beneath pant legs forming a solid rectangular surface. The frame was suspended horizontally at eye level in the center of an empty room. Two people dressed and undressed their way through it. It was done as naturally as it could be done. A normally vertical activity performed horizontally and reshaped by the pull of gravity. It was strenuous. (Brunel et al. 1987: 34)

The audience either watched from below by squatting or sitting on the floor or studied the intricacies of this playground apparatus from above (Figure 5.2).[3] In performance, the dancers wrestled to get into jeans or wriggled into T-shirts that were stretched to accommodate a leg or torso. The dancers had to navigate the matrix of ropes, and familiarize themselves with each garment's capacity to let them enter or not. Some of the most satisfying moments for spectators came when a dancer was tightly suspended between a couple of items mismatched to their bodies, and the garments must sag or stretch in response to their weight. At times, the dancers hung, heads down and toes tucked in, resting a while. With the bulbous shapes, the strange blockages, and flapping movements, the dancers appeared like fish or monkeys, and the performance generated ripples of laughter.

Floor of the Forest became an exposition of the ways in which a body might be held by a garment and how our bodies reconfigure weight, shape, and comfort in different items of clothing. A decade later, in a review of Douglas Dunn's performance, *Echo*, the New York dance critic Deborah Jowitt (1980a) observed: "Perhaps the exchanging of clothes points out that movement can be shared or exchanged and that [clothes] hang differently on different people." In addition to reimagining the horizons of movement from the vertical to the horizontal, *Floor of the Forest* makes the exchange of clothes between dancers an active navigation of trying out, and trying on, examining the possibilities of altered form in a garment. This economy of bartering, adaptation, and making-do also represents an ethos in which what was "found" became an essential aspect of art and dance.

The title, for instance, invokes the litter, leaves, and debris that fall onto the floor of a forest, and from within which new life emerges—seedlings that poke through the mulch, smells that come from the rotting materials, and the replenishment of the soil itself. First performed in Brown's studio apartment and working loft, with textile fragments "not cleaned up" from "the preceding manufacturer," the space was already littered. In that

FIGURE 5.2 *Floor of the Forest,* 1970 performance at Coffman Union, University of Minnesota, Minneapolis, April 30, 1979. Courtesy Walker Art Center Archives.

sense, the secondhand clothing also recalled the detritus of the building, and its now-absent workers, as a place of garment manufacturing.

The art historian Susan Rosenberg in her book *Trisha Brown: Choreography as Visual Art* describes a remaking of the piece a year later, in which Brown added a *Rummage Sale*, so that people were "actually trading and exchanging clothes" under the installation (2016: 89). By 1979 for another reconstruction, Brown was explicit that pristine garments were not to be used: "The clothes were familiar to me; I had collected them from friends. The piece, therefore, continues to this day through my seeing or being told of one of those bargains" (Livet 1987). By connecting the experience of art with the transactions of everyday life, Brown took pleasure in the ways in which trying on garments produced new sensations, as well as reconnecting with "clothes [that] are artifacts of history" (Rosenberg 2016: 89).

The phenomenologist Iris Marion Young is attentive to these forms of "bonding" that take place between women. She writes that when "the clothes flow among us, so do our identities . . . we do not just exchange; we let or do not let each other into our lives" (2005: 71). Figure 5.3 shows how feet and hands in *Floor of the Forest* elaborated

FIGURE 5.3 Audience bartering for clothes, *Floor of the Forest,* 1970 performance at Coffman Union, University of Minnesota, Minneapolis, April 30, 1979. Courtesy Walker Art Center Archives.

a choreography of gestures associated with touching and exchanging garments on the "floor" as well as in the leaves and branches of the garment frame above.

For Rosenberg, this composition also bore "the marks of impoverished SoHo living with the selection of clothing merely functional, holding no appeal to the eye" (2016: 89). Functional clothing was however a deliberate part of an aesthetic during this period, especially in places like New York's downtown, where "second-hand and vintage clothes were worn with hippie pride" (English 2007: 96). Rather than determined by visual appeal, the performance reflects on the material conditions of a lived reality, in which the history and memories of garment "recycling" included "consequent changes in sexual [and social] morality" (English 2007: 96). Making visible the awkwardness of dressing in, or removing, a recycled garment celebrates the fecund transformation of an everyday choreography. The not-forgotten movements in the body of each garment imprint a layered, sometimes invisible, process of transmutation to personal memories of clothing hidden in the *Floor of the Forest.*

The material conditions of Brown's early performances mostly involved "found" situations, including works made in the street and on rooftops, in and around Brown's residence, like that of other "loft-dwellers" in downtown New York City. The area known as SoHo (South of Houston Street) was named in 1962, when a group of town planners, urban activists, and community members began to reclaim these relatively abandoned streets. The new residents occupied the grand nineteenth-century buildings that were constructed a century before to house the expanding garment industry. Textile firms owned these large warehouses, and their workers had lived alongside them in tenement buildings, where a single room housed a family, and in which all members made coats and suits for the growing city.

After World War II, with industrial rights gaining a hold in the textile industry and growing mechanization of sewing and cutting, the manufacturers moved the industry out of the city into provinces such as New Jersey. With cheaper labor, they could employ the "low-skill assembly line" methods of "section-work" that had become the norm in product manufacturing (Wilson 2003: 84). Between 1947 and 1956, 22,000 workers from the garment industry left New York. Many large buildings stood empty, while others were pulled down or converted into garages, printing plants, or auto-repair shops. By the 1960s, small stores began to sell cheap, mass-produced, and imported clothing. Pictures from Greenwich Village streets in Figures 5.4 and 5.5 provide a sense of the energetic activity that was focused on this circulation of clothing merchandise.

Artists, students, and communes seeking cheap accommodation were attracted to "the Village," because warehouses and tenements, which previously housed machines or multiple tenants, offered tall ceilings, big windows, and large rooms for studio living. "Time can make the space efficiencies of one generation the space luxuries of another generation," observed Jane Jacobs, author of *The Death and Life of Great American Cities* (1961: 202).[4]

The Greenwich Village zone was however under constant threat from developers in the City Council who wanted to carve it up with two large freeways (Lax 2018: 21). In this struggle for urban space, activists and writers such as Jacobs began to argue for mixed-use developments, community neighborhoods, and "walk-able streets."[5] Notably, Jacobs framed the sidewalk as a central mechanism for maintaining the social fabric: "This order

FIGURE 5.4 Lower East Side street scene c. 1965. Photograph by Gerald Silverman. Image: Tenement Museum Collection, New York.

FIGURE 5.5 Clothing stores operating out of a tenement building at 96 Orchard Street, 1992. Photograph by Jerome Liebling. Image: Tenement Museum Collection, New York.

is all composed of movement and change, and although it is life, not art, we may fancifully call it the art form of the city and liken it to the dance" (1961: 60). For Jacobs, an "intricate sidewalk ballet" occurred on this quotidian stage in which everyone had a distinctive role that "never repeats itself from place to place, and in any one place is replete with new improvisations" (1961: 60–61).

Many of the downtown artists took their inspiration from the streets, the structures, and the activity around them, and their dress aesthetic, as Charlie Porter points out in his book *What Artists Wear*, included found clothes or work clothes. "Clothing was either practical or sociological," he writes (2021:118). For the visual artist Gordon Matta Clark, also Brown's friend, this choice meant wearing "Practical clothes. Dressing for protection and warmth." Concerned about basic survival, Matta experimented with the idea of "wearing your house," selecting a clothing style adapted to living on the streets.

During this period, Brown created *Leaning Duets* (1971), which involved two people holding hands, leaning sideways, and balancing down a cobbled street, and the acclaimed *Man Walking Down the Side of a Building* (1970), which made the cast-iron fire escape and rear windows of a warehouse the subject and partner of the performance. In those works, the "dancers" wore their own clothes—the cast-off jeans, the ready-made T-shirts, and sneakers. The dancers in Brown's *Roof and Fire Piece* (1973) wore "red sweat suits," but the film documentation by Brown's collaborator, Babette Mangolte, shows some variations; one performer wears the T-shirt and trousers, and another has platform sandals (Rosenberg 2016: 102). Red was chosen so that people "could pick them out," according to Brown, but the color is also indicative of the "fire" element in the work's full title and reconnects the costume with local garment history (Livet 1987).

In 1911, the notorious Triangle Shirtwaist factory fire in Greenwich Village killed 146 garment workers, predominantly women, according to local history (von Drehle 2004). Most could not escape; some climbed onto the roofs, but many fell to their deaths. The silent and stationary signaling of female dancers in *Roof and Fire Piece* (1973) has eerie echoes of these mostly invisible narratives of the warehouse roof. Seeing the water tanks that feed the buildings, with the women calmly wearing red, is a reminder of the impact fire has had in such an environment.

The sweatsuits were also a classic garment socialized in this period. Designed for comfort and ease of movement, the shaping of a sweatsuit is loose, combining a top with no darts and basic sleeves with pants that have an elasticized or drawstring waist; the fabric is mostly cotton jersey. These low-cost constructions are made to standard sizes and do not require exact measurements. They are manufactured in sweatshops where workers are given the segmented pieces of the garment and repeatedly cut or sew hundreds of units with the same fabric every day. Whether in a factory in New Jersey, in the Caribbean, or in Vietnam, sweatsuits have become appropriated as a reward for leisure time in the capitalist system; they are mass-produced garments for mass culture. With the trickle-down effects of excessive consumption, cheaper recycled versions of the T-shirt or sweatsuit eventually return to the class that made them. Before that, they became components of the costume "look" for an avant-garde creating postmodern dance.

T-shirts and Mass Clothing: Grand Union (1971)

Forti, Brown, Paxton, and Yvonne Rainer, among others, were members of a group that formed to create experimental performances in and around Judson Church. Loosely identified as a collective called Grand Union, these artists "used pedestrian movement, participatory explorations, scores, and unusual performance contexts to disturb the normative performer–spectator relationship, creating new terrains for shared sensation" (Henderson 2011: 75).

In her ground-breaking book *Terpsichore in Sneakers* (1980), Sally Banes labeled these experimental dance practices postmodern, as distinct from modern. She also considered using blue jeans in her title, so the reference to "sneakers" was somewhat anomalous; in reality, the dancers were often barefoot (Kourlas 2020). Tom Berthiaume's photograph (Figure 5.6) shows the abandoned footwear—lace-up sneakers, hiking boots, leather-thonged sandals, and tangled socks—removed by the Grand Union artists during a performance. Their casual style rejects dance costume as a form of dressing up, yet it too is affected; the seemingly "pedestrian" style of dress is nonetheless conceptualized for performance. "The wearing of blue jeans may express counter-culture ideology," Hollander observes, "but they are still worn for their looks" (1975: 313). And since this book investigates the materiality of dance costumes, the history of even the most informal or everyday components of dress becomes significant.

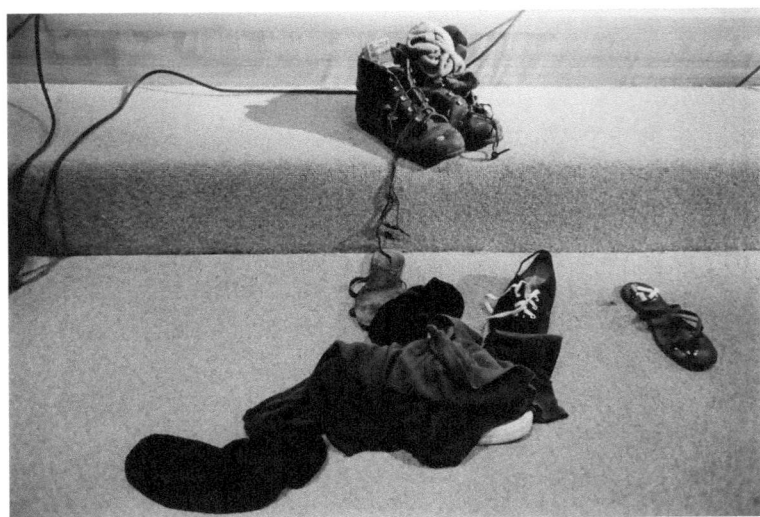

FIGURE 5.6 Shoes from Grand Union performance in Walker Art Center Auditorium, May 1971. Photograph by Tom Berthiaume. Courtesy of Walker Art Center Archives.

The white T-shirt has been identified with the youthful heroes of postwar Hollywood film. Figures such as Marlon Brando in *Streetcar Named Desire* (1951) and James Dean in *Rebel Without a Cause* (1955) appropriated this item of clothing to brand a new form of "rebellious youth" as the popular style of 1950s masculinity (Figure 5.7). Of equal significance, the white T-shirt was worn by male African American boxers such as Sugar Ray Robinson, whose fame was unparalleled in this period; the white T-shirt soaked in sweat became almost an emblem of his heroism in the boxing ring (Figure 5.8). Earlier accounts attribute the white T-shirt to the sailors returning from the war who adopted this cotton undergarment as a form of flirtatious masculinity visible from the ship's deck. The derivation of the word with its descriptive T perhaps belongs to F. Scott Fitzgerald in *This Side of Paradise*: "So early in September Amory, provided with 'six suits summer underwear, six suits winter underwear, one sweater or T-shirt, one jersey, one overcoat, winter, etc.,' set out for New England, the land of schools" (1920: 16). From this list of appearances, the T-shirt became an essential fashion item in a young man's wardrobe.

In her *Cultural History of Fashion*, Bonnie English views the "inexpensive T-shirt" as a "blank canvas" that offers "diversity and changeability" by allowing for printing, painting, and the expression of social or political beliefs or affiliations. A T-shirt, she writes, could be "worn to street marches . . . bridging language and cultural barriers . . . as a means of protest and propaganda" (2007: 92). Because of their cheap production, they also rapidly became commodified with slogans and contemporary branding.

At the same time, "taste in T-shirts" includes "fabric, cut, [and] embellishments" that add distinction, including those "other associations one wishes to make or makes unconsciously: suggestions of regional origin, social style, sexual and moral outlook,

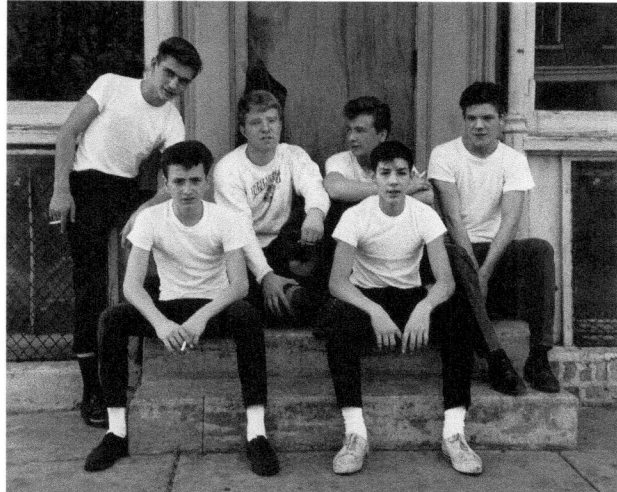

FIGURE 5.7 Group of urban teenage boys sitting on a step, 1953. Photo: Underwood Archives/UIG/ Bridgeman Images.

FIGURE 5.8 American boxer Sugar Ray Robinson, 1921–1989 training in Paris on November 20, 1950. Photo © AGIP/Bridgeman Images.

attitudes towards work, money, leisure, and pleasure, and above all, the other people one's clothes associate one with" (Hollander 1975: 347). As Hollander observes, two T-shirts that "resemble each other closely" may differ in price by a factor of twenty (1975: 347). As a "non-fashion" item, the T-shirt may claim the "concept of comfort" and gender-neutrality, both concerns of importance to second-wave feminism, but as Hollander observes, "They don't simply look comfortable and casual, primarily, they look like all the other people of their sex and age who wear the same garments" (1975: 348). They therefore do not escape being part of a fashion system.

In 1971, Grand Union spent three weeks as artists in residence at the Walker Art Center, where they offered classes, created installations, and hosted improvised performances. Documentation of these events shows a gallery housing a large timber box frame, mountains of cardboard, and yards of cloth awkwardly draped from the ceiling (Figure 5.9). Members of the ensemble can be seen climbing up and over the timber structure while others sit on a sofa surrounded by lamps and televisions. The group's clothing is eclectic: patterned skirts, denim jeans, gloves, men's shirts, a dust coat, with one holding a Japanese umbrella.

At the heart of this style are off-the-rack T-shirts or sweatshirts and mass-produced or homemade trousers—a style adopted by youth culture during the 1970s, now entering dance aesthetics. The stretchy 1960s unitard persists in some Judson performances, alongside naked bodies, but this new outfit changes the visibility of movement while accommodating gender neutrality and more diverse bodies. Wearing the T-shirt for dancing aligns with this moment of egalitarian promise—the unadorned blank canvas adopted by students, artists, and writers—and rejects materialist and conventional, indeed synthetic, forms of dress. Dungarees and T-shirts, or hippie alternatives such as faded blue jeans and handmade items using printed and flowered fabrics, were acquired from secondhand clothing or discount shops, or as in Brown's *Floor of the Forest*, often also bartered or exchanged between men and women (English 2007: 96). In the disheveled outfits of Grand Union, whether climbing on slant-boards, throwing balls, rolling on floors, or reciting

FIGURE 5.9 Grand Union performance in Walker Art Center lobby, May 1971. Photograph by Tom Berthiaume. Courtesy of Walker Art Center Archives.

poetry, the performers looked, smelt, and felt much like the assembled audience. They were practicing a form of social democracy by adopting a non-hierarchical attitude toward the body—in which every little movement matters—and their rejection of spectacle required a limiting of adornment in dress.[6]

During this countercultural moment, as in other social insurrections, gender-neutral clothing becomes a potent sign of political change. Ulrich Lehmann argues in *Tigersprung* that "the revolutionary garb of male and female sans-culottes and the unisex long shirts made from calico" were central to the visualization of the French revolutionary subject (2000: 313). Another form of unisex revolutionary dress—the dark trousers and buttoned jackets of railway workers—became the dress code of Maoist China. Such revolutionary ideologies infect the dress codes of postmodern dance in different ways, not least through their adoption of "working clothes" as fashion, the massification of a "look," and later the usurpation of Eastern aesthetic values related to clothing.

The genre of "pedestrian" performance, with its improvisatory logics and attention to somatic experience, has led to claims and counterclaims about the "democratization" of dance in Judson Dance Theater (Burt 2006). Dance historians such as Danielle Goldman (2010) are critical of the liberatory ethos aligned with the conditions of improvisational dance, and the curator Thomas J. Lax identifies a "subliminal racism" in the postmodernists' quest for an egalitarian dance (Lax 2018: 21). Despite the geographical proximity in New York, the downtown experimental art scene had little interaction with African American artists; even if black dancers, such as Eleo Pomare discussed in this book's Introduction, also performed in T-shirts as a continuation of street style.

On an economic level, the informal dress codes associated with cheaper methods of fabrication and design were neither more nor less democratic in their "anti-materialist bias" (English 2007: 94). The availability of such clothing was the result of mass production techniques in the "world market factory" of clothing manufacture (Wilson 2003: 85). One result of this mass production system is that there are few remains; and yet, the minimalist aesthetic depended on the redundancies of excess consumption because every low-value T-shirt was substitutable for another. The postmodern dancers who adopted these unadorned garments were delivering their rejection and refashioning of the "industrial or technological processes" that had built the architectures, clothing systems, theatrical forms, and exchange practices of modern capitalist societies. Nonetheless, they were complicit with changes in modes of dress production that enabled access to cheap clothing, and the flexible stylization that accumulated from racialized systems of postwar representation. The very neutrality of the T-shirt, and its redundancy, appears supercharged with potential—sensuous and simple, replaceable and iconic, form-fitting and comfortable—and in color, white or neutral, it produces a calculated minimization of the corporeal surface. This flexible and replaceable commodity can easily become excess and waste.

When Robert Whitman invited Brown to perform with her husband in *Flower* (1963) at Judson Church, layers of street clothes were pulled off their bodies with accumulating tension (Rosenberg 2016: 85). The corporeal politics served as a reminder that these art-ists "lived and worked" in precarity, "on the periphery of the world's economy, stimulated by the labor and productions of that economy, with no support, no place in the struc-ture of the market" (Annette Michelson cited in Rosenberg 2016: 108). In the critical spirit of the Judson Church, Jennifer Monson later made a T-shirt performance called *ode to summer*, that was presented in Melbourne in 2000. The piece begins with Monson "screaming into the room midst the noise of smashing glass. She rolled on the ground with what at first seemed like a lot of padding but subsequently was revealed to be the many T-shirts she was wearing. The subsequent removal of each was like the removal of layers peeling back to the kernel, an autobiography of T-shirts" (McDonald 2000).[7] The European conceptual choreographer, Jerome Bel's work, *Shirtologie* (1997) also "peels off layers of T-shirts and sweatshirts with words, brand names, imprints," displaying as Andre Lepecki suggests, "the vast image archive" of our everyday saturation in clothing as commodity form (2006: 55–56). The dialectical costume—some carrying slogans, others brand advertising, some too large and others too tight—therefore functions as both parody and protest at the role the T-shirt has played in postmodern dance, as synecdoche for democracy, as alternative community, and residue of labor history.

Aikido Uniforms and Contact Dance (1972)

The casualization of dance costume was never static. By the late 1960s, American post-modern choreographers were not only rejecting virtuosic movement in the concert space but experimenting with the physical training systems and philosophy informing mar-tial arts, especially Aikido. If the "mass clothing" of the T-shirt became one uniform for dance, then the formal neutrality of waist-tied, loose-legged pants reflected further changes in the transnational formation of dress codes in dance.

America's postwar rapprochement with Japan generated a global flow of ideas that influenced writers and artists as diverse as Allen Ginsberg and Yoko Ono, and Paul Reps's (1957) book *Zen Flesh, Zen Bones* became a manual for the counterculture. By the early 1960s, Steve Paxton, a young dancer from Merce Cunningham's company, had begun learning Aikido in New York. At the time, most practitioners teaching this martial art were Americans who had lived in Japan during and after the war.[8] Paxton and the artist Robert Rauschenberg were some of the first students at the New York *dojo* (studio) estab-lished in 1961 by Virginia Mayhew. Mayhew had studied Judo and then Aikido in Japan at Morihei Ueshiba's Aikikai Hombu Dojo under the instruction of the revered master Koichi Tohei Sensei (Figure 5.10). She was the only non-Japanese female to have learned Aikido directly from O-Sensei, according to Guillaume Erard.[9] Following successful Aikido demonstrations at the World's Fair in Queens in 1964, Mayhew was joined by a full-time Japanese instructor, Yoshimitsu Yamada. He assumed control of the New York Dojo and became a leading figure in the dissemination of Aikido in the United States.

FIGURE 5.10 Virginia Mayhew practicing with student. Unknown photographer, c. 1970s. Courtesy of New York Aikikai.

This studio in the Village attracted artists, journalists, and intellectuals seeking alternative paths and lifestyles.

Paxton may have studied with Mayhew, but must certainly have trained with Yamada. Philosophically grounded in ideas of balance, the practice of Aikido involves redirecting resistance, and release through falling. Beyond the physical training, the spiritual ethos was directed toward non-violence, or how "to adopt a peaceful stance" (Patel 2013).[10] The political implications of redirecting violence when meeting the energies of a rival warrior originated in samurai forms in traditional Japan. As Japan began recovering from the devastation of war and atomic bombing, many military training regimes were translated into new philosophical systems by master practitioners. Between 1942 and 1948 (Holiday 2013: 64–65), Aikido emerged as a way of reaching out to the West— "making one with the opponent." When these training practices were adopted by dance practitioners such as Paxton, the political diplomacy was transformed into a sub-branch of postmodern dance called Contact Dance (Holiday 2013: 107).

At Oberlin College in 1972, Nancy Stark Smith, a co-founder of Contact Improvisation, confirmed that connections between Aikido teachers and students in New York had seeded the formation of new approaches to weight and flow.[11] This duet form depends upon two partners using contact between their bodies to identify subtle shifts in weight that might propel motion, whether small adjustments or becoming airborne. The frequent experience of falling in contact dance requires "a dynamic balance" that is practiced through repetition, so that, according to Stark Smith, an experience of "enjoyment took the place of fear and disorientation" (cited in Albright 2013: 372).

In (Figure 5.11) Paxton is performing an Aikido roll at the Walker Art Center— falling backward, head down with toes and head counterbalancing the force of gravity.

FIGURE 5.11 Steve Paxton performing with Grand Union, Guthrie Theater, Minneapolis, October 5, 1975. Photograph by Boyd Hagen. Courtesy of Walker Art Center Archives.

The ripple down his spine embodies the exuberant articulation of corporeal disequilibrium adopted by Contact. The dancing is enhanced by Paxton's basic attire—a T-shirt scored by a printed motif and flowing pants.[12] To minimize friction between surfaces in a duet, Contact practitioners typically wear soft, loose clothing modeled on the garments of Aikido.

Aikido's formal but loose white garments have a very particular Japanese historicity and materiality. The trousers, the *hakama,* are tied at the waist with strings and reinforced at the knees, a protection for kneeling actions (*suari waza*). A loose-fitting jacket, cut short at the sleeves and hem, known as *keikogi* or *gi,* covers the torso and is secured with a belt of cloth called an *obi.* Traditionally, this garment included the embroidered insignia of the local samurai, and still today, a medallion marks out a particular lineage and unifies the troupe.[13] Similar in structure to a kimono, the jacket is cut from four lengths of fabric manipulated into folds and has a serial multiplicity; its characteristic patterns—sleeves, fronts, and back panels—are encoded in a ritualized folding taught to novice students during their training. In dance rehearsal rooms, this process is often de-ritualized, but strands of continuity exist between these martial arts garments and the advent of loose-fitting clothing in dance.

These same principles of costume construction appear in the fashion of the Japanese designers Issey Miyake, Rei Kawakubo, and Yohji Yamamoto, whose philosophy of fabric craft includes advocating for the "poverty, simplicity, and imperfections" of traditional clothing (English 2007: 122). For them, the kimono is distinctive as a structure that uses simple shapes, but also because of the "space between the garment and the body and its general flexibility" (English 2007: 124). As a companion to movement, this aesthetic form of fabric drapery corresponds to the kinesiology of somatic practices—such as yoga and tai chi—that entered dance in the early 1970s. Mabel Todd's pioneering book *The Thinking Body*, for instance, developed movement imagery linked to anatomical alignment, with a "constructive rest" exercise inviting practitioners to lie on the floor and visualize the leaking of sand from the seams of a "suit" (1968). Experiencing the quality of space between the body and the loose fabric worn during training activates a qualitative change toward a more released, fluid, and softer dynamic that supports a "collapsible body" (Perron 2013: 14).

In terms of fabric, this chapter can be linked with calico, an unbleached, "natural" use of cotton, although calico and cotton are by no means the exclusive fabrics of postmodern dance costumes. T-shirts differ widely in their cotton fiber counts, and knitted cotton jerseys may be chemically treated to make them softer, colored, or blended with synthetic fibers. The loose pants, however, whether fabricated in the heavier styles of Japanese *gi* or made from hand-sewn calico or linen, will soften with washing to bend at the knees and yet remain strong enough to knot and fall easily from the hips. The stylization of such cotton garments involves a lack of markings, retaining an apparent anonymity of origins. But their manufacture always happens somewhere with material implications.

After the cotton industry developments outlined in Chapter 3, in 1966, "cotton growers in the United States successfully petitioned Congress to pass the Cotton Research and Promotion Act" (Hancock et al. 2016: 23). This led to the formation of Cotton Incorporated, an organization that "would lobby fiber mills and the general global public to reap the benefits that cotton had to offer the American consumer with the tag line 'the touch, the feel of cotton, the fabric of our lives'" (Hancock et al. 2016: 23). It was backed by new trade protection laws aiming to recover the market share lost to Asian economies such as India, Japan, and China. These trade subsidies were valued at more than 100 per cent of production costs and directed billions into the use of pesticides and new technologies (Thanhauser 2022: 54). According to Sven Beckert, the cotton grown in the United States "is so uncompetitive on the world market" that it relies on subsidies equal to the GDPs of entire developing nations (2014: 429). Still, the United States remains one of the world's largest exporters of cotton goods, even though the industrial protections achieved in advanced economies have been replaced by systems independent of state regulation elsewhere. The fabrics of the dance studio are thus either produced by subsidized industries, or by other countries using exploitative methods. In either case, dance maintains its dialectical relationship with the global flow of goods and ideas.

The rest of this chapter unfolds from these historical narratives, of localized avant-garde transmission and transnational politics, that have shaped the cotton uniform of postmodern dance. It examines more closely the choreographic representation of this semantic unit, T-shirt and loose trousers, in works from the repertoire of Trisha Brown and her company. With her interest in minimalist repetition, Brown configures this costume multiple times. Even when her more theatrical works differ from this ideal, the "pajama" silhouette remains a referent for movement.[14] And later, when the fibers cease to be cotton, the significance of the fabric becomes more complicated.

"Neutral" Clothing and *Line Up* (1976)

In the signature piece *Accumulation* (1971), Brown stares into the camera and repeats a set of hand gestures that commence with hands outstretched, thumbs up. She wears a long-sleeved pale top and wide floral-patterned pants in pinkish-red tones. After a while, she begins to rotate her hips and turn her torso. With this, the dance veers onto another plane. The trousers flare out around her like a skirt so that traces of the spinal rotation linger. The beauty of her choreography lies in these understated qualities and her use of an immediately recognizable hand gesture. Is she hitchhiking? Turning a tap? Winding something up?

In *Accumulation with Talking*, she adds a spoken autobiographical narrative, sometimes a deceptively short memory, at other times a long, rambling story. Brown describes the primary gestures of her dance vocabulary as "fold, extension, and rotation," and these actions are relayed and repeated through the soft weaves of her costume. In a subsequent version of the same work called *Primary Accumulation*, Brown lies prone on the floor, one foot artfully bent upward while the other arm rests languidly by her side. The sequence of gestures is familiar, and she often turns her head and torso away from the viewer. She is wearing what Rosenberg calls "neutral" clothing, loose pants and a long-sleeved cotton top (2016: 124). In many of these works, Brown's costume appears to do very little: Does it say anything? Or more performatively, does it do anything? As the earlier part of this chapter indicates, Brown also participated in Grand Union, wearing a range of clothing types from the informal to the dancerly (leotards and tights), but her interest in costume was far from "casual." Indeed, attention to dress, like the details of her thinking about the micro-movements that accumulate in the body, always informed her visual and choreographic aesthetic.

In *Group Accumulation* (1973), the choreography of the former variations is magnified by four female performers lying on the floor together, lifting their legs, rolling their heads, and upper torsos. Their plain soft clothing deflects attention away from individual dancerly identities toward their actions, and the rolling and recumbent shaping of spaces between them. The T-shirts and knotted waists draw attention to the contours, and the fabric folds, wrinkles, and buckles, occasionally twisting on the chest and arms as they rotate. In a quiet and dignified manner, the choreographic actions arouse other connotations—sleeping, corpses, swaddled children, hysterics in hospital gowns. When they roll together, the dancers become a landscape of snowy mountains, hills, and valleys. They lift their heads and chest in an awkward cresting action, and the relaxed splaying of their legs is erotic and vulnerable.

This modest garment's signification in Brown's choreography reaches its apogee in the ensemble piece *Line Up* (1976), a work that includes the segments *Spanish Dance* (1973) and *Structured Pieces* (1973). Methodologically, this dance is a critical study in Brown's incremental approach to the sudden fluctuations that generate movement for dancing. It was created through improvisation with dancers in her first company. They were asked to memorize and "accumulate" the movement vocabulary generated in twenty seconds in response to the instruction "Let's begin again" (Perron 2013). Adding sticks and corner formations, making lines and breaking them down, determined the structures and prepared the architecture of the performance space.

In *Spanish Dance*, a powerful movement motif emerges from a task in which five dancers shuffle across the stage, eventually snaking into a line one behind the other (Figure 5.12).[15] Performed to a Gordon Lightfoot song, *Early Morning Rain*, sung by Bob Dylan, the sentiment is a nostalgic story about feeling stuck "on the ground" at an airport a long way from home. The guitar chords whine along to a steady 4/4 beat, and the dancers move with the rhythm. The erotic pleasure, and perhaps joke, of this dance is that as one dancer shuffles into another, their wiggling hips merge, crotch cupped in pelvis, with knees bending in time. Slowly, they become a pulsing train—a midnight rolling along—while seductively their arms are lifted into high *port de bras*. Any subtle elevation of the ankle is replicated, transmitting an upward pulse until the dancers find "their sultry siren

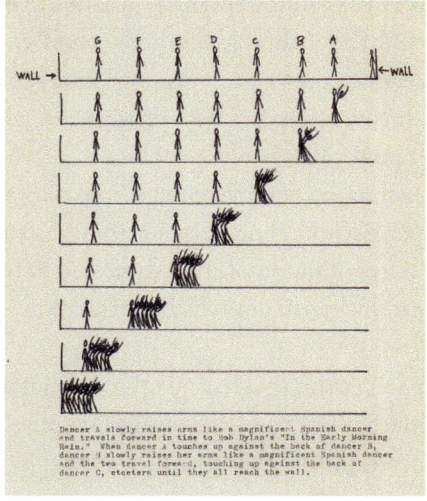

FIGURE 5.12 Trisha Brown, *Spanish Dance*, part of *Accumulating Pieces*, 1973. Walker Art Center.

selves" in the (silent) bravado of flamenco (Kraus 2011). Without the egoism of a duet, the seductive gestures of the "line-up" seize the plaintive notes of the song and transform the self-pity of the singer into a manifestation of feminist jouissance or feminine desire.

In its earliest incarnation, *Spanish Dance* was performed in everyday clothes, like those of Grand Union. A 1973 photo by Babette Mangolte shows the dancers wearing dark trousers (possibly colored), at least one pair of jeans, track pants, and printed fabric tops in various lengths and colors (Rosenberg 2016: 141). The movement in the image is also asynchronous. According to Rosenberg, the dancers "adopted long-sleeved white T-shirts and white drawstring pants" during the Festival Automne in Paris in 1973; these were later "formalized as costumes" for performances of the collected work, *Accumulating Pieces*, at the Walker Art Center in 1976, to represent "signature qualities of Brown's 1970s choreographies—their neutrality, purity, and abstraction" (2016: 150).

Lisa Kraus, one of the original co-creators, describes the relationship between the choreography and this seemingly innocent, unadorned outfit in these terms: "It was a dance for all women, simply and uniformly clad, strong and smart, but reflecting the non-heroic performer ethos of its time. Its virtuosity was brainy rather than flashy; it's tongue-in-cheek with a fresh breeze (2011)." The iconicity of this silhouette also appears in company correspondence, which features the flexible S-bends of the white T-shirt and pants on three dancers in profile. In the culminating accumulation of *Spanish Dance*, the waistlines and variegated folds visibilize how minimal differences in a garment can be relayed in dance (Figure 5.13). In more recent performances and exhibitions of *Accumulating Pieces* by the Trisha Brown Dance Company, the white cotton long-sleeved T-shirts and loose white pants tied at the waist are always reproduced.

In *The Fashion System*, Barthes describes the shift of an iconic garment from the level of manufacture to its role in the plasticity of an image system as a process that involves the "accentuation of a movement, enlargement of a detail, [and] angle of vision" (1990: 6). The repetitions of this costume ensemble accentuate Brown's patient excavation of corporeal sensations, and the malleable fabric becomes enlarged by the subtlety of wrinkles. When the dancers enter into close relations, body to body, the angle of vision infills the choreographic imagination: the field of white on white, moving in costumes and walls, has an aesthetic power that invites attention. Like white sheets in the wind, the dancers reflect the pure abstraction of movement, eliminating all but the energetic pulse.

Throughout her career, Brown's choreographic thinking sought to illuminate a fragment or a single point in the continuum of space-time and to transmit the immediacy of a gesture, turn, or lift by producing an unpredictable iteration:

> Pure movement is a movement that has no other connotation. It is not functional
> or pantomimic . . . Mechanical body actions like bending, straightening, or
> rotating would qualify as pure movement, providing the context was neutral.
> (Brown cited by Rosenberg 2016: 115)

FIGURE 5.13 Trisha Brown Company dancers Lisa Kraus, Mona Sulzman, Trisha Brown, Elizabeth Garren, and Wendy Perron performing *Spanish Dance*, 1973, at the Brooklyn Academy of Music. Photograph by Nathaniel Tileston, 1977. Courtesy of Trisha Brown Dance Company Archives. © The Estate of Nathaniel Tileston.

The repetitions of bodily actions and the neutrality of the costume repertoire as "context" exemplify this belief in pure movement.[16]

In terms of serial modification, Brown's approach to the incremental effects of minimal variation has parallels in the minimalist music and visual art of the 1970s. These ideas, as with task-based improvisation, underpinned a shift away from expression and technical abstraction to modes of production that visually or audibly copy a tone or pattern. The musicologist Robert Fink says that minimalism in music relies on repetition, which is "sometimes experienced as pleasurable and erotic, but more often as painfully excessive, alienating, and (thus) sublime" (2005: 4). For Brown, the minimalism of the clothing, its capacity for serial repetition, and its visual diminishing of dress as an arbiter of expression have produced a minimalist dance aesthetic; this may seem "alienating," but with the haptic qualities of the dancer's clothing transmitted through folds and rotations, the choreographic experience also becomes sublime.

In 2011, Brown's choreography was shown at the Museum of Modern Art, and stark white new costumes were worn for the pristine modernism of *Line Up* in the context of visual culture. According to rehearsal director Diane Madden, the subtle differences of Brown's "modernist" line accumulate from the embodied knowledge and eloquent movement of the dancers, realizing the potential of repetition (Madden 2011).[17] This refabricated line up and the vertical kinesthesia therefore align the dance costume with discourses on art that have the "clarity and generalized texture of antique drapery . . . undoubtedly most perfectly realized in uncolored marble" or rather a transmission through loose white clothing (Hollander 1975: 77).

Before moving on from this specific configuration of the postmodern dance costume, I want to interrogate the color allusions of these fluid garments. Like the tutu, the T-shirt and pants are often "white," even when gray, beige, or muted by other tones. Whiteness is a reminder of the purity of movement as "Art." In art history, white paint appears in elaborate tribal ochres as well as in the thick gloss of Renaissance painting, and its intensity depends upon the materials from which it has been constituted—bone white, shell white, chalk white, lime white (which can look milky), and the much desired but toxic lead white (Finlay 2002: 120). Lead white, now replaced by zinc and titanium white, has the brilliant sheen of a white that stands apart from other hues. "White paint is white because it reflects most light rays away from it. The penalty it pays for this apparent purity is that it absorbs no light into its own body" (Finlay 2002: 120). It is "pure" because it is non-absorbent, reflecting light back into the eye of the beholder, a minor blinding of perception. For natural fibers to remain white, however, chemical intervention is essential, since calico absorbs stains and particles of dirt with alacrity. The use of bleach and other chemicals breaks the chemical bonds of chromophores within a fiber and releases oxygen molecules. This molecular change prevents the absorption of light and hence the material represents a rejection and absence of color. In choreography, white costumes, in this absence, are mostly seen on stage through the movement of illuminated shadows on a surface.

The color white has not always been symbolic of purity. The white shroud has long been associated with death, and "in China and Japan the color represents death and sickness in general and funerals in particular" (Finlay 2002: 119). From the nineteenth century, white clothing developed its connotation as a mark of distinction; "in Western culture, a woman wearing white so often represents purity that it is easy to imagine the paint itself having that squeaky clean reputation as well" (Finlay 2002: 119). In the United States, James Whistler's painting of "White No. 1: The White Girl" precipitated a fashion for white dresses, white handbags, white lilies, and even what were called "white waltzes" (Finlay 2002: 141). If one translates this color to the "white ballets," wearing white may represent purity, but it is also romantically associated with a morbid sensibility and the "dying swan." One might also recall material associations with "white paint" in the facial mask (often disfigured by lead poisoning) of the "sad clown" or of "white powder" as the toxicity of morphine in the drug underworld. And the white suits worn by music stars can be a flashy statement that has at times carried fascist connotations. For feminist politics, a white dress references the suffragettes who marched in white when campaigning for the vote. These many connotations of a white costume are a reminder that the wearing of a white dress or suit is a fashion choice.

Laboring the extent to which the T-shirt and loose pants represent a costume constellation, its ongoing presence in dance uncannily fabricates attitudes toward movement across rehearsal rooms, workshops, and performances. When Steve Paxton created *Audible Scenery* (1986) for the London-based Extemporary Dance Theatre, the dancers wore a neat, white, and slightly tighter version of this outfit, made by Isabella Hargrave with more transparent fabric and visible seams.[18] With sporty jumping and running in the choreography, the athletic dancers appeared like a deconstructed English cricket team: cool, fast, and calculated. In *Aether* (2005) by Australian choreographer Lucy Guerin, male and female dancers appeared in a brown-toned variation of the T-shirt and trousers, with the serial repetition sublimating gendered differences into a rhetorical strategy.[19] These copy costumes, with their blurry boundaries, make the dress code citation a potential pantomime in a larger historical pattern. Much like the minimalist music incorporated into sound reproduction by the culture industry, these "pure" costumes of postmodern minimalist choreography become dialectical, not through their distinction but by their repetition in mass choreographic formations that produce a disturbing sense of "sublime" detachment in the artwork.

Brown's 1981 work *Son of Gone Fishin'* almost signals an end to this period. Made in collaboration with the visual artist Donald Judd, the minimalist costumes were constructed by designer and sculptor Judith Shea for the ensemble of male and female dancers (Figure 5.14).[20] With Brown's choreography remixing movement motifs on a grander scale, Judd experimented with a color field of "dark blue cloth dropped halfway down in

FIGURE 5.14 *Son of Gone' Fishing,* 1981, Trisha Brown Dance Company performance at Hamline University Theater, Saint Paul, Minnesota, March 9, 1984. Courtesy of Walker Art Center Archives.

front of a light blue one" (1985: 72).[21] Instead of white, the outfits were jaunty singlets, T-shirts, and trousers, defying the fashion maxim that shades of "blue and green should never be seen without a color in between." Dance critic Deborah Jowitt, reviewing the work, remarked on this novelty: "you barely notice that their easy-going dance clothes are made in various combinations of dark blue, light blue, and pale virulent green, before Brown enters in an all-green outfit" (1985: 72). With the fluid blues and greens enveloping each other, the dancing bodies are glimpsed as they twist past, flicking and turning in contra-motion, and with this cool-toned color palette, the spectator follows the turbulence of the river, winding and rewinding, and the unleashing of flow. The loose costumes enact a further trick of perception by releasing the transfer of individuation as differences in shape design, rendering the experience of the choreography as an intricate, if unpredictable, surface of movement rippling through cloth.

Augmentation: *Lateral Pass* (1985)

Brown reworked the T-shirt and loose pants ensemble many times, and even in her later choreographies for European opera houses, there is a consistency of costume style and flow. Not all her costumes were demure or minimalist, particularly when her design collaborators added shiny fabrics, printed surfaces, or bodily attachments, but for the most part, they do not encumber the movement. In *Opal Loop/Cloud Installation #72503*, an emboldened Shea dressed Brown in shot silk, glinting blue and mauve; for Jowitt, this was an "inspired choice," and a "metaphor for Brown's dancing and her current compositional processes. Now you see it, now you don't" (1985: 72). In *Foray Forêt* (1990), Rauschenberg selected fabric of "gold and silver with markings of magenta, green, rose, and yellow," making the dancers appear as if they had stepped from a Byzantine mosaic (Lucas 1990). Brown herself wore a two-piece consisting of sunray pleated trousers and a loose jacket with bow-shaped extensions on the upper arms that folded beneath her gestures, quite literally like wings. The inherent theatricality of these costumes augments the lucid, articulate vocabulary of Brown's compositional structures; the more expansive dancing remains enigmatic, with the additional layering of fabrics not unlike the gilding on a bas relief. Beyond these design experiments, Brown reverts to unitards as a base costume, while remaining faithful to modest clothing in rehearsals: "She likes seeing the dancers throw on ratty sweatpants over gleaming costumes to warm up for a performance" (Perron 2001).

When Brown engaged female artist and friend Nancy Graves to collaborate on *Lateral Pass* (1985), however, a unique exception to the minimalist aesthetic appeared. In her own work, Graves created dynamic gestural paintings using multiple colors and textures to generate a sense of animation across the canvas. They have an intentionality toward expression that is sympathetic to dance, if not entirely congruent with the embodiment of choreographic meaning. The set design for *Lateral Pass* resembled her paintings—squiggly colored tubing suspended on stage with multi-colored leotards and

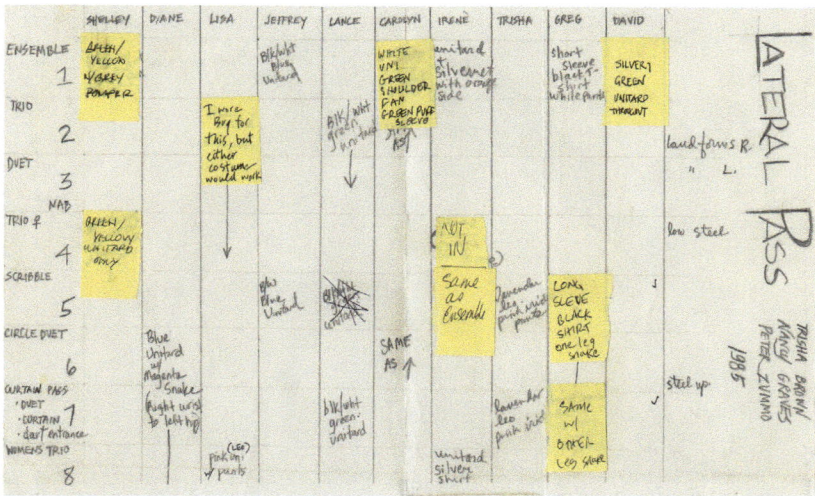

FIGURE 5.15 *Lateral Pass*, 1985. Costume Score. Courtesy of Trisha Brown Dance Company.

tights decorated with swirling lines, appendages, and props. In the costume workshop, Graves became excited by the possibility of different fabric swatches: "It was better than Christmas. . . fifty blues in all kinds of kooky textures. . . And then I tried to consider the reality of using them" (Teicher 2002: 132). Figure 5.15 shows the "reality" of her intricate plotting of costume variations for the first half of the dance, with the yellow notes identifying which colored unitard was to be worn and how it was "different" from the performer's previous costume.

In the end, the company's costume inventory included list such as, "1 grey romper, 1 silver sleeve, 1 green and yellow unitard, 3 lace ruffs, 1 lace skirt," or, "1 cream unitard, 1 silver net 'romper', 4 orange cords, 2 plastic shields," and more (1986). For the dancers, this involved multiple costume changes, and various objects collected to accompany different choreographic sequences. The striped decorations on the unitard in Figure 5.16 bear an uncanny resemblance to Ted Shawn's water costume in Chapter 1, but in the giddy assemblage of colors and ornamentation, urban rather than nature allusions existed in this *Lateral Pass*.

Inside a circus-like atmosphere, the dancers swung on ropes, adding to the swirling lines and illuminated decorations (Figure 5.17). And the augmented costumes required spatial negotiation and adjustment to Brown's fluid, quick movement pathways.

Often dancing in elevation, with elongated arms and legs, Brown wore a pale pink, fine-fitted, and hand-sewn leotard with pink iridescent gauze trousers (Figure 5.18). The form of this garment, representing a compromise between modern and postmodern costume, was rendered in the finest fabrics. Its translucence suited her nymph-like movement quality. Her "prop" was a tightly pleated two-tone cape in metallic fabric that flickered from side to side as she danced.

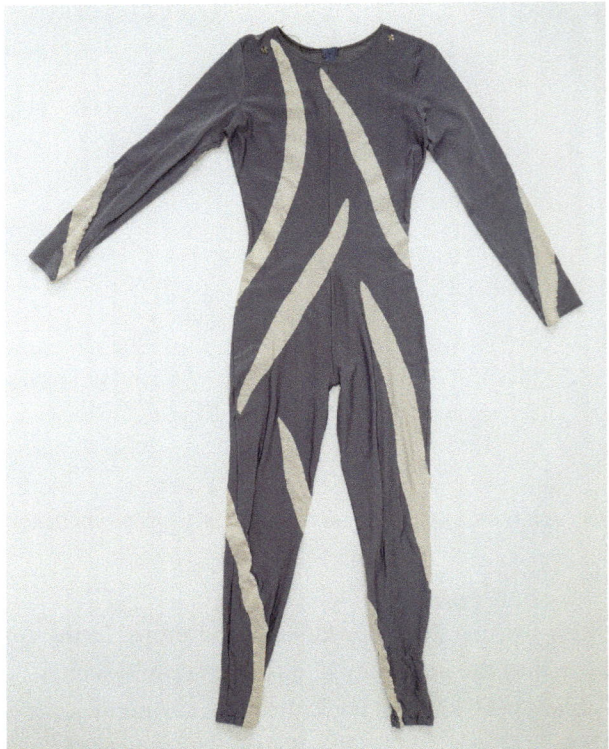

FIGURE 5.16 Unitard from Nancy Graves, costumes for Trisha Brown Dance Company's *Lateral Pass*, 1985. Photograph by Cameron Wittig. Walker Art Center. Artwork © Nancy Graves Foundation. ARS/ Copyright Agency, 2025.

FIGURE 5.17 *Lateral Pass,* 1985, rehearsal close-up, Hamline University Theater, Saint Paul, Minnesota, 28 August1985. Courtesy Walker Art Center Archives.

FIGURE 5.18 Cape worn by Trisha Brown from Nancy Graves, costumes for Trisha Brown Dance Company's *Lateral Pass*, 1985. Photograph by Cameron Wittig. Walker Art Center. Artwork © Nancy Graves Foundation. ARS/Copyright Agency, 2025.

FIGURE 5.19 Trisha Brown rehearsing *Lateral Pass*, 1985, Hamline University Theater, Saint Paul, Minnesota, 28 August 1985. Courtesy Walker Art Center Archives.

Figure 5.19 shows Brown exploring the scope of her wings, with the curvature of the pleats unfolding down her sides and creating the angle of vision. Her concentration is on how this sophisticated extension to her torso modifies her gestures. The garment renders Brown as part-bat and part-fairy godmother, no less fantastic than the composite picture of the ensemble inhabiting this intricate choreographic fairytale world (Figure 5.20).

When *Lateral Pass* was performed at the Teatro San Carlo in Naples in 1987, a strange twist occurred in the costume repertoire. Neither the set nor the costumes arrived in the company shipment, so Rauschenberg, a long-time friend of Brown's who was traveling with them, agreed to improvise substitute costumes (Figure 5.21). Taking the black rehearsal unitard as his template, he cut jaggedly into the sleeves, making each of them individual and irregular (Teicher 2002: 139). He then explored local markets for found textiles and located a stall selling vintage football flags, so he purchased a bundle. The dancers would attach these large bold-colored banners bearing local club emblems loosely to their unitards. The dancers were free to move as if playing a game of soccer, at times letting the flags fly behind them, each representing a different team (Figure 5.23). The "lateral pass," a sporting move that involves throwing a ball sideways or behind to a teammate, therefore gained significance that was not evident in the former costumes.

For the Italian audience, this distillation of the physicality and playfulness of competitive sport was a highlight. The choreography in a large circular stadium—with broken debris collected from local streets assembled as the set—took on an entirely different meaning from its New York premiere. Both sets of costumes have been retained in the

FIGURE 5.20 Trisha Brown and company in *Lateral Pass*, 1985. Photograph by Mark Hanauer. Courtesy of Mark Hanauer Photography.

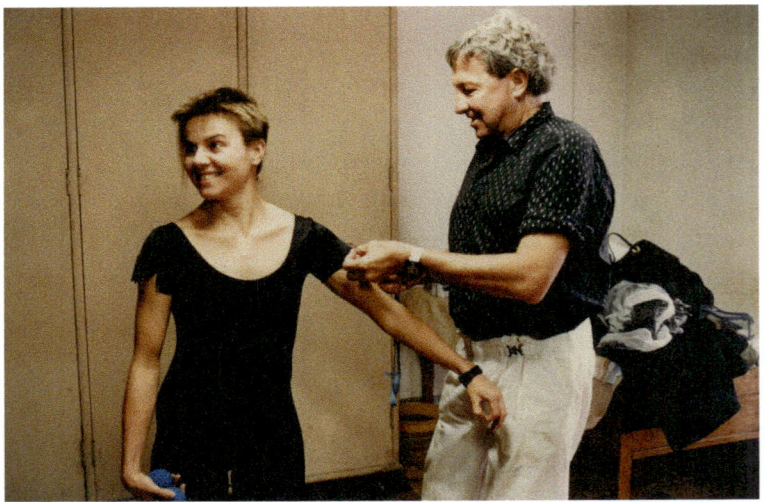

FIGURE 5.21 Diane Madden and Robert Rauschenberg backstage before performance of *Lateral Pass*, 1985, Teatro di San Carlo, January 2–7, 1987. Photograph by Luciano Romano. Courtesy of Trisha Brown Dance Company Archives. © Luciano Romano/Teatro di San Carlo Photography.

FIGURE 5.22 Unitard and Roma flag from Robert Rauschenberg, costumes for Trisha Brown Dance Company's *Lateral Pass*, c. 1985. Photograph by Cameron Wittig. Walker Art Center. Artwork © Robert Rauschenberg Foundation. VAGA at ARS/Copyright Agency, 2024.

FIGURE 5.23 Lisa Schmidt and Shelley Senter in *Lateral Pass,* 1985, in performance at Teatro di San Carlo, January 2–7, 1987. Photograph by Luciano Romano. Courtesy of the Trisha Brown Dance Company Archives. © Luciano Romano/Teatro di San Carlo Photography.

archive, but these differences are a reminder of the extent to which "what is worn" in "the framework of the immediate environment" can transform the qualities, semantics, and orientation of a precise choreography (Taylor 2003: 3).

Allegory and Angels: From *Glacial Decoy* (1979) to *Set and Reset* (1993)

In this concluding discussion of the costumes that appear in Brown's choreographic repertoire, I propose a shift in horizon from the pure minimalism or repetition of bare essentials in postmodern dance. While resistant to representation, especially when reducing explicit narrative or context, all costumes provoke material associations with fabric, form, and fashion culture. And dancers must animate the ways in which different garments move, making their qualities more or less present on stage. When Brown lifts a leg or points a toe in her famous solo, *Water Motor* (1976), her tied pants balloon and flutter from the narrowed waist, and the haptic properties of a soft cotton jersey T-shirt ripple in diagonal folds from the scooped neckline over breasts and torso. The folds show the dancer turning away, always a little off-center. From the perspective of art history, there is an ideality of portraiture associated with folds. "Nothing in the cloth," as Hollander writes, "must distract attention from the subject. The positive value of any fabric in a picture must be confined to showing either the movement of figures or the pull of gravity on them and always in the service of lofty expression" (1975: 76).

For Brown, the ensemble costume of the loose top and trousers that has been shaped by layers of production and reproduction has a flexibility toward elevation. In one moment, a simple knee bend produces a knot of bunched cotton; in another, the arc of a falling back inflates the cloth with air. This versatility of drapery presents a figurative movement that condenses into allegory; at once, the folds of simple fabric resemble "the pull of gravity" in the chiton of a Greek statue, or they appear "in the service of a lofty [perhaps inscrutable] expression." The costume, as Mark Franko notes in a different context, becomes "a site of exchange between material and immaterial culture" (2020: 48). The draped top and trousers amplify the contours of the postmodern dancer, with the visible weight of cloth down and from behind, while the "compulsive performance of gesturing" reconnects the dancing figures as an ancient chorus for a contemporary moment (Fer 1998: 13).

In a final example from the costume archives, we will see how Brown's friendship with Rauschenberg allowed him to further transform the stylization of postmodern dance. For *Glacial Decoy* (1979), in Brown's words, he made "white A-shaped dresses with one-inch vertical pleats from collarbone to ankle" accompanied by similarly styled upper arm puffs, the classic bell sleeves used in ballet to represent nascent wings (Figure 5.24). Fabricated from the nearly transparent calico "used for silkscreens," now faded to cream, they were tied with white cord at the neck, and "during the course of the dance bent in angular lines" (Teicher 2002: 102). These tunics are elegant in their design and construction, and with only the neck as the anchor for motion, the costumes are utterly responsive to changes in weight or direction.

For Barthes, the stylization of woman as "wearer of the garment" connotes the romantic: "a noble art sufficiently rhetorical to let it be understood that it is acting out beauty or dreams" (1990: 302). Jowitt described the dresses as "icebergs" that "blurred into flings and swishes," obscuring the body; in a critical review, she argued that postmodern dancers should wear "simple pants and blouses," lest the costumes "make the audience concentrate more on the form of the dance and less on the dancing itself" (1980b). The Judson dancer and feminist Yvonne Rainer also tried to reconcile Brown's composition for *Glacial Decoy* (Figure 5.25) with her impressions of the female dancer returning to representation of the sylph: "one goes back and forth in seeing movement-as-movement, body-inside-dress, dress-outside-body and image of woman/dancer" (Brown and Rainer 1979: 32).

In this multiplicity, the creamy whiteness of this delicate costume hovers between pure form and deathliness, an enhanced image of a threshold where light erupts in the darkness. Its immateriality is immanent and vital, as well as absent and figurative, because the garment resembles the flight of angels. The pursuit of evanescence resides not in reaching for pure light in a fluid, near-transparent costume, but in the form and expression of motion in Brown's choreography. Philip Bither, Senior Curator of Performing Arts at the Walker, recalled her self-confessed capacity to "levitate"; and her interest in departure from the vertical is well-documented (Eleey 2008: 12). The early *Equipment* performances, which used ropes and harnesses, including *Man Walking Down a Building*, gave practical shape to movement that disrupted the relationships between gravity and ground.

FIGURE 5.24 Dress and shoulder details from Robert Rauschenberg, costumes for Trisha Brown Dance Company's *Glacial Decoy*, c. 1980. Photograph by Cameron Wittig. Walker Art Center. Artwork © Robert Rauschenberg Foundation. VAGA at ARS/Copyright Agency, 2024.

FIGURE 5.25 Flying Angel, 17th Century. Image © The Museum of Modern Art, New York/Art Resource/Scala, Florence, 2025.

While many choreographers simulate birds, Brown is less interested in animals than in the ambiguity of the human with the androgynous or non-human being. In her dance repertoire, another theme emerges from the aesthetic potential of flowing garments, their modesty of body display, and the "silky" movement in her choreography that is both feminine and other worldly. This mixture, alongside Brown's love of flight, suggests memories of childhood play and structural invention as well as the revelation of angels (Brown 2004).

An angel, of course, has no gender and no absolute form, although they may appear to resemble humans. They exist fleetingly as messengers between worlds; they may guide but not direct intention. The flying angel in Figure 5.26 is a Baroque sketch full of disconcerting dimensions, and the angel's backward glance makes it uncertain whether they belong on earth or somewhere more elevated. The fall of the folding cloth makes it more certain that the figure would like to fly.

In Brown's work, the religious conception of the angel is turned upside down since she aspires to be an imperfect transmitter while remaining an absolute servant of movement. Such pure movement arises as an immaterial experience, when the corporeality of dancing—the navigation of gravity or flight, weight, or weightlessness—is transformed into its most elemental form. In a barely graspable gesture, the fleshy encounter becomes a fleeting vision of spiritual departure.

FIGURE 5.26 Flying Angel, 17th Century. Image © The Museum of Modern Art, New York/Art Resource/ Scala, Florence, 2025.

FIGURE 5.27 Trisha Brown with Steve Petronio in *Set and Reset,* 1993. Photograph by Jack Mitchell. Image: Jack Mitchell/Archival Photos via Getty Images.

Brown's desire to assume embodied flight became more than metaphorical in *Set and Reset (1993),* when she hovered on the horizontal against the dancer Stephen Petronio's shoulder (Figure 5.27). The ensemble performed in "gorgeous filmy white transparent costumes, silkscreened with pale-gray-to-black urban industrial images. No blue jeans. No underwear either. [Rauschenberg] did not want the lingerie lines to interfere with the body as a body" (Teicher 2002: 292). The allusions to the angel persist in these loose, white, flowing garments, even if any overt figurative reference is shadowed by the printed surface.

FIGURE 5.28 Trisha Brown in *If you couldn't see me,* 1994, premiere performance at The Joyce Theater, May 3–8, 1994. Photograph by Julie Lemberger. Courtesy of Trisha Brown Dance Company Archives. ©Julie Lemberger.

In her final solo, *If You Couldn't See Me* (1994), Brown wears "a very scoop-backed dress with two long panels front and back, open on the sides, with a pair of shorts underneath" (Teicher 2002: 186). The fabrication of this costume emerges from her ongoing dialogue with Rauschenberg. Brown finds an advertising image of a backless dress by Ralph Lauren with looped ties across the back and writes to him, "Bob, I'm now in a state of dorsal infatuation so send this suggestion. I probably should have drawn it clinging to the body which it would do if made from a silk fabric. . . love love love Trisha."[22] Beneath the floating silk panels of the resulting tunic, she dances with her back toward the audience, and both feet flutter while her swooping ribs lift her limbs into a fine arc (Figure 5.28). Repetition on repetition, white on white, fold on fold, the interval between space and time is embodied by the dancer in the soft cloth. If the philosopher Gilles Deleuze (1993), reading Leibniz on the baroque, found in the "fold" a representation of mobility, then the sculpture of the body in filmy white garments, like the flying angel, combines ecstasy and erotic transfiguration, with antecedents in a pre-modernity covertly imparted by Brown's dancing.

Looking back, Brown's *Roof Piece* could be regarded as the first sign of "the dancer as reconfigured minor angel" (Lepecki 2018: 311). Earlier in the chapter, the young female dancer and new mother, Brown, choreographs in the borderlands of the postindustrial city. Her dancers appear as fallen angels or "neutral" subjects, adrift in a silent rooftop world. We glimpse them only in part; in the semaphore of open and closed actions, torso bends, and attention to relaying a sequence, they transmit an obscure language system. Imperfect angels, bound to earth, this choreography seeks to loosen the chain of dance from reproduction, for women, as dancers, as industrial agents, and as laborers.

In 2011, a German–Iranian artist, Anahita Razmi, filmed a re-enactment of Brown's work as *Roof Piece in Tehran* for Frieze Art Fair.[23] Inspired by television footage of Iranian women protesting on their rooftops during the general elections in 2009, Razmi understood the potentiality of this space in the city's material history. Traditionally, a place out of public view and used for communal prayer, the rooftop is also where women take their children and hang their washing. Since dancing is forbidden in public places in Iran, contemporary dance does not exist. However, women can share messages if out of sight. With local women wearing red versions of a postmodern dance costume—loose trousers, long-sleeved tops, suitably modest, with red headscarves—a new form of radical choreography emerged. The red precipitates novel associations—blood, flags, signs of danger or warning, even socialism. In this repressive culture, their folded gestures transmit a torrent of messages between women into the sky. In Razmi's video, *Tehran Roof,* the red costumes signal a quiet intent toward life, toward the fabrication of an ongoing presence.

Conclusion

In Benjamin's epitaph for this chapter, the textual fragment examines how men's fashion differs from that of women in late nineteenth-century modernity. He is struck by the emphasis on the suit, in its gray or blackness, as a marker that rejects overt or classical beauty in favor of a cooler, more intellectual outfit. In terms of postmodern dance dress, the discussion has attempted to consider how neutrality and white (rather than "gray . . .running to black") function in the stylization of the T-shirt and loose pants, which under late capitalism was also the adoption of men's clothing that rendered dancing bodies gender neutral or "colorless." This minimalist "suit" often also rejected beauty, the sensory or pictorial, in favor of the critical and "more cool."

The chapter analyzes two objects—the white T-shirt and loose trousers—as they evolved from the milieu of postmodern dance to become signs for the pedestrian reinvention of choreography. In terms of new materialism, habit formation accrues vitality when enacted in "an ontologically diverse assemblage of energies and bodies, of simple and complex bodies, of the physical and physiological" (Bennett 2010: 117). The continuous iterability of this aesthetics and these garments has become a powerful production technology, rendering this ensemble a major constellation in the histories of twentieth-century dance, contemporary performance, and women's art practices. As repetitions within specific choreographic events, they hold memories of pleasure and falling, disorientation and adjustment, for the bodies that wore and witnessed them. And, over time, they have accumulated values to which we have become habituated—the comfortable familiarity of this "suit" affords ease of movement in legs and torso, even if it eventually falls out of favor or fashion.

The choreographic emphasis on pure movement patterns involving repetition, line, and flow assembled must now be attached to an appreciation of cotton, calico (and sheer) garments fabricated in exchange with other systems of meaning—mass production, sexual modesty, Japanese martial arts, and the affordance of wings. Combining rebellion with gender, class, and race mobility, this dialectical potential has given occasion to a wide range of performances—those that release improvisation and group cohesion, as well as those that offer critiques of industry, masculine pathos, and environmental destruction. Its flexible conditions of production and replacement can however obscure differences, given the extent to which whiteness and the historical materialism of cheaper garments can undermine the radicalism of dance gestures.

Writing about contemporary art, Briony Fer suggests that "repetition cuts both ways, both shoring up and shattering its fragile and precarious hold. It is a means of organizing the world. It is a means of disordering and undoing" (2004: 71). So too, the repetition of a dance costume registers almost imperceptibly; it amplifies a fragile sensation on the body and organizes the choreographic world in relation to an uncertain outside. In its motion, the "suit" becomes less solid, less constrictive as the dancer reaches toward a spiritual undoing of material constraints.

I will close this chapter with Jowitt's revised assessment of the "angel" costumes in a later season of Glacial Decoy: "I even liked Rauschenberg's pleated white tent dresses with bells for sleeves. Emmon's lighting rendered them lighter and more transparent, and the combination of their prettiness with the gentle rambunctiousness of the movement became quite engaging" (1985: 74). Faint praise, perhaps, but looking again, the "engaging" qualities that accumulate in association with the dialectical costume of loose clothes have a distilled and deliberative beauty.

Feathers and Sequins

Josephine Baker

> I forgot to tell you that last Wednesday I saw on the boulevards an old
> dowager dressed in mirrors stuck to fabric. The effect was sumptuous in the
> sunlight. You'd have thought it was a gold mine out for a walk. Later it started
> raining and the lady looked like a silver mine.
>> Guillaume Apollinaire, cited in Benjamin (1999: 70)

Josephine Baker's final secretary and confidante, Michèle Barbier, rhapsodizes about
the impression Baker created at a concert in Mexico, sketching the costume: "Radiant,
wearing a coat superbly decorated with gemstones, embroideries, and sequins. On her
head, a rhinestone and feather headpiece" (2022: 52). Feathers, rhinestones, sequins, and
embroidered fabrics, repeated over and over in performance, are the primary elements of
an ornamentation used to illuminate dance as spectacle.

This final chapter considers the materials—feathers and sequins—that produce the
fashion silhouette of variety entertainment. Tapered yet curvaceous, a stylized hourglass
shape represents the female body before glimpses of the flesh beneath the dress get revealed. Adornments, whether shiny, slippery, or fluffy, can be obsessively added to a costume or enlarged and recombined to make the complete ensemble. Once confected into a
dress that fulfills a fantasy, such costumes do not define the dance vocabulary—it is often
a pastiche of movement styles—nor a choreographic signature. Instead, the assemblage of
feathers and sequins becomes aligned with a quality of undulating flow through the surface that constitutes the choreographic presence of the artist. Such a costume is designed
not merely to seduce but to entrance the spectator.

Baker's own dance and singing career in Paris has come to symbolize everything
from the celebrated transformation of the music hall to the heights of jazz-era deca-
dence, from the scandalous plight of the racialized and gendered showgirl to the skillful
black artistry of Baker herself. There has also been long-overdue recognition of Baker's
work as a spy and activist for peace and justice (Lewis 2022; Dudziak 1994). Such myriad

Fabrications. Rachel Fensham, Oxford University Press. © Oxford University Press 2026. DOI: 10.1093/9780197699638.003.0007

representations of Baker—the black entertainer, also a woman, mother, and patriot—exist alongside a double consciousness of her historical reception and continuous circulation as a racialized subject in the transatlantic world. If one reads between the French and American literature and, as the authors of a critical reader suggest, one examines the innumerable images, narratives, performances, and exhibitions generated by Baker, and her "interstitial positionalities" become endlessly bifurcated (Henderson and Regester 2017: 6).

In regard to performance, the dance scholar Hannah Durkin (2019) undertook a comparative study of the filmic and literary careers of Baker and Katherine Dunham, contributing to a reassessment of Baker's agency as one of the many African American artists who made Paris their stage in the face of racial discrimination in the United States. Some scholars, such as Brett Berliner (2002), have examined the racialized and gendered stereotypes that constrained black entertainers in Paris, while others, such as African American sociologist Bennetta Jules-Rosette, have evaluated her unique theatrical stylization as an "icon" (2007). Moreover, Jules-Rosette has proposed five "performative strategies of image and identity construction" that Baker deployed in her use of "spectacular dress" to reverse cultural codes and display difference to her audiences (2013: 205). Felicia McCarren, on the other hand, examines the "use value" of those dance moves and gestures that give Baker agency within her cinematic performances (2008). Baker's life intersects with so many spheres of diasporic geopolitical performance in the mid-twentieth century that every new telling offers another perspective. The task of this book is to consider how what Baker wore carries forward a fashion ideology for dance entertainment. This historical discussion of her costume legacy will thus locate Baker in relation to the specialist industries that fabricate the shiny "frocks" that she and other performers have worn (Figure 6.1).

The chapter engages, of necessity, with the contradictions that accrue in the evanescent materiality of "glamor." It examines how a choreography dependent on an excess of flimsy materials affords the potential of luxury, disguise, and self-presentation for so many artists. Central to the political fashioning of modernity, it suggests that entertainment costumes remain complicit with non-human forces such as the flow of commodities, images in advertising, and the consumption behaviors of mainstream culture. But the feathers and sequins also do something more, since such adornments affect a kind of power for those who wear them: one that can be, at times, troubling in performance.

To begin this discussion, the distinctive assemblage of silhouette, feathers, and sequins in a cabaret or variety costume can be located at the confluence of three or more abstract systems that produce dance-specific forms of subjectivity. These three systems are those of the popular stage; the surrounding artistic milieu; and the visual representation of fashion through photography, illustrations, or film. The structural dimensions of these systems need to be considered, but not because the "showgirl" is passive in her choice of dress. From the 1920s to the 1970s, the strategic uses of costume in the French entertainment industry, or in the United States, were sophisticated and varied, even when

FIGURE 6.1 Josephine Baker on the Olympia stage on April 24, 1964. Photo © AGIP/Bridgeman Images.

the spectacle was mass produced. Fragile "things" like the wearing and choreography of feather boas or sequined thongs were in tension with the gendered and racialized affordances that need inserting into the dialectics of modern entertainment and dance fashioning.

As this chapter argues, entertainment dress also concatenates with other aspects of material culture, including the colonial forces that harvested exotic birds into fashion items, and the transformation of precious metal sequins into plastic discs and glitter. The sequins—little bits of shiny stuff—and the feathers—their harvested tendrils—confront dance studies with what social anthropologist Daniel Miller (2005) calls the efficacy of "stuff." The person making, dancing, or thinking, about an item of sparkly clothing is conventionally regarded as the active subject. Yet, as Miller suggests, many facets of materiality are bound up with formless phenomena, and he gives the example of money or the Internet. In relation to dress, he observes that "we are not just clothed but we are constituted by our clothing," hence what we wear is both a material, affective reality and an immaterial, imagined or ideological reality (2005: 22). As this book has shown, dancers are constituted by both material and immaterial things: they are dress consumers who move with their costumes in particular ways, but they are also fashioned by the economic and social mobility that circulates with shiny textiles, slippery silhouettes, and frivolous ornamentation.

In costume archives, the scope of this chapter has been confined by the limited number of surviving costumes that Baker wore on stage.[1] The primary resource has been a selection of garments housed at Baker's former residence, Chateau Milandes, in the Périgord region of southern France, owned and managed by Madame Angélique de Labarre. This collection represents, for the most part, Baker's later career, although it includes Baker's famous banana skirt and her military uniform, as well as ensembles from the Olympia and Bobino theatres in postwar Paris, where she was a leading *chanteuse*, and frocks from concerts in Monaco. Given how few complete Baker outfits (dresses, shoes, head-dresses, and props) survive, the chapter compares this wardrobe with a collection belonging to Line Renaud, Baker's French friend and dance peer, at the Centre National du Costume de Scene (CNCS) in Moulins. Renaud was a next-generation entertainer and actress who shared Baker's mantle in Parisian cabaret, and some Baker costumes may have been passed to her. Renaud donated her costume collection to the CNCS, where they have been carefully preserved and stored. The chapter includes an elegant dress cared for by a private collector in St. Louis, identified with one of Baker's "returns" to the United States. In a museological sense, these Baker artifacts demonstrate an accrued exchange value, because they are aesthetic objects that relay the labor and pleasure associated with modes of creative invention.

In terms of twentieth-century performance, the chapter concludes that the form, construction, and lingering agency of a shapely silhouette multiply the corporeal potency of a popular entertainer or singer-dancer—an alluring legacy that continues in the dresses of the Supremes, Divine, and RuPaul.

The Banana Belt, Surrealism, and the Ziegfeld Follies (1938)

Resting on a stool covered in russet satin inside a glass vitrine is a unique fabrication— twenty-four pendulous objects suspended from a twisted cord of woven metallic fabric. Each tubular object is about 8 inches long, pointed at the lower end like a crescent moon. Made from silk lamé, an ancient "cloth of gold," a neat seam of golden sequins follows the contour of each stuffed prong. Even at rest, they look phallic, swollen, and badly behaved in the irregularity of their curvatures. This object is the infamous banana belt worn as a "skirt" by Josephine Baker around 1926 at the Folies Bergère, a year after her premiere season in Paris.

In *Second Skin: Josephine Baker and the Modern Surface*, Ann Anlin Cheng argues that whether Baker was "celebrated as icon and decried as fetish," regarded as "a groundbreaking performer or a shameful sellout," she "would be identified" with this outfit "for the rest of her life" (2011: 39; 43). Adopting a psychoanalytic lens, Cheng interprets the

FIGURE 6.2 Banana skirt, 1927. Photograph by Karen McLeod. Courtesy of Château des Milandes.

banana skirt as a fetish object that is potentially homoerotic, in that the substitute "black dick [is] masking the hunger of the white imperial phallus" (2011: 46). Cheng contemplates the possibility that wearing it gave Baker a sense of power, and from her actions with the skirt, Baker understood the costume's multiple significations even if she later disdained its use in her performances. While acknowledging the banana skirt's potency, particularly as a phallic symbol, this costume will not dominate this chapter's analysis of Baker's body, her subjectivity, or her consummate theatricality.

In material terms, the skirt is not a singular thing. There have been at least three, and there may be several replicas. According to Madame de Labarre, the banana skirt in the Salle des Robes at Chateau Milandes is a surviving "original" that she located in the family home of Baker's former companion and manager, Pepito Abatino.[2] This "belt," which has visible signs of wear and tear, could have been constructed in the late 1920s when it may have supported thirty bananas.[3]

The conceptualization of the banana skirt has a similarly vague provenance; it has been variously attributed to the fashion designer Paul Poiret, the surrealist Jean Cocteau, and the artist and illustrator Paul Colin, who produced posters for the Revue Nègre depicting Baker's angular body in a highly animated banana skirt. Another theory includes the Mexican artist and set designer Miguel Covarrubias, who often painted exotic women with flowers and fruit.[4] All these artists were affiliated with the surrealist circle that attended the Paris cabarets, and their art practices used the "formal aspects of collage or assemblage" to produce "contradicting, heterogeneous, and often pre-existing forms within one work" (Lehmann 2007: 20). The extent to which the surrealists realized their ambition through fashion, photography, and the "new media" of reproduction confirms Benjamin's observations on the affiliations between capitalist modernity and art.

Whoever suggested that Baker replace an ostrich-feathered costume with a belt of bananas, there are clues in the surrealist Giorgio De Chirico's (1913) painting "The uncertainty of the poet" (Figure 6.3).[5] The image depicts a bleak urban landscape with a colonnade leading to a port; a sailing ship is arriving while a steam train departs on the horizon. In the overcast foreground, a female plaster bust—bare-breasted, sharply angular, with no head or arms—is ambiguously placed in front of a large bunch of bananas. The stalk is thick, muscular, and brown, while the mottled yellow bananas bring light to the somber scene. The ship and train represent capitalist flows from colonies to and from the metropolis, with bananas—and exotic fruits more generally—symbolizing colonial commerce. Cheng notes, "In the 1920s banana plantations were being promoted as a supplement to and replacement for the sugar plantations in the French Antilles" (2011: 45).[6] In De Chirico's representation, the exploitation of French colonies is juxtaposed with classical art's dismembered female body. The painting thus acknowledges that the modern colonial project co-existed with the ruins of European history, a thesis made by Benjamin himself.

A decade after De Chirico creates his sober painting, Baker reanimates this trope in her routine. The black performance writer Hanif Abdurraqib reads Baker's hip-twirling

FIGURE 6.3 Giorgio de Chirico, *The Uncertainty of the Poet* (1913). Artwork © Giorgio De Chirico. SIAE/ Copyright Agency, 2025. Photo: Tate.

of the bananas as "secondary to the body tasked with carrying them," describing how she "swings her arms and widens her eyes, crossing them briefly before thrusting out her back, bending over and doing a brief Charleston" (2021: 150). In this way, Baker revivifies the "ambivalent desire" for exotic black bodies in the French imaginary during the "jazz age," but she also asserts her own agency (Berliner 2002). Baker's literary memoirs, according to Durkin, provide evidence of her "intervention in interpretations of her body as a colonial commodity." As Baker wrote, "it was a very painful job to be a curiosity" (Durkin 2019: 15, 28).

During Baker's 1938 return to the United States, a more disturbing version of the "skirt" appears when she is hired by the Ziegfeld Follies under the direction of Vincent Minelli. Abatino and her French collaborators were sidelined by Broadway, and she was required to wear a "skirt" designed by Raoul Pene Du Bois and execute choreography by a young Georges Balanchine (Figure 6.4).[7] In a sketch labeled "the Antilles," she performs a conga, representing a wild Caribbean woman in a skirt and bra with "sharp and menacing" spikes "cut like daggers in silver fabric." These "bananas" were intended to "bristle and hide her breasts, stomach, and buttocks," according to her French biographer Gérard Bonal (2021: 196).

FIGURE 6.4 Josephine Baker in a banana skirt in Ziegfeld Follies, c. 1936. Photographer unknown. Courtesy of Billy Rose Theatre Division, The New York Public Library.

In a quartet of production photographs from this New York season in Figure 6.4, Baker contorts into alarming profiles that exaggerate this prickly "skin," in dancing that replicates the primitivist imaginary of America's mid-century popular stage. Statuesque, sharply angular, and leaping widely, Baker is forced by the choreography to bury the erotic potential of the skirt along with any critique of its colonial legacy. With the gendered violence writ large, this costume variation degrades the athletics of her performing body.

The New York press greets the show with withering scorn, and Baker quits her home country again, fully alert to the barbarism of its racialized gaze.[8] Thereafter, her performances discard "the sexually suggestive banana belt" in favor of a "look that more closely reflected her status as a member of Parisian high society" (Durkin 2019: 16). The rest of this chapter addresses the costumes that defined this "look" during her later career.

Feathers from the *Revue Nègre* (1925) to Olympia (1968)

Baker's appearance in the first all-black Parisian cabaret for the *Revue Nègre* at the Théâtre des Champs-Élysées in 1925 was exceptional but contiguous with other Parisian cabarets, such as Le Chat Noir in the Montmartre quartier.[9] As with many entertainment precincts, an informal night culture began at dusk and ended in the small hours of the morning. The venues had individual proprietors who maintained rules of conduct but tolerated borderline transgressions induced by alcohol or drugs, debt, or desperation. In a culture replete with cancan dancers, Dada performers, gymnasts, and exotic circus acts, many artists and musicians from around Europe and the Americas tried their luck.

Each novelty act required new décor and costumes, so bedecked like the dancer Maud Allen in "a delicate assemblage of beads, paste jewels, gauze, and sequins," Baker was launched on stage (Schweitzer and Zerdy 2014: 42). For *La Danse Sauvage*, Baker's "string of beads" was apportioned to dangle across the breast and pubic region in her first "jazz dance." Following that, she wore "a waistband of ostrich feathers attached to satin panties, and a collar of red feathers around her neck" (Bouillon-Baker 2021: 21).

Photographs of this costume show Baker bent double with a startled expression and blackened feathers sprouting from her rear, like a large bird caught mid-strut. Reviewers exulted in her imitation of "a bird from the islands" and elaborated their praise in stereotypes of the "black woman" as African grotesque (Bouillon-Baker 2021: 22–24). She was an immediate sensation, using her comic sensibility to render the feathered costume as a prop, an object to exploit through improvisation. At the slightest wiggle of her hips and tilt of her pelvis, the fan of feathers flapped back and forth like a peacock's display. This choreography inverted the creaturely seduction, tempting the male to chase and identify his fantasy "bird." This feathered and beaded costume, infinitely more than the bananas, haunted and configured her future stage presence.

The ostrich-tail in dress history belongs in the savage fantasy world of plumage, in which the application of feathers to different body parts transforms the wearer into an avian ensemble, part-bird, part-human. The capture of live birds for fashion, however, involves an extensive trade that has often been more brutal than the hunting of mammals for their pelts.

In Europe, elaborate ornamentation created from plucked feathers appears in fashionable clothing, as stage accessories, and alongside flowers in decorative household displays. In the sixteenth century, a range of feathered hats and cloaks were worn by the wealthy as colonizing powers registered imperial conquests in their clothing. An expanding colonial trade in the next two centuries collected ever more exotic birds specifically for fashion; and by the nineteenth century, decorative feather headdresses became a bourgeois trend in Paris and London. According to costume historian James Laver, "There was a rage for feathers, hats being adorned with one or more plumes, [and] feather boas were worn around the neck." The best boas made of ostrich plumes could cost as much as ten guineas each (1995: 216). The millinery industry refined its skills in shaping fabric and created head-coverings decorated with cascading and variegated feathers. These distinctive hats became status symbols in the expanding mass market of women's fashion.

Feathers arrived from the furthest reaches of imperial trade to the large import markets operating from London and Paris. Ostrich feathers farmed in Southern Africa were sold at an alarming rate, with two harvests a year yielding feathers that could be sorted into different classes. The male feathers—"prime whites"—were prized for their ornate, stiffened structure, while the soft tendrils of the "feminas" were plucked from under the wings of female birds. In 1900, an ounce of feathers was worth almost twice as much as an ounce of gold.

After an auction in London, feathers were deployed to factories around Europe, where they were dyed, curled, layered, and combined with exotic feathers from "hummingbirds, egrets, and birds of paradise" collected in Asia or South America (Munro 2009: 280). Feathered accessories were "taken to ever greater extremes," the historian Jane Munro notes, citing instances where "whole birds were perched in mid-flight on hats and accessories such as fans" (2009: 281). The merchandising of exotic feathers continued apace until legislative change was enacted in the United States in 1900 amid accounts of the cruelty inflicted on birds for theft of their plumage and mounting evidence of entire species disappearing (Munro 2009: 281).[10] No similar legislation was concurrently achieved in France.

The natural scientist Charles Darwin interpreted this "craze for feathers," particularly male "plumes," as replicating animal mating behavior, but he was puzzled by a social behavior that to him seemed "purposeless" (Munro 2009: 276). Fashionable adornment involving the "conspicuous" display of heightened colors in dress, ornamentation, and "plumage" was beyond his expertise as a naturalist, but he was curious about how sensitive fluctuations in taste had evolved in the female of the "human species" (Munro

2009: 278). Perhaps, he speculated, women wore conspicuous ornamentation to enhance their "beauty" to attract a sexual partner.

Notwithstanding Darwin's "obscure and obscurantist" ruminations on gender and display, by the time Baker performed in Paris, feathers were prized theatrical items of display, particularly for women. Costume designers for the popular stage were adept at realizing the power of feathers in both sexual and aesthetic terms. One example is the large Baker headdress on display at Milandes (Figure 6.5), with its spray of green and blue-black dyed feathers stitched on a fountain of "prime whites" secured to a crown laden with ostentatious jewels. Another exotic outfit worn by Baker was constructed in white feathers tipped with a dramatic orange and attached to paisley-shaped metal panels, with feathers spraying from her hips and a pointy hat (Figure 6.6). Performing at the Royal Orfeumban in Hungary in 1928, Baker's costume included a feathered umbrella. This representation of an "Asian" bird of paradise recalls the Cambodian dance influence in Paul Poiret's fashions; and, given his closeness to Baker's early circle, the designer may have concocted this outfit (Cassin-Scott 1971: 198).

In Paris, feather theatrical costumes had their own specialist manufacturing atelier, known as *Les Maisons Fevriers*. This studio provided advanced training in design and construction, teaching apprentices how to manipulate the delicate feathers and to fasten them securely for performance. For dancers, a crafty stage apparatus was secured by a specialist "carcassier" to a frame, a structure of fine carbon steel, flexible yet unbreakable, that could support the feathers and rhinestones (Vergès 2021: 128).

A mannequin dressed in Line Renaud's black velvet bustier for her revue, *Plaisirs* (1959–1963), in Figure 6.7 shows the extreme silhouette of the ostrich outfit as costume; the headdress towers above the performer's diminutive body, and the wings and tail

FIGURE 6.5 Blue and black ostrich-feathered headdress. Photograph by Karen McLeod. Courtesy of Château des Milandes.

FIGURE 6.6 Josephine Baker at the Royal Orfeumban, 1928. Photographer unknown. Courtesy of Hungarian Museum of Trade and Tourism.

FIGURE 6.7 Black velvet bustier worn by Line Renaud in the revue *Plaisirs* at the Casino de Paris, 1959 to 1963, designed by José Luis Vinas. Collection of the National Center for Costume and Stage (Moulins, France)/gift from Madame Line Renaud. © CNCS/Terminal 33.

FIGURE 6.8 Headpiece from black velvet and feathers ensemble worn by Line Renaud in the revue *Plaisirs* at the Casino de Paris, 1959 to 1963, designed by José Luis Vinas. Collection of the National Center for Costume. and Stage (Moulins, France)/gift from Madame Line Renaud. © CNCS/Terminal 33.

FIGURE 6.9 Interior view of black velvet bustier worn by Line Renaud in the revue *Plaisirs* at the Casino de Paris, 1959 to 1963, designed by José Luis Vinas. Collection of the National Center for Costume and Stage (Moulins, France)/gift from Madame Line Renaud. © CNCS/Terminal 33.

FIGURE 6.10 Feathers with sequins from black velvet and feathers ensemble worn by Line Renaud in the revue *Plaisirs* at the Casino de Paris, 1959 to 1963, designed by José Luis Vinas. Collection of the National Center for Costume. and Stage (Moulins, France)/gift from Madame Line Renaud. © CNCS/Terminal 33.

extend in three directions. Fabricating as well as wearing such high plumage requires an intense awareness of how its structural components engage with the anatomy of movement. Secured by a wig or headband, or encased in a turban, the frame serves as the fulcrum for the plumes. In this instance, Renaud's five-foot black feathers (Figure 6.8) were attached to a brass cup decorated with rhinestones and silver beads, and yet firmly embedded in a circular horsehair headband.

The interior of the tailpiece in Figure 6.9 was a belt on which metal studs secure the wires, with leather padding used to stop friction against the skin, and a reinforced strap to ensure that the performer can make vigorous sideways movements. To each glossy black feather, sequins were individually stitched for added luster (Figure 6.10).

During performance, such items of stage plumage need adapting or replacing; afterwards, the feathers need cleaning and time "to breathe" (Pinasa 2023). Because of their fragility and the expense of repair, revue production companies often retained the hundreds of headdresses they commissioned, each made by hand, especially those ostentatious crystals and jewels belonging to the star performers.

Most of Baker's costumes involved elaborate headdresses, and she often appeared "wearing the feathers" on her body. For the 1968 Olympia show sponsored by entertainment entrepreneurs, the Coquatrix family, new dresses were designed by Lucien Berteaux and fabricated by Paula Coquatrix, who managed her own costume atelier. The performance began in spectacular style with Baker emerging from a newspaper booth as if stepping out from the Paris Metro. She wears a black velvet gown with black tulle at the neckline and sleeves ringed by white, red, and blue rhinestones. From a neatly curled black wig, her rainbow-colored feather headdress billows in beehive formation, while her eyes are heavily lidded with a rainbow makeup that befits the swinging sixties.

Given the lurid adornment, Baker's face seems distorted, mask-like with enlarged eyes and solid lips. At the time, she was facing severe economic problems, and mounting debts had forced her to leave her home at Castle Milandes in 1967. Hoping to relaunch her theatrical career, perhaps the impasto face was intentional. The elegant black sequined dress is also deceptive; from the front, its "slit aesthetic creates the image of the sexy clothed body," while the sheer fabric and sequined bands substitute for bare skin and bracelet decorations (Young 2005: 67). Behind the sculptured dress rises an ignominious tail of rainbow feathers (Figure 6.11). The bright synthetic dyes on organic matter almost mock her "rainbow" family, the adopted children from different countries that she was supporting through her performance.

FIGURE 6.11 Josephine Baker on stage at the Olympia, April 5, 1968. Photo © AGIP/Bridgeman Images.

FIGURE 6.12 Detail of pale orange feathered headdress. Photograph by Karen McLeod. Courtesy of Château des Milandes.

FIGURE 6.13 Coral satin gown worn at the Olympia, 1968. Photograph by Karen McLeod. Courtesy of Château des Milandes.

In a film recording of this revue, Baker smiles charmingly and waves to the audience's applause before swinging her hips, humming, and belting out a tune (Tartz 1968). When she turns to walk down stage for the rhythmic section, the prime tail feathers are in full jostle, her buttocks waggling, and the audience laughs and claps. She exhibits the fake nature—"an-other" bird—with a false turn. In profile, her body knowingly exaggerates the dance joke, establishing herself as its producer. At other times, she is cheekily conscious of appearing like a dancing "Christmas Tree" (Barbier 2022: 52). A film close-up shows Baker's companion, the dressmaker Marie Spiers, watching with her children and clapping loudly; a sudden reminder of the intimate domestic labor involved in maintaining appearances (Tartz 1968).[11]

This elaborate production never recovered its expenses; indeed, the atelier closed shortly afterward and consequently fell out with Baker. From this Olympia show, the Milandes collection has located one headdress (Figure 6.12), with a bejeweled topknot and pale orange "femina" tufts joined to a short-bobbed wig. The feathers accompany a fitted sleeveless gown of coral silk chiffon that is embellished at the V-neckline with a gold pendant chain and rose-shaped medallion (Figure 6.13). It artfully creates the allure of an ornate kaftan while maintaining the silhouette.

With the down-like "femina" feathers around her head and flowing curves around her body, the gown exudes warmth in performance rather than boldness. From long, shiny cuffs in the sleeves, her hands grip the jewel-studded microphone and she sways back and forth, rustling the soft cloud of feathers on her head. Having secured her position with a turn of the head, Baker gives the electrical lead a tug, a small gesture that allows her to scan the audience, then begins a rhythmic bending of the knees, gently

FIGURE 6.14 Josephine Baker in Monaco on April 19, 1968. Photo © AGIP/Bridgeman Images.

lifting her hips up and down and swinging ever so slightly from side to side. The swiveling makes the rhinestones sparkle and the tallest reach of her plumage twitch. Baker ensures that all the feathers remain visible and that their quivering amplifies every beat in the choreography as she lifts her arms in ritualized greeting and triumph (Figure 6.14).

The feminist phenomenologist Iris Marion Young argues against reading dress in terms of the gendered coding of a "pictorial aesthetic." Her essay about "women's pleasure in clothes" is applicable to ordinary women as well as female entertainers, particularly when imagined from within the costume (2005: 64, 69). Renaud's collection includes multiple fluffy jackets and boas made of "feminas" dyed in fluorescent colors. These light feathers are suitable for lavish embellishment around necks and shoulders or for trailing down the torso. A feather boa, after all, has no actual utility—lacking any warmth and even the weight of silk to support a fully realized gesture. One jacket in pale pink, purple, and yellow feathers is made of hundreds of fine tendrils (Figure 6.15); they produce a glamorous drape but also offer a sensuous pleasure, that of nest-like comfort to the wearer.

In the analysis of a feathered stage persona, should we decry the dancer's inner experience of the "pictorial aesthetic" associated with a tall and feathered bird charming its audience? What makes the adornments attractive to wear is their light playfulness; the feathers float, and each tendril unfurls in volume around the body. A halo of softly curling feathered headdresses, collars, and cuffs in pale blue (Figure 6.16) beckons toward the fluidity of a cloud, as a wrap that offers delicate comfort and radiates its own allure.

At a grander scale, the fanciful elaboration of feathers as a costume type fabricates and enlarges these effects of seduction in performance. Still today, massive appurtenances are created for the Carnival in Rio de Janeiro, and exotic, now mostly fake or farmed, feathers remain formative in the trans-species pleasure that similar costumes animate in show business and fashion.

FIGURE 6.15 Detail of long coat in pink worn by Line Renaud for Las Vegas show, 1974. Collection at the National Center for Costume and Stage (Moulins, France)/gift from Madame Line Renaud. © CNCS/ Terminal 33.

FIGURE 6.16 Detail of long coat in blue chiffon worn by Line Renaud for Las Vegas show, 1974. Collection at the National Center for Costume and Stage (Moulins, France)/gift of Mrs. Line Renaud. © CNCS/Terminal 33.

Sequins and Glamor in Monte Carlo (1969)

In his discussion of the fashion system, Barthes identifies the "variants of existence" determined by opposing features, such as soft textures with hard adornments, or feathers with sequins in dance entertainments. The story of sequins, which comprise the shiniest of skins, is wrapped around Baker's body from her earliest performance to her last. During her first season in Paris, she learned the Charleston, which was all the rage in

FIGURE 6.17 Josephine Baker, 1926. Photograph by Stanislaw Julian Ignacy Ostroróg, known as Walery. Courtesy of National Portrait Gallery, Smithsonian Institution.

the local jazz clubs. By 1926, she had made this dance her own—with bodily contortions and facial expressions—and versions of its choreography stayed with her throughout her career. In front of a backdrop advertising Cunard, the shipping line that had transported her African American troupe to Paris, Baker—herself a new commodity—appears in an unsophisticated dress of ruffles and fringing, with tinsel around her ankles and tap shoes (Figure 6.17). With an energetic swiveling of feet, alternately turned out and in, she danced with flicking heels and low-down body weight, her costume flickering rapidly. Her slim shape maps the syncopated form of the jazz dancing body, but its surface is increasingly adorned by sequins—round shiny discs—sewn onto a base textile structure.

In her cultural history, *The Shining Cloth*, Victoria Rivers writes that "massed accretions of sequins, beads, shells, and mirrors" served multiple purposes beyond the obvious identification of status or wealth. In many societies, the prized quality of luminosity "encapsulates soul-force, attracts or deflects spirits in unseen worlds, and provides protection" (1999: 7). The "flashing energy" of shiny objects possessed value as signs of beauty, rarity, or protection in ancient trading networks and inspired fascination. When worn as bodily adornment, reflective objects—a bead, a crystal, a piece of shiny metal—accrued power and influence for its wearer. Rivers explains: "Sequins, originally small rounds of flat gold money, serve a dual purpose in textiles: to display wealth and to ward off the evil eye. . . garments and objects embellished with sequins create dazzling kinetic effects, as well as tinkling sounds which further distract the evil eye" (1999: 13).

Dating back to ancient Egypt and Persia, *sikka* or sequins were stitched to stately robes to inspire awe and add luster to their owners. Originally heavy coins, they evolved into smaller and lighter objects constructed from wires of gold, silver, or copper coiled around a thin rod, cut into sections, and beaten flat. Later, when thin sheets of rolled metal could be produced, circles were cut out and punctured. These handmade sequins often retained hammer marks and were cupped to reflect more light. The finer the quality and the greater the shine, the sequins would signal wealth and status. These metallic or-namentations began to appear in rugs, cushions, and jackets, not only in India and Persia but also in the clothing of European imperial courts.

Sequins as signs of beauty, wealth, and power accumulate significance in Baker's costume history, particularly as "variants" of the desire for "shiny skin." The graphic designer Colin, who had been Baker's lover during her first years in Paris, introduced Baker to Boris Lipnitzki, a Russian émigré renowned for making photographic portraits of the Parisian demi-monde.[12] Under unknown circumstances, the young Baker posed nude in his studio against a white sheet and with crude electric lighting; she appears both bold and fearful, both subject and object of the male gazes in attendance and off-screen (see also Durkin 2019: 39–40). In one image, she lounges in the odalisque style of a Matisse painting; in another, she huddles against the wall like a coquette.[13] Contrary to her stage history as a comedic performer, she adopts the ecstatic pose of German modern dance, torso thrown back, one leg bent forward at right angles, and the other raised on a flexed foot. Without the adornment and privacy of beads or feathers, the male artists are fashioning her shiny (probably oiled) body to become modern. These embodiments affirm her sleek gestural articulation of a pose, but she is also learning how to please and become a subject of reproduction. Baker does not smile, nor is she fully defined by the beholder, but her accomplishment as a nineteen-year-old entertainer under scrutiny in a foreign city is impressive.

By 1928, following success in Paris and Berlin, her entourage booked a season in Vienna, but it became plagued by controversy led by the Catholic Church, and early signs of racist xenophobia were directed at the presumed immorality of her show (Durkin 2019: 30). The portrait in Figure 6.18, taken in Vienna, depicts a pensive Baker whitening her face and wearing a rosette headband, beaded shorts, and a blouse made of rhinestone crystals.[14] The scant costume is stylish with its cut-away sleeves and plunging V-neckline, and has become more than a "string of beads" and feathers. Flesh is subtly exposed, and under the lights, the costume would emit plenty of dazzle. Her fully-robed, black attendant's determined face and pearl-drop earring are the visual punctum of the image, existing in tension with the racial dissembling to which Josephine was subjected.

FIGURE 6.18 Josephine Baker with an assistant, Vienna, 1927 (1928). © KHM-Museumsverband, Theatermuseum.

Whether the showgirl becomes aware of it or not, the sequins add more than luster. They might function, as Rivers suggests, as a protective surface warding off evil spirits by deflecting the audience's gaze. With its shiny objects and overlapping surfaces, the garment actualizes a form of defense, heavy to wear and repellent to touch.

At the time of Baker's debut, sequined dresses were still made of fine metals fastened securely to a base fabric. In fashionable dress, the cloth was often silk, but for performance, the sequins were attached to a resilient yet flexible cotton tulle that would not add to the overall weight. The inside of a sheath dress belonging to Renaud in Figure 6.19 demonstrates fine rows of sequins and beads attached to a ribbed bodice. The tiny, weighted objects are evenly distributed so as not to distort the tight fit of the garment, which has a metallic surface like chain mail. Artisans working with sequined and beaded fabrics can produce extraordinary designs spun into spirals, flowers, and leaves, or geometric patterns. On dark fabric, the sequins appear like pricks of light, while on softer colors, they infuse the surface with a glow. Precious metals, used sparingly, were therefore interspersed with diamantes or rhinestones—faceted glass beads—that reflected the gold and silver sequins as molten light.

FIGURE 6.19 Interior view of long strapless sheath dress worn by Line Renaud in the revue *Plaisirs* at the Casino de Paris, 1959 to 1963, designed by José Luis Vinas. Collection at the National Center for Costume and Stage (Moulins, France)/gift from Madame Line Renaud. © CNCS/Terminal 33.

One can imagine the curvaceous silhouette of this long strapless dress illuminated under lights by the layered rows of sequins, tiny beads, tubular pearls, and rhinestones. Its elaborate armature is sculptured off the shoulder, and with its side slit below the hips, the spectator's attention is directed by design to an oblique area of leg flesh.

This duplicity between tensile sharpness and sparkling elegance is particularly impressive in the costumes Baker wore in Monaco in 1969. By this date, the revue genre, with its nostalgic tone of idle luxury, was out of step with contemporary politics. In May 1968, Paris had seen student and worker uprisings whose radical rejection of establishment values contrasted with Baker's passionate support of the nation. African independence movements and postcolonial intellectual activism had produced a populace more ashamed of French colonial histories, while rock'n'roll and the cinema of the French new wave were transforming the entertainment world. All these changes in fashion and social values ensnare Baker's reputation and appeal. Bereft of an audience, she reverts to staying in hotels until the principality of Monaco provides an opportunity for more glamor and fantasy.

In 1969, Levasseur invited her to perform for a Red Cross fund-raising gala in Monaco. He adapts his designs from her Olympia costumes and adds new costumes responsive to the hues of 1960s pop fashion. Respectfully, they collaborate on the spectacular staging, which is a fund-raising event as much for Baker as for charity (Figure 6.21). In an evening-length performance in the casino ballroom, she performs "tableaux [that]

FIGURE 6.20 Long strapless sheath dress worn by Line Renaud in the revue *Plaisirs* at the Casino de Paris, 1959 to 1963, designed by José Luis Vinas. Collection at the National Center for Costume and Stage (Moulins, France)/gift from Madame Line Renaud © CNCS/Florent Giffard.

FIGURE 6.21 Joséphine Baker and André Levasseur, 1969. Photograph by Robert Oggero © Archives Monte-Carlo S.B.M.

follow, one after the other . . . [and] for each, she dons a new costume, paired with breathtaking headpieces" (Barbier 2022: 32).

One sleeveless sheath dress is covered in "vert anis" sequins—the lime more yellow than green—with front and back panels encased by vertical rows of pearls and rhinestones.[15] The "flesh" bands of skin-colored netting are outlined by silver sequins to create an hourglass effect. This glamorous Egyptian-style tunic remains seductive, but the fine beading would have required hours of labor. In its simple form, it realizes the psychedelic trends, popular with French designers such as Pierre Cardin, and the side vents elongate the slim line of an A-line shift, while offering the illusion of exposure. These modest variants to the silhouette belie the scale of the overall impression this chartreuse costume created on stage.

While the original dress hangs at Chateau Milandes, Levasseur's design illustration includes a massive circular tailpiece extended by a large hoop of lime green feathers surrounded by an even larger spray of black and white ostrich feathers. In the choreography, Baker descends a wide circular staircase, carrying the towering tailpiece and acidic glittering costume. Each component of this ensemble is dialectical, the residue of time and place; the black ostrich feathers hark back to Baker's first Paris costume; the striped armbands emphasize the "Sauvages" body of 1925; the acid green sequins reflect the swinging sixties; the flesh panels accentuate midriff and legs; and the coiffed wig and careful comportment reflect a black bourgeois respectability.

Dancing in this costume requires specific choreographic skills to manage the weighty dress and towering headdress. Agility must be combined with deportment. Baker and Renaud shared advice on how to descend a staircase with the head erect and looking toward the back of an auditorium. The formality of stage choreography, with its full-frontal

FIGURE 6.22 Green sequined panel dress, designed by Andre Levasseur, Monte Carlo, 1968. Photograph by Karen McLeod. Courtesy of Château des Milandes.

address to the audience and central positioning of the star, must create a spectacle to accompany the massed bodies in the backing chorus. Figure 6.23 of Baker's 1959 Revue shows how sequins and feathers dramatize the lines of attention from chorus to star as she begins her performance.

By minimally turning the head from side to side, the female entertainer projects her singing voice and embraces the wide audience with waving gestures.[16] Once stationary at the center of the stage, her shifting of weight creates a constant, subtle dynamic that travels through the upper body and outward through the feathers. Shimmying the shoulders or rippling the torso excites the faceted surface of the sequins, allowing the dancer to hover for effect or emphasis while finishing the delivery of a verse. At these peak moments, she will be surrounded by the swirling movements of the accompanying singer-dancers, who wear less encumbered versions of the costume theme—smaller hats, looser dresses, fewer sparkles. Their dance patterns will amplify the musicality of the event, but Baker in costume must produce the synchronicity and radiating halo of the spectacle.

The next two sections of this chapter discuss the reception of Baker's costumes in Paris and the United States, with a view to understanding how she harnessed fashion to negotiate her bifurcated identities in performance.

FIGURE 6.23 Josephine Baker during the revue *Paris Mes Amours* revue in Olympia Theatre, Paris, May 23, 1959. © Keystone Press Agency/ZUMA Wire/Bridgeman Images.

Fashion in New York (1951) and *Paris Mes Amours* (1959)

Glamor allows a woman, as Jennifer Sweeney-Risko observes, "to travel between. . . supposed celebrity and the class and gendered actualities of her life." Moreover, the performance of glamor underpins "the spectacle of celebrity in a synecdochical way to that of her clothes" (2015: 311). In 1951, with the war over, Baker returned to New York in partnership with the French couture houses, which were intent on rehabilitating their reputations in America. She wanted to support France and to reconcile with the United States, and her promoters were keen to benefit from her transatlantic fame. Under the tutelage of then husband-manager, Jo Bouillon, she agreed to perform her Paris repertoire as well as musical numbers that included Broadway songs, and she arrived armored with her own designers and costumiers.

From Poiret in the first decades to Dior, Balmain, Balenciaga, and Jacques Griffes, Baker maintained close personal relationships with many French couturiers (Sweeney-Risko 2018: 510). Indeed, an entire genre of Baker photography depicts her being fitted with floor-length skirts, embroidered jackets, satin trains, plunging and ruffled necklines, layered chiffons, and oversized coats. There is an apocryphal story that she casually discarded mounting piles of designer dresses on her apartment floor because more would be delivered the next day (Barbier 2022: 70). Whatever the relationship with fashion houses, they "dressed her" much like contemporary celebrities at the Met Gala, and she did not own the dresses.

Having completed a season in South America, Baker reluctantly committed to sing at concerts in Miami. She was however persuaded to return to New York, with the backing

FIGURE 6.24 Poster advertising Josephine Baker at Carnegie Hall, October 12, 1963. Courtesy of Carnegie Hall Rose Archives.

of influential sponsors from the black civil rights movement—the National Association for the Advancement of Colored People, Congress of Racial Equality, Student Nonviolent Coordinating Committee, and the Southern Christian Leadership Conference—and offers of support for her own charity for refugee children. The Carnegie Hall concert poster (Figure 6.24) featured the black silhouette of a slender woman with a narrowed waist in full-length dress, her bangled arms reaching upward. Into this black keyhole, the viewer projects the eponymous black female entertainer—Joséphine Baker—with the acute accent marking her French *différance*.

The poster strap line promoted her "fabulous wardrobe" and estimated its material worth with a string of zeroes. Some reviewers described the concert as a fashion parade, with eager stylists copying down the details of French design styles for remaking in local salons. The visual artist Marcos Cotti Lorango Jr. saw Baker perform in New York; with her permission, he followed her across the country, sketching her dresses; and the Cotti collection in the Smithsonian documents their extravagance and diversity (Smoot 2012).

His drawings include a full-skirted dress with a strapless bodice by the House of Balmain (Figure 6.25), its purple velvet lavishly embossed with gold braid and beading and extended by a long green train. Restrained and regal, the adornment speaks to the style of the British Princess Margaret, who was a celebrity in the Caribbean jet set at this

FIGURE 6.25 Marcos Cotti Lorango Jr., *Josephine Baker,* 1952. National Portrait Gallery, Smithsonian Institution. © Marcos Cotti Lorango Jr.

time. "Its heavy warmth and textured depth," Young reminds us, communicate "the way the fabric hangs and falls around the body" (2005: 70). The royal velvet dress with its accompanying black mantilla had the desired effect of assisting Baker's wider acceptance in the United States. The successful tour also provided a stage for recognizing Baker's accomplishments as a vocalist.

During this visit, Baker reconciled with her family in St. Louis. As an international celebrity, she also spoke with political leaders and became increasingly critical of media representations of black experience. Moreover, her travels in the Southern states made her attuned to the diminished conditions of minorities. Mary Dudziak recounts that during the Cold War, Baker would "speak about justice at a press conference in the afternoon and then don a feathered gown and headdress for the evening show" (1994: 555). At one community event in Harlem, she spoke wearing a glittering white evening gown; a photograph from this day shows her mid-sentence, with one arm raised like the Statue of Liberty.

She aspired to unite her fellow citizens, even if she did so from a position of distanced privilege. For the State Department and FBI, however, she was a potential threat; her brother Richard Martin found these allegations ironic: "Imagine Josephine a Communist when you think of the way they dress in Moscow" (in Dudziak, 1994: 552). Caught between conflicts, some black activists found the gap between her glamorous reality and their local struggle too great, although she later became a figurehead in the struggle for black rights. Speaking at the March on Washington led by Martin Luther King in 1963, she wore her French military uniform. Dressing sensibly in solidarity with protests against racial injustice, she knew on that occasion which costume would speak to the crowd.

At Chateau Milandes, the velvet Balmain gown is on display alongside the military uniform, both with shiny decorations (Figure 6.26). Together, they mark a significant period in Baker's career, when the elegant diva and the political figurehead were combined in one person. "With her sophistication and couture wardrobe," Phyllis Rose noted, "her act now in every way called attention to her artifice, the triumph of art over nature" (Dudziak 1994: 555).

Adam Geczy and Vicki Karaminas suggest that Baker's ability to "shape-shift" in this couture phase secured her "libertine ways" (2020: 126). I disagree; the 1950s could be considered Baker's most conservative period, in that she endorsed fashion values aligned with domesticity, status, and capitalist entrepreneurship. Her willful adoption of French haute couture was not libertine but a weapon that gave her the license to assemble a politically powerful Josephine in a fractured United States. Her anti-racist activity included visits to Mexico and Argentina, and her determination to campaign against injustice cost her financial support from the United States in the 1950s, even as she embarked on adopting her refugee family. Not yet, had her dress-ability provided restitution and a secure future.

In 1959, Baker performed in *Paris mes Amours* at the Olympia Theatre, sponsored again by the Coquatrix family (as in Figure 6.23). Her reappearance on the French stage benefited from her wartime support for France, and in 1961, she was belatedly awarded the *Croix de Guerre* (Lewis 2022). With this respected status, she accumulated wealth, rented Chateau Milandes in the Dordogne as her home, and gathered her American and "rainbow" family together, but she desperately needed reliable income. With better personal stability, she wanted to entertain on her own terms, and this program marked the apogee of Baker's success in using her voice and rhythmic movement to communicate.

Supported by another glittering array of costumes, the ode to Paris comprised multiple musical segments, including a reprise of the Charleston with Baker dancing "on a drum" and wearing a short-skirted white sheath dress. This exquisite costume, adorned with layers of white tulle petals decorated with blue teardrop beads encased in pearl white sequins, still exists in the Milandes collection.[17] Its fine beadwork, creating an eye-shaped motif, is three-dimensional with rows of sequins supported by over-stitching on the backing cloth (Figure 6.27).

Baker was in her early fifties, but her dancing body harnesses the theatricality of glamor so that the layered eyes catch the light in all directions. With the slightest wriggle, her ensemble shifts its reflective attachments, and the blue lights flicker and flash across the body's surface and into the audience. The dancer appears to have "a second skin scarred with sparks," in the hyperbolic discourse of more recent fashion; and the result is "a body radiating with inner beauty."[18] Shifting between androgynous flapper and flirtatious mistress, the slim-fitting, glowing dress illuminates Baker's luxury appeal, and perhaps wards off evil spirits. In these fashion gowns, her performances are at the vanguard as she models the more voluptuous femininity of postwar European culture.

FIGURE 6.26 Purple velvet gown with gold embroidery and green train, designed by Balmain. Photograph by Karen McLeod. Courtesy of Château des Milandes.

FIGURE 6.27 Detail of sequined flapper-style dress worn for *Paris Mes Amours*, Olympia, 1959. Photograph by Karen McLeod. Courtesy of Château des Milandes.

Shimmering in New York (1973) and Paris (1974)

According to the sociologist Rebecca Coleman in her book, *Glitterworlds*, the shimmering of shiny metal or plastic objects has purposes beyond ornamentation or fake glamor in contemporary life. In alignment with the new materialisms, Coleman argues that "glitter"—tiny bits of plastic that sparkle when they catch the light, that are thrown in the air, stuck on a surface, or worn on the body—possesses a liminal quality that generates powerful moments of luminosity and superfluity. In its ephemerality and lightness, glitter helps young women to fabulate community, to imagine new alternative worlds. This "worlding" propensity of glitter extends to having a material and "political value for feminist and anti-racist work" (2020: 7). Artists today from Beyoncé to Taylor Swift mobilize glamor and glitter in performance; and, as Elyssa Goodman asserts, drag artists in "lush feathers floating through elegant theaters or sequins sparkling under tiny barroom stage lights" throw glitter as "gender punks and outlaws" (2023: 3–5). Glitter is another commodity form with a distinct history that follows from the rise of sequins in American manufacturing.

In the mid-twentieth century, the availability of sequins for costumes was transformed when synthetic plastics replaced metallic goods. Earlier experiments with acetate decorations in fashion failed because cellulose melted or cracked, but once robust plastic sheeting could be manufactured, trademark Mylar® sequins could be mass produced with a variety of finishes—multi-colored, metallic, and fluorescent (Rivers 1999: 59).[19] In the United States, the dominant manufacturer of sequins became Meadowbrook Glitter, a company that patented the technologies for stamping out tiny, punctured circles. Today, Meadowbrook's sequined textiles for the dance world are pre-stitched flat by machines across a backing cloth.[20] This reduction in factory production costs has facilitated the rapid spread of shiny cloth in competitive dance outfits; sequins appear in outfits for ballroom and hula-hooping, and glittery patterns emblazon sweatshirts and sneakers as often as fancy evening wear. The mythic glamor of ballroom dancing in "performance and presentation," as Jonathan Marion argues in his study *Ballroom: Culture and Costume in Competitive Dance*, depends on the "minutiae of experience" navigated by dancers moving with "the weight of rhinestone encrusted dresses and the sound of a dress's beaded fringe" (2008: 60, 136). In these diverse settings, a little bit of sparkle has become a lot of bling.

In 1973, Baker appears in London at the Coliseum, and the following year she performs at Carnegie Hall in New York. Now in her mid-sixties, Baker works to support herself and her family, many of whom are now university students. Still a celebrity, she is relatively unmoored and travels for concerts across Europe. As Baker aged and her body lost its svelte androgyny, the evening dress contours of her silhouette became longer, and the quilled outfits more extreme. At the Coliseum, Baker wore a white gown with long cuffed sleeves fringed with soft curling feathers that flounced with every gesture, almost drowning her facial expressions and her dancing body.

At Carnegie Hall, she opens the concert in a net bodysuit, credited to Levasseur, now a design attaché to Dior. The costume copies an earlier outfit, created by Berteaux, and resembles a net bodysuit worn by Renaud under a decorative bikini (Figure 6.28). The silhouette with its loose weave of flesh-colored net is like the fleshings of Chapter 1, which reveal and mask the body beneath. Dotted, specular sequins peer from the net (Figure 6.29), once again featuring as protective eyes on the skin-like surface.

In this performance and later in Monte Carlo (1974), Baker removes a fluffy, overblown feathered cloak and bares the sparkly, netted jumpsuit, drawn tight at the waist to emphasize her curves (Figure 6.30). The costume seems innocent but beckons the imagination. Do the studded sequins and feathered turban provide plausible escape or safeguarding from the audience's gaze that judges the entertainer? As an artist who seeks to please, Baker waves in exultation as if to exploit the costume's absurdity. She looks exposed, with a sense of fragility like an awkward chick, newly hatched.

Changing costumes frequently, Baker speaks in English and sings mostly in French. With stiffened elegance, she maintains her gift for repartee with the New York audience. In

FIGURE 6.28 Net bodysuit worn by Line Renaud in the 1960s. Collection of the National Center for Costume and Stage (Moulins, France)/gift from Madame Line Renaud. © CNCS/Terminal 33.

FIGURE 6.29 Detail of a rhinestone stitched into the fishnet of bodysuit worn by Line Renaud in the 1960s. Collection of the National Center for Costume and Stage (Moulins, France)/gift from Madame Line Renaud. © CNCS/Terminal 33.

FIGURE 6.30 Josephine Baker in net bodysuit performing at Gala de la Croix-Rouge Monégasque—Monte-Carlo Sporting Club, 1974. Photograph by Robert Oggero © Archives Monte-Carlo S.B.M.

Figure 6.31, she wears a long pale cocktail dress studded with jewels, with a short black wig as disguise, and perches on the edge of the stage. Encased but close, intimate but restrained.

From this concert, another outfit at Milandes is a dialectical costume to the "second skin" of glittering net. Fabricated in silk crepe, this faded black garment resembles the smart pantsuits that Baker increasingly wore as personal attire during the 1960s (Figure 6.32). Fitting the body closely, fine rows of silver sequins are neatly spaced down the legs, but there are "no feather[s] or gems, her long golden chain barely visible" (Barbier 2022: 52). Unlike the shiny surface or dense pattern of a sequined fabric, the small discs are individuated, barely visible, like the pinpricks of stars in a dark sky. Since they do not connect, they illuminate only discrete points, producing a delicate skeletal outline.

With this costume, Baker wears a large curly wig, more bouffant than her usual tightly coiled style, yet befitting of the Afro looks popularized by 1960s figures such as Angela Davis. Along her arms are jeweled armbands, and around her neck is the single gold drape (Figure 6.33). When Baker sings Bob Dylan's anthem, *The Times They Are a-Changin'*, the ornaments resemble the liberating beads of a hippie goddess. Secure in this outfit with its lack of ostentation, Baker inhabits the lyric sentiments with some pain in her voice. The vitality of a material reality exudes from the unadorned dress and it fits with her subjectivity. Her remark that year to Norwegian journalist Eric Bye, "I personally am not too much fond of jewels!" might accompany this change in attitude (Bye 1971).

FIGURE 6.31 Josephine Baker performing at Carnegie Hall concert, 1973. Photographs and Prints Division, Schomburg Center for Research in Black Culture, The New York Public Library. Photograph by Austin Hansen; used with permission of Austin Hansen estate.

A final dress belonging to Baker's second visit to St. Louis on this tour produces a different narrative: this beautifully crafted white evening dress was worn with high white boots and a white feather headdress. Embroidered with hearts and trefoils and appliquéd with gold braid, tiny glass beads, bronze sequins, and large colored rhinestones, the costume is both glamorous and regal (Figures 6.34 and 6.35). An archival photograph shows Baker surrounded by young black women, smiling in delight and admiration (Figure 6.36). Contrast this photograph with the young Baker in Vienna: her direct gaze demonstrates the agency, acquired through her efforts, to take pleasure in the effects of a decorative costume.

After her return from New York, Baker commences intensive rehearsals for a final show at the Bobino in Paris. Simply called *Josephine*, her own life has become the music-hall subject.[21] Baker was unwell, but close collaborators gathered around her, including the musical choreographer Jean Moussy and the costumier Mine Vergès. Vergès ran a Paris theatrical costume atelier, and had earlier met Baker at the *Winter Circus*, an artists' fund-raiser. She was responsible for preparing the new wardrobe, including "a blue satin stretch combination, a grand cape cut from the same fabric as well as a turban headdress

FIGURE 6.32 Black sequined pantsuit worn at Carnegie Hall in 1973. Photograph by Karen McLeod. Courtesy of Château des Milandes.

FIGURE 6.33 Josephine Baker performing in black sequinned pantsuit at 21st Gala de la Croix-Rouge Monégasque, 1969. Photograph by Robert Oggero © Archives Monte-Carlo S.B.M.

to be covered in diamonds and large jewels" (2021: 160). This confection fastened to a headscarf consisted of hundreds of dyed "femina" feathers that radiated into a conical shape. As the workshop sewed "diamonds onto her turban," Vergès recalls, "we were permanently watched by two minions that never stopped watching us, even escorting Josephine to the toilet. This drove me crazy!" (2021: 160).[22]

Despite these difficulties, Vergès remembers Baker's kind professionalism, as well as a stoicism about her stage presence. "At nearly 70 years," Baker confessed, "I have never been seated in a *robe-de-scène*. Sometimes I would cry because I would like myself to have become a queen" (Vergès 2021: 163). The dialectical potency of Baker, through her incessant mobility and costume repetitions, is contained in Vergès's response: "Her wish would have been granted. When she placed her feet on the stage, with her ostrich feathers, her fake diamonds, and her train, she was beautiful and certainly a queen" (161). On the second evening of this final show, Baker returns home and dies of heart failure.

In the archives, the black pantsuit is torn at the knees, and the regal dress from Balmain is ragged. These traces remain from Baker's lived experience and from wearing them to perform. Curator Delphine Pinasa from the Museum of Costume understands

FIGURE 6.34 Josephine Baker dress, c. 1973. Photograph by JJ Lane, Be Lovely Photography. Courtesy of Mary Strauss.

FIGURE 6.35 Detail of Josephine Baker's dress, ca. 1973. Photograph by JJ Lane, Be Lovely Photography. Courtesy of Mary Strauss.

FIGURE 6.36 Josephine Baker with young women, c. 1973. Photographer unknown. Courtesy of Mary Strauss.

FIGURE 6.37 Detail of black sequined pantsuit worn at Carnegie Hall, 1973. Photograph by Karen McLeod. Courtesy of Château des Milandes.

FIGURE 6.38 Detail of purple velvet gown with gold embroidery and green train, designed by Balmain. Photograph by Karen McLeod. Courtesy of Château des Milandes.

this decay of illusion in dress: "For the spectacle, for the show, all is possible, but afterwards the costume is very fragile" (2023). The dialectical image of Baker's costumes is thus a material fragility that echoes the immaterial spirit of her dancing world.

Coleman argues that the use of glitter in social and creative practices enables imagination, and rather than decrying its wasteful abundance, she affirms that sparkly things afford a diversity of embodiments. While more stable than glitter, I would argue that Baker's appearance on the concert stage in sequined outfits of elite and glamorous style was always a form of affirmative and disruptive politics. Baker knew how to embody a "look" and a "style," and what it means for a dancing body to be rendered mute, expressive, or powerful. Importantly, the sequins adorn a corporeal intelligence harnessed by women in repeated formation as a matter of survival. Feathers and sequins—acting alternately as display, as cocoon, as theatrical prop, or as protection against evil—become essential agents in a mode of dress that has inspired many black and queer entertainers, with a selection discussed in the next section.

Glittering Gowns: The Legacy

From Baker, sequins and feathers, both together and separately, spiral forwards in endless repetitions. The luxury and the cheap, the real and the fake, become intermingled in small and large entertainment venues. And the costume technologies of glamor fabricated by dancers can be politically and artistically transformative.

In 1959, just as the Civil Rights movement gained momentum and as Josephine Baker concluded her successful US tour, a new black girl group was formed in Detroit, Michigan, by Motown Records. From an initial group called *The Primettes*, a trio consisting of Mary Wilson, Diana Ross, and Barbara Martin emerged as *The Supremes* in 1962. In their first television appearances, they wear modest dresses with cinched waists and short gathered skirts while innocently cooing into microphones. Portrayed as modern urban women wearing tailored suits and A-line shift dresses, these singers were the respectable face of a Middle America that had also become black.

By the mid-1960s, however, a more glamorous costume choreography became a signature part of their performance. Designers such as Michael Travis (who was creating for Liberace), Pat Campano, and Bob Mackie (the "Sultan of Sequins" working for Cher, Elton John, and many others) shape and construct the glittering "look" of the group. The three young women were also closely involved with the choice of outfits, often selecting and purchasing items while on tour. With their beehive wigs, miniskirts, lapelled jackets, and pantsuits, the Supremes stimulated a rising awareness of the sexiness of black style that was a counterpoint to the Civil Rights movement.

In performance, the Supremes' costumes were quite literally multiples of the same dress—women inside a template or silhouette, given variation by a unique decorative surface. Their dancing was tempered to the slim costume: the celebrated Motown "Director of Artist Development," Maxine Powell, instructed the Supremes in how "not to protrude the buttocks, but to roll under," and "if they did not know their step, then to smile" (Dickinson 2008).[23] When the Supremes were introduced to the Queen Mother in identical dresses embossed with beads and gemstones that weighed 35 pounds each, their training in comportment was indeed tested.

The Motown dance coach, Cholly Atkins, prepared the choreography, composed of sensual movements in unison—beginning with the feet, traveling through the hips and torso, with a shimmering out through arms and fingertips. As with Baker, this subtle shifting of weight gave the sparkling costumes extra volume and interplay. With the fashion silhouette of "glamor goddess" in triplicate, the Supremes also transported op art to the stage—brown, gold, and orange discs splitting into fractions, overlapping segments of lime green, black, and citric yellow. Pushing these optical effects, their dresses exploited this period's interest in hallucinatory experience. As the group sang, the circular forms would move, causing emerald reflections, frosty lights, and rippling oceanic blues, while their sweet voices would soothe their listeners. Not soul singers, these entertainers were ready for the "baby love."

By the end of the 1960s, the glittering trio was sadly torn apart by rivalries and mismanagement. Reviews of their last performances riffed on the expectation of shine: the Supremes had "lost their spark," or even more dismissively, were only "gin and fizz." Musically, their solo careers continued, and decades later, Mary Wilson assiduously located and collected the slim-fitting gowns of chiffon, satin, and silk studded with sequined scrolls and diamonds to organize *Supreme Glamor*, an exhibition in celebration of black diva style in the era of psychedelia (Wilson 2019).[24]

If *The Supremes* replicated the sparkling dress, the transvestite entertainer Glenn Milstead, performing as the raucous Divine in the 1980s, upends its iconicity when they belt out the line "you think you're a man but you're only just a boy." In "shoot your shot," Divine wears a tight-fitting costume with a red sequined body and black sequined phalanges hanging from an off-centered neckline (Figure 6.39). The sequins do their work, flicking in the intermittent lighting from the side and overhead, while they clutch the microphone and hurl the words. The choreography empowers the male entertainer, both inviting adoration and mocking the normative reception of the erotic female singer. Subverting the "silhouette" but in thrall to the spangles, the dress distorts the feminine hourglass with its pointed breasts, thickened middle, and Divine's stretched buttocks wiggle and twist.

This sparkling look of stardom is rendered by Divine as a monstrous feminine. The film-maker John Waters, Milstead's collaborator, argues that this character "was thought up to scare hippies. And that's what he wanted to do. He wanted to be Godzilla. Well, he wanted to be Elizabeth Taylor and Godzilla put together" (Jung 2019). Singing *I'm so Beautiful* with "jiggling breasts" in a sequined silver and hot-pink mini-dress, Divine puts hands on hips and pulses, then swipes down their curvaceous body. From a contemporary perspective, the performance celebrates body positivity for differently sized women, and much cosplay with fake feathers and plastic sequins in queer and queen fashion continues to ward off evil spirits and quite literally "dazzle."

The global popularity of the long-running television show *RuPaul's Drag Race*, with its extreme competition for trans-fashion, is another legacy of the florid use of sequins. Created by RuPaul Charles and American–Filipino costume designer Zaldy (Zaldy Goco), RuPaul combines a stately walk with wiggling hips and a "super model" figure—"big

FIGURE 6.39 Divine. Photograph by Greg Gorman. © Greg Gorman.

blond hair, a teeny-tiny waist, and long, long legs" (Lautens 2022). In Season 14, he performs in a black sequined outfit consisting of a black off-the-shoulder bodice cut on the diagonal, with one arm exposed and the other in tufted feathers, accompanied by classic black net stockings and scooped apron skirt cheekily edged with a ruffle of black feathers.

In a low-grade version of this black and white uniform, RuPaul could be serving tables in a nightclub; so, the costume deliberately combines sophisticated glamor with cheap titillation. But the effect is belied by the polish of the wig, the toned muscles, the manicured nails, and the confident swagger and swish of the dance that follows. Zaldy merely exclaims: "I'm honestly addicted to sparkles! I'm surrounded by them all the time, and I love them" (Lautens 2022).

Given the role of such shiny things in popular dance, subaltern fantasy, and gender play, we might recall Iris Marion Young's argument about how pleasure extends to the imaginary: "The very multiplicity and ambiguity of the fantasy settings evoked by clothes and by the fashion imagery of these clothes contributes to such pleasure" (2005: 73). As objects that attach to the dancing body, feathers and sequins invent a potential "Utopia" for the entertainer—whether male, female, transgender, aged, body-inclusive, black, or hybrid. In the hyper-capitalism of entertainment, the dancer must however "transform . . . into a bewitching object that will capture his desire and his identity," especially if the desire for shiny [black] skin is the commodity at stake (Young 2005: 67). The dialectical costume of feather and sequins supports thus a fiction that has a deep, and complicated, material history that reaches into the future. As the glamor silhouette mutates, expands, flashes, multiplies, and becomes monstrous, or glittering waste, it will be dancers who manifest its power in performance.

Conclusion

In the Benjamin epigraph, Apollinaire is struck by the sumptuous dress of an "old dowager" that at one moment dazzles like a "gold mine" in the sun but loses value to "silver" in the rain. The flickering values of feathers and sequins in entertainment costumes illustrate the variable currency of a glittering dress in dance. It implies a fantasy of transformation, but its silhouette is rarely crafted for the unique subject, and its repetition furthers the global flows of the entertainment economy. At the same time, the survival of an individual artist depends on a marvelous capacity to wear this costume and make it tickle and dazzle.

A costume archive of feathers and sequins is a non sequitur; everything we know about an archive—its authority, its cataloguing system, its preservation of records and artifacts—is undone by such ephemeral adornments. These materials rot and disintegrate, crack and melt, and the garments end up stored at the back of cupboards.[25] The production companies for whom Baker performed disposed of most of her costumes; the couture gowns were repossessed or destroyed; others were given to fellow entertainers; and when she lost Chateau Milandes, the contents of her wardrobe were seized by police (Barbier 2022: 26). Except for the Balmain dress, on loan from a private collector, there is little evidence of the many glamorous gowns created at great expense by French fashion houses.[26]

Mysteriously, there is a hidden Baker costume archive, acquired by private collectors who jealously guard the provenance; smaller items, such as shoes and design drawings, are scattered across collecting institutions in the United States and Europe. One apocryphal story, perhaps true, is that Baker sent three taxi-loads of gowns to Lynn Carter, a successful 1970s female impersonator, because she admired his parodies of Baker and other female artists such as Bette Davis. Carter passed away in 1984. In one photograph in the *Queer Music Heritage* archives, he wears a sequined Dior outfit, one of the "fabulous gowns of the woman being mocked" (Doyle, n.d.).[27] Many other dresses presumably reappeared in underground shows, disappeared into wardrobes and flea markets, or were discarded in waste bins.

To understand the dialectical costume through this "stuff," one confronts the carefully fabricated illusions of the entertainment industry, the reification of dress, and the precarity of women's excess labor in both manufacture and performance. In this world, Baker herself is everywhere and nowhere—since 2021, she has been "officially" interred in the Pantheon (one of only six women to have this honor) and has become a symbol of respectability for her contribution to France as an entertainer and Resistance ally.[28] She is celebrated as a fashion icon, having inspired the 2023 Dior haute couture collection. She has become a cause célèbre for Paris—the dialectical image of a modernity that embraced a black stranger in an affirmation that remains beyond the capacity of the current French state to welcome its immigrants. In strictly economic terms, however, it is easily forgotten that Baker only had financial independence—or her own dressmaker—for a very short time.

In this book, the relationships between subject and object, between material and immaterial, are transitive in choreography, but never more so than in the costumes of dance entertainment, which are not easily reconciled with the agency or affective potential of the dancer. "Many of our clothes never attain this privileged status of the beloved," says Young, "perhaps because our motives for having most of them are so extrinsic: to be in style or to give our face the most flattering color, to be cost-effective, or to please others" (2005: 70). From the perspective of dance studies, in terms of corporeal agency and self-awareness as a black artist and entertainer, Baker's remarkable resilience and adaptability made her style attract attention and "please others." In her own words, she echoes those of Young, "the costume, the stage outfits, the make-up are of crucial importance and the first sign of respect for your audience" (Barbier 2022: 140). In the complexities of that life, this persona, the assemblage, and fabrication of the shiny dance costume exhibit an active consciousness of a modernity whose time is still coming.

Conclusion

Fabrications: Dance, Costume, and Material Culture has been concerned with the relationship between dance costumes and modernity (meaning "recently" or "right now") under capitalism. For most of the twentieth century, modernity has been shaped by the world's largest economy, with the United States being a global leader in the production, innovation, and consumption of manufactured materials as well as a powerhouse of dance dissemination. Rather than focusing on subjectivity or identity in dance, the book has aimed to explore the technologies of production and reproduction that influence the construction and availability of costumes, and therefore shape the fashioning of the dancing body.

During this period, flows of capital, marked by colonial relations and industrial inequalities, have affected the availability of raw materials, domestic goods, and production methods. How dancers are dressed is therefore directly aligned with economic trends, which have in turn influenced choreography, stage design, and the development of dance-related industries. Fashion, with its role in disseminating dress codes and values, has contributed to the representation of dance as an exemplary art form for the expression of changes in modernity.

In this context, dance costumes deserve more detailed study in fashion and clothing histories. The performative body may exemplify processes of standardization and control, but it also produces insight into creative relationships with dress and dressing. Adopting a material cultural studies approach, this book has focused on how a series of objects—archival costumes—were created by different modes of dance practice. And it has been proposed that, over time and in multiples, standardized types of costumes produce exemplary patterns and silhouettes for the embodied movement of dance aesthetics.

To place parameters around the raw materials of each chapter, I have proposed three ways in which a typology of costumes connects choreography to the fashion system: by textile, by silhouette (ideal shape), and by formal design techniques (drapery, cut, color, stretch, and ornamentation). The basic silhouettes repeat regularly in key genres of expressive movement and choreography, although diverse characteristics permit variations within a dance repertoire over time, depending on the artists, the available resources for making costumes, and the contexts in which they perform. The specific characteristics become significant when the choreography requires specific qualities such as flow, tension, or dazzle.

Most importantly, the forms of dance costume represent a constellation of ideas about movement in a historical moment, what I have termed, after Walter Benjamin, the

Fabrications. Rachel Fensham, Oxford University Press. © Oxford University Press 2026. DOI: 10.1093/9780197699638.003.0008

"dialectical costume." As such, a dance sartorial style can illuminate an attitude from the past, a crystallized view of social conduct, but also orientate the imagination as a choreographic thought, a potential animation, that leans toward the future. Each chapter has provided detailed examples of how costume types evolved in the work of a particular choreographer; in the process, it has illustrated the unique and novel forms of costume experimentation in dance. Throughout the century, design innovation has been generatively linked to the creative thought that takes place in the embodiments of dance and choreography. A dance costume, however, is not only a visual statement about the body or about fashioning the self but is fundamentally about how clothes move and what the moving body can express through dress.

The early years of modern dance exemplify the eclecticism of small companies such as those led by Ruth St. Denis and Ted Shawn in creating fantasy worlds from tunics and trousers, employing fabric in dimensions that reached beyond conventional norms of sexual expression. As artisans, they employed the latest construction technologies, notably in the use of fasteners to make robust garments that have been used by generations of future dancers. Coming after them, Martha Graham asserted the necessity of fabric sculpture, using cuts and torsion to mold the wool jersey robe and the internal body in ways that placed her choreography at the vanguard of fashionable modernity. Her dance designs used the weight and volume of skirts to produce an articulate shaping of passionate ideas about the female subject.

At a different scale, Katherine Dunham, in her collaboration with John Pratt, produced an extensive wardrobe using the latest fabrics in radically theatrical designs. Their complex layering of adornments in a wide range of dances developed the integration of dress styles from a multitude of cultures and contexts. This creative repertoire led to a formative representation of Caribbean and African American fashion on stage and the elaboration of an energetic dynamics that was an articulation of black dance labor.

Mass manufacture on an industrial scale became the hallmark of postwar industrial capitalism, sparking widely different choreographic responses. On the one hand, Merce Cunningham and his collaborators embraced spandex and other synthetic fabrics and extended their design potential, developing a gender-neutral uniform of leotards, tights, and unitards that dominated their intricate, expansive choreographies. With costumes dyed in bright colors shown under increasingly sophisticated lighting, the company acted like a laboratory on the affordances of color in the dance industry more widely. On the other hand, the dance artists of Grand Union rejected artifice in favor of mass-produced clothing that was pragmatic in style. Their use of everyday clothes was intended to make a political statement rejecting artifice, which also meant making use of secondhand clothing and outfits that were assembled for flexible uses.

A similar approach to the singularity of materials can be seen in the work of Trisha Brown, but it was used for quite different artistic ends. Brown pursued a minimalist approach, favoring light, fluid textiles in which postmodern dancers could signal movement rather than experiencing the costume as an encumbrance. Her aesthetic of transparent, almost floating, costumes lent itself to the play between visibility and invisibility in dance. And at the other extreme of the political power of dress, Josephine Baker and her collaborators worked the surfaces of glitter and the flick of feathers to create a glamorous stage presence that gained her international fame. For each of these artists and companies, the dance costume is both material and immaterial, worked and reworked, to influence the imagination of the dress in motion.

These case studies are not exclusive. Similar or wildly divergent types of costume exist for artists working in the same locations or perhaps separated by time, ideology, or geography. One challenge in writing this book has been deciding how to exclude the variants, no matter how fascinating. Each thread left hanging leaves much more to be explored.

Beyond the cultural history of materials and methods of fabrication, the costume is always material in another sense, because its distinctive properties matter to what the dancers do with their bodies. The haptic qualities of a textile, the fit of a garment, and the complexity of structure in a dress impress themselves on the person wearing the costume. This book has given limited attention to the phenomenal perspective of the wearer, whose use of the costume, even when resistant to the garment, is essential to performance. Dancers wearing a costume transform it from a static thing into something changeable, because their bodies manipulate and activate its structural properties. They modify fabric that hangs too loosely or stretches that are too tight. They also make the costume fit with gestures and steps that will animate original perceptions in the dancing. The costume is no longer an inert shape, but a bearer of meaning beyond its material objecthood. There is more to be written on the living dimensions of dance dress.

At the same time, this research sheds light on the networks involved in costume production, including those of producers, companies, designers, and artists. These networks have also influenced the disparate practices applied to the archiving of dance and its physical traces. The costume as a material artifact will often endure well beyond the performance, but they are difficult to conserve. This book, therefore, was dependent upon those costumes that have been saved, preserved, and stored in archives, museums, and private collections. Pragmatically, it takes time, specialist knowledge, and practical expertise to identify the costumes that warrant preservation and ensure the retention of records that document the memory of works in production.

The flip side of this is that many costumes remain unrecorded in photographic form, and many more are unlikely to be retained or displayed in the future. Viewing the span of twentieth-century experience, the preservation of costumes and dance company records has inevitably been influenced by a mix of personal, economic, and ideological factors, not to mention the occasional climate catastrophe. In the case of the Denishawn archive, for example, a personal breach between the principals led to a literal bonfire of costumes and other items; the remaining items were split between several different sites until thirty years after Ruth St. Denis's death, when the university library that held her costumes decided to reunite them with the rest of the Denishawn collection; even so, there is a secondary repository for Ted Shawn in Florida.

There are numerous active dance companies where the daily requirements of creative production and economic survival leave no time for undertaking the work of managing a legacy. This situation applies to the informal alliance of dancers with Grand Union, where the use of secondhand material and cheap, disposable clothes also militated against constituting a costume archive. At the other extreme, Merce Cunningham ensured that his collection was managed with an eye to posterity, establishing a trust with a dedicated archivist and a standing relationship with a collecting institution to support the cataloging of items, and guaranteeing that a full suite of costumes and notes were was assembled and preserved. Somewhere between the two is Trisha Brown, whose reputation in both the United States and Europe gives ongoing life to the company, which has an in-house archivist facilitating documentation; at the same time, some of the original costumes have been relinquished to various collecting institutions. Martha Graham, whose archive and repertoire were the subject of legal battles, has a resource collection that is carefully controlled by a network of supporters and former company members. Hurricane Sandy inundated their repository in 2012, but what is left of a costume collection has been reconstructed and stored on higher ground.

It is impossible to ignore the influence of racial discrimination in this collection history. The two African American choreographers whose work features in this book were both subject to the vicissitudes of commercial survival, which included expanding their reputations outside the United States. Katherine Dunham spent more than a decade traveling internationally after World War II, while Josephine Baker left for Europe when she was in her teens. Both refashioned themselves multiple times, and for long periods, they did not own the costumes in their wardrobes. Both were dependent on the availability of financial backers, and the exigencies of touring required costumes to be continually repaired and adapted. Dunham returned to the United States for her later career, and most of her company records, including the immense costume collection, are held in public institutions, largely thanks to her own commitment and that of her close supporters, but her personal artifacts are housed in an un-resourced and isolated building in East St. Louis. And in the case of Baker, official disapproval of her civil rights activism left her with limited support when she began adopting refugee children after World War II. She died in financial straits, although supported by industry friends in Monaco and Paris. Few traces of her remarkable stage presence survive in North American archives, and only fragile records of her costumes exist in France.

The chronology of the book ceases in the late twentieth century, when the iconicity of dance costumes mutates once again. In 2023, when I was in New York finalizing research for this book, the Fashion Institute of Technology held an exhibition called *Fresh, Fly, and Fabulous: Fifty Years of Hip Hop Style*.[1] It recognized how this popular dance genre has proliferated, not only producing new forms of music and dance but also stylizing whole communities, from black kids on the street to wealthy entertainers on the global circuit. Its clothing has a unique silhouette, characterized by oversized clothes: baggy jackets, sweatpants that hang off the hips, plus caps and trainers. The variations are many—in color, textile, layering, and adornment—and some of the more extreme outfits on display were decorated with thousands of sequins. Like the costumes worn by Ted Shawn's Male Dancers or the dancers of Grand Union, most of those on display were constructed from ready-made sportswear, although often with additional customized features.

The flexible moves the street dance body can make, on and off the floor, are intertwined with these clothes, and the contemporary reality of social and economic survival for the dancers, often from marginal communities, is identified with the meanings they circulate. One distinctive feature of the exhibition was the ubiquity of prominently displayed brands. In its celebration of dance as production and costume as commodity, the exhibition marks the ongoing entanglement of dance, fashion, and capitalism. As we have seen, this assemblage has a long history. With greater resistance to consumption culture, there are also choreographers working today with costumes made from recyclable clothing or found materials in their attempts to produce a sustainable dance practice and, hopefully, remove the costume from waste bins.

Whichever approach to costume curation unfolds in the twenty-first century, we need to be aware of the garments that have been lost, sold, stolen, or thrown away. They are potent reminders of the dance that has disappeared, the bodies that wore them, and the possibility of an alternative history. Their very absence, however, lingers in narrative traces as a reminder of an historical dialectic that is creative and political, material and immaterial. With care, and with respect, for these threads of a worked and embodied object, there is always the potential for the costume to reanimate the historical as a form of now-ness. This dialectical costume may be thought of as a series of folds, fabricated in the repetitions of the past, turning both forward and back. When lifted out of its costume box and given a shake, this material "thing" helps us to consider why dance matters in studies of culture.

Coda

The concept of *Fabrications* that has guided this book borrows from the philosopher Hannah Arendt, who extended Marxist thought—including Benjamin's own formulations of cultural history—into the late twentieth century. In this coda, I offer a brief reflection on her writings about fabrication, as the products of labor, in relation to the persistence of dance.

In her study of *The Human Condition,* written in the rebuilding of societies after World War II, Arendt examines how actions affect political change and rethinks whether work is a precondition for a meaningful life. For Arendt, fabrication is the product of labor, an activity that takes a given material and makes something for use, which can also be exchanged. Any process of fabrication requires an activity of human thought, and she writes that "the image or model whose shape guides the fabrication process not only precedes it, but does not disappear with the final product, which it survives intact, present, as it were, to lend itself to an infinite continuation of fabrication" (1998: 141). This emphasis on the image, or model, and its endurance as a repertoire is pertinent to my arguments in this book about silhouettes, dialogical images, and the multiplicity of ways in which a costume becomes replicated in dance and choreography.

Arendt also reasons with the extent to which an artwork in human society differs from other kinds of labor. The activity of art, according to Arendt, is a manifestation of thought, rather than the mere product of scientific development or cognitive processes. Making an artwork is an action that can produce a tangible form, such as an item of clothing, but equally works of art may be "useless things, objects which are unrelated to material or intellectual wants" (1998: 171). Art objects involve some degree of reification, the abstraction of ideas, or a conceptual direction, which are, uniquely, a "fabrication" that persists as an immaterial thing as much as the tangible instance of a given form of work.

Following the materialist analysis of this book, the dancer's costume remains an object of interest not only because it is the body of a commodity, the reified product of a recent fashion, but because it is a thing that returns attention to the sensuous and material work of dance performance. Alongside the determinations of labor, practice, and other social distinctions such as class or race, there is imagination, desire, and aesthetic pleasure in the art making of a choreography. The image form of the costume endures

Fabrications. Rachel Fensham, Oxford University Press. © Oxford University Press 2026. DOI: 10.1093/9780197699638.003.0009

then as a materiality also in its aesthetic value as a work of art. A dancer's dress is thus a fabrication, in the fullest sense, of an object that has been made and transformed, used and exchanged, through the actions of human creativity.

Insofar as dance—like paintings, music, or poetry—derives from fabrication, it will persist in things that may have no intrinsic functional value. Yet Arendt says these material things have "permanence" because they retain their association with creative acts of thought. When the costume in concert dance stimulates imagination, it paradoxically offers a limited kind of freedom from the demands of work itself (1998: 169). Once the costume has been fabricated and has found its life in the fabrications of a choreography, it remains open to modes of thought about the freedoms and ideas produced by the act of dancing. The plural fabrications of the costume are therefore the "tangible things" of that thought and its embodied labor, both in manufacture—in the broadest sense of the sensuous, material objects that are made—and their ephemeral, yet enduring, presence in imaginative acts of dancing.

Notes

SERIES EDITOR'S FOREWORD

1. See *The Oxford Handbook of Dance and Reenactment,* edited by Mark Franko (New York: Oxford University Press, 2017).

INTRODUCTION

1. Queer, black, and digital scholars, such as Thomas De Frantz, Ananya Chatterjea, Harmony Bench, Melissa Blanco Borelli, and many others, are expanding conceptions of dance history and theory.

2. In addition to the archive of documents and media reproduction (recordings, videos, etc.) that support historical interpretation, or the related systems of training, design, and rehearsal that transmit repertoire, as defined by Taylor, the embodied trace of dancing in the remains of a costume will enrich knowledge of the performance (2003: 22–26).

3. Elna Matamoros (2021) in her book, *Dance and Costumes: A History of Dressing Movement,* considers dance genres a defining aspect of the historical interpretation of costume in ballet.

4. Since their Paris inception in 1909, the Ballets Russes have excited the dance stage and captured attention in multiple exhibitions, reviews, and books. Their distinctive costumes have featured in exhibitions that celebrated the centenary of the Ballets Russes, including *Diaghilev and the Golden Age of the Ballets Russes* (2011) at the Victoria and Albert Museum and *Diaghilev and the Ballets Russes, 1909–1929: When Art Danced with Music* (2013) at the National Gallery of Art in Australia.

5. Hanna Järvinen's materialist examination of archival costumes challenges received interpretations of the 1913 production of *The Rite of Spring* by the Ballets Russes (2020: 153–173).

6. Sekula identifies the genesis of social classification in the identification of criminals from nineteenth-century photographic archives. He argues that these systems form the basis of modern archival cataloguing methods, in which individuals were "both an object and means of bibliographic rationalization" (1986: 57).

7. Benjamin's influence on theories of art, literature, and theater is well known, but he seemingly showed little interest in dance. In *The Arcades Project,* one dance entry appears in the section on "Prostitution, Gambling" and is a reflection on vulgarity, gender, and surveillance from 1844 (1999: 492).

8. Queer costume historians Adam Geczy and Vicki Karaminas draw upon Benjamin when they suggest "garments contain the past in some form, either in their technological development . . . or in their aesthetic component" (2016: 83).

9. In another variation, Pomare's costume included "jeans, a black beret, and a turtleneck sweater" (Wells 2020: 10).

10. Concerts at the Apollo Theater in Harlem featuring James Brown in 1962 and his record release in 1963 are linked to the emergence of "funk" music, establishing a distinctive dress code for black artists, musicians, and radicals. This funk style became commodified and mainstreamed in the 1970s.

11. Barthes's analysis of modern fashion as a system borrows considerable insight from the German cultural historian George Simmel, whose 1904 essay on social class distinction proposed the now discredited view that elite fashion trickles down to the masses until a new form emerges; see McNeil (2016: 75).

12. From the Frankfurt School to contemporary media studies, the critique of mass production and consumption has been aligned with the expansion of capitalism and its ideological formation in the "culture industry" (Adorno 1975).

13. Coole develops this phenomenological understanding of the fold through the writings of the philosopher Gilles Deleuze in her essay "The Inertia of Matter and the Generativity of Flesh" (Coole and Frost 2010: 92–115).

14. New journals such as *Studies in Costume and Performance*: *Textile: Cloth and Culture* and networks such as *Critical Costume* support contemporary scholarly research.

15. See also Victoria Finlay's *Fabric: The Hidden History of the Material World* (Profile, 2021) and Virginia Postrel, *The Fabric of Civilization: How Textiles Made the World* (Hachette, 2020).

16. Prarthana Purkayashna extends the material analysis of the imperial archive in *The Archives and Afterlives of Nautch Dancers in India*, Cambridge University Press, 2025.

17. Curator Roger Leong produced an early example of this exhibition genre in *Fashion and Ballet*, National Gallery of Victoria (2012); and the Paris Olympics cultural festival included the exhibition, *Fashion and Movement*, at the Palais Galliera (2023–2025).

CHAPTER 1

1. Isadora Duncan's dramatic death occurred on September 17, 1927, in Nice, France: the circumstances are disputed and subject to frequent reinvention (McAuliffe 2016: 26).

2. Nevin and Wyman were vanguard experimentalists in the early twentieth century, with research collections at the University of Pittsburgh and Brown University, respectively.

3. Program for Duncan–Damrosch tour, Carnegie Hall Susan W. Rose Archives, February 15, 1911.

4. Raymond's wife, Penelope Duncan, is photographed wearing a raw-edged tunic with hand-printed shawl by Imogen Cunningham in 1910. https://www.imogencunningham.com/.

5. *La Danse* by Matisse was first exhibited at the Salon d'Autonne of 1910 in the Grand Palais des Champs-Élysées, Paris, before being donated to the Hermitage in St. Petersburg, and Duncan performed in both these locations.

6. Isadora's "adopted daughters" were students from sister Elizabeth Duncan's dance school in Berlin and presented under the aegis of Raymond Duncan.

7. In 1981, Owen commissioned a costume inventory, and later organized to exhibit Shawn costumes in *Ted Shawn: A Centennial Tribute to the Father of American Dance* for the National Museum of Dance at Saratoga Springs, New York, from May 1991 to October 1992.

8. The exhibition, *Dance We Must: Treasures from Jacob's Pillow 1906–1940*, at Williams College Museum of Art included thirty costume ensembles with related ephemera (Murphy and Hamilton 2023). The digital catalogue is available from the Pillow website: https://www.jacobspillow.org.

9. Barney cultivated a lesbian literary and artistic salon in Paris and was friends with St. Denis, Sikelianos, and Duncan. With her various lovers, she experimented with wearing fashionable tunics, posing and dancing naked (Dorf 2018: 60).

10. The first Paterson mill in 1840 produced thread and employed French émigrés, but later owned multiple weaving mills (Schoeser 2007: 95).

11. A report of the *National Industrial Conference Board* (1919) investigated employment conditions, since the silk worker's specialist skills were of vital interest to manufacturers' profits. In 1913, Paterson was the site of major industrial action supported by the Industrial Workers of the World, which closed 300

mills for seven months. The strike led to short-term gains in conditions, but probably hastened the relocation of silk production offshore in the 1920s.

12. Victoria Finlay links Japan's mastery of the silk trade to the technologies and finance that led to its military dominance of the Asia-Pacific in the early twentieth century (2023: 373).

13. Originally presented in Tokyo in 1925 as part of a suite called "American Sketches" and entitled *Dance of the Volcano Goddess*, the work was retitled *A Legend of Pelee, Hawaiian Volcano Goddess* for the cross-country tour of 1926–1927. It became a free-standing dance known as *A Legend of Pelee* on the 1927–1928 Ziegfeld Follies tour.

14. The apocryphal account of St. Denis's conversion to "Oriental" choreography inspired by a cigarette package decorated by an Egyptian dancer is less relevant than her paid employment as a skirt dancer for Belasco. In 1904, he produced *Madame Butterfly*, its central character a seductive geisha who charms her American military "husband" dressed in kimonos. St. Denis would have known of this show's popularity and have mixed with the multiracial entertainers Belasco presented at the Louisiana Purchase Exhibition, also in 1904.

15. Mumaw describes the use of Denishawn ethnic costumes as adding the "flavor of authenticity," and retrospectively justifies St. Denis's role in usurping the "proper dress" of other cultures as a step toward the recognition of diversity in modern dance (1984: 3).

16. Sherman (1984) provides details about the purchase of saris and other items for use in the Denishawn Nautch dances and their adaptation for choreography. This exchange value of the commodity form counters St. Denis's naive narratives about their role as pure "inspiration."

17. The complex histories of Jacob's Pillow costumes are debated by Munjulika R. Tarah, Erica Dankmeyer, Thandi Steele, and Panalee Maskati in "Contentious Histories in Emergent Archives, a Dialogue" (Murphy and Hamilton 2023: 103–120).

18. The 1902 Mt. Pelée eruption stimulated the scientific study of deadly volcanos that continues to this day.

19. Scolieri describes another dance performed by Shawn and St. Denis, called *The Wind* (1922), that involved a "huge swath of rose-colored Indian silk" (2020: 155).

20. For more on Stebbins's influence on physical training systems in the United States, see Foster (2011: 105–110).

21. Mariarden was a private estate and hosted an annual summer school for actors and dancers in the 1920s; see https://monadnockcenter.org/m-is-for-mariarden/.

22. In rehearsals, the Ballets Russes dancer Lydia Sokolowa wore a similar garment made from three and a half meters of "*crêpe-de-chine* . . . caught in with one bit of elastic under the breast and another around the thigh . . . that fell in pretty draperies just below the knee" (Buckle 1989: 33).

23. Scolieri identifies this work as *The Peacock: A Legend of India* (2020: 79).

24. Shawn speculated on a latent homosexuality in the relationship between Wheeler and St. Denis (Scolieri 2020: 236).

25. Net originated in fishing, but net fabric is frequently used as a form of stiffening under skirts. In the layered skirts of a tutu it migrates as gauzy fabric, or, in black stockings to the legs of cancan dancers.

26. Techniques linking physical education with moral virtue—healthy bodies, healthy minds, healthy societies—were reinforced by the eugenics movement, whose precepts were adopted by Shawn (Scolieri 2020: 75–152).

27. Correspondence and notes from Sherman and Mumaw were typed up as an article, titled "The Costumes of Denishawn," probably unpublished (Norton Owen, Email correspondence, April 10, 2024).

28. The Hollywood code that restricted "undue exposure" made an exception for "documentary" performances; this censoring of the body pushed choreographies toward ethnographic style and content (Scolieri 2020: 323).

29. Zips first appeared at the Chicago World's Fair in 1892, with the hook-lock joint rapidly popularized for use in domestic clothing after 1926.

30. For notes on Aldrich and Aldrich's production of sportswear, see *The Vintage Traveler* blog, July 4, 2022, https://thevintagetraveler.wordpress.com/2022/07/04/aldrich-and-aldrich-exercise-suit/.

31. In a 2018 reconstruction of *Dance of the Ages* by Adam Weinert for Jacob's Pillow, the male dancers wore lycra copies of the green minimalist "slacks." His Water choreography placed emphasis on upper

body elongation, and the sleek costumes stressed the virtuosic dancing of each individual, so the impressions of a "fluid" mass were more limited.

32. According to the dress historian, Robert Ross (2008), the tape measure, paper pattern, and sewing machine are three commodities that dramatically impact clothing history, to which should be added the diverse fasteners discussed in this chapter.

33. Palmer-Sikelianos was married to the Greek poet and nationalist, Angelos Sikelianos, and his sister was Penelope Duncan married to Raymond. In partnership with the Duncan family, she advanced knowledge and appreciation of ancient Greek textiles, fashion, and performance (Leontis 2019: 45). Whether in Europe or New York, they all regularly wore woven tunics "in defiance of convention," much to the horror of Palmer's wealthy American mother (2019: 52).

34. Shawn initially valued Sikelianos's deep experience in Greece, but they clashed over the role of music as an authentic contribution to theatrical choreography (Scolieri 2020: 352–353).

CHAPTER 2

1. The angular geometric sketches of Graham drawn by Carlos Dyer in the 1930s illustrate these opposing dynamic lines in her choreography (Armitage 1937: 7, 23, 34).

2. Some costumes were recovered, dried, and stored in a secret location, others most certainly exist as the property of company associates. Unfortunately for this research, it was difficult to ascertain further information about the archival value of these "lost" items.

3. In 1999, my students at Monash University in Melbourne, Australia, learned the opening sections of "Steps in the Street" from a Graham-trained dancer. Regrettably, I cannot recall her name.

4. County records include the Pittsburgh Wool Company Documentation Project Records, 2000.

5. For a history of industrial work sites, see Spaulding (1990); and for the revival and history of Germantown yarns, see Kelley (2018).

6. Whitted's thesis contributes to the textile history of the USA; although German stocking production was replaced by English machines in 1864, the principles of circular interlocking for stocking fabrics still applied.

7. Premiere of *Lamentation*, January 8, 1930, at Maxine Elliot's Theater, New York City: choreography by Martha Graham, costume by Martha Graham, and music by Zoltán Kodály. The woolen reference appears in an advertisement for a WGN concert in New York, under the title, "Martha Graham Emerges from 'Woolen' Period with Dramatic Dances on Eve of Tour," December 7, 1941, Carnegie Hall Susan W. Rose Archives.

8. Tamiris and Graham shared a debut concert in 1926 and later danced together; but for most of their careers, they were not artistically or politically aligned. In the 1930s, Tamiris and her Group used dramatic and rhythmic structures to represent America's underclass and exiles in choreographic works for the Federal Theater Project.

9. The Bennington film by Simon Moselsio, a Russian-born sculptor, is variously dated as 1937 or 1939, but the film release date was 1943. During the documentation, his wife Herte Moselsio took serial photographs of *Lamentation*, now held by the Library of Congress.

10. Early technicolor was created by projecting separate reels of black-and-white film through colored filters that overlapped to create the illusion of color diffusion, hence the instability of this footage on screen today.

11. Many modern artists wrestled with the conflict between a maternal identity and an artistic career. Both the painter Käthe Kollwitz and the sculptor Barbara Hepworth also created intense works about the deaths of children. By 1930, Graham herself was at child-bearing age and grieving her lack of motherhood.

12. Hobbes is best known for formulating the idea of the social contract, wherein individuals have obligations to the collective life of a society.

13. Graham opened her first studio at the rear of Carnegie Hall, 881 Seventh Ave, corner 57th Street, and then moved to 316 East 63rd Street, New York. Calder and Noguchi met in Paris through Brancusi and initially shared a studio in Carnegie Hall and then at the Arts Students League in 215 West 5th Street; between 1931 and 1933, Noguchi established studios at 58 West 57th Street, in the Sherwood Studios;

then in a storefront space at 446 East 76th Street; and then in the artists coop at Hotel des Artistes, One West 67th Street, New York. The Hawes dress shop was located at 8 West 56th street.

14. Brancusi's influence on American art began with his participation in the International Exhibition of Modern Art at the Armory, New York, in 1913; and subsequently, at the Chicago Art Club in 1927.

15. The Carnegie Hall dance studio known as Studio 6 became the crucible for many modern dance rehearsals over multiple decades.

16. The location of Isamu Noguchi, *Bust of Martha Graham*, Bronze, 1929, is unknown, but it may be in the New School collection: https://archive.noguchi.org/Detail/artwork/9625.

17. Two sculptures were cast; the one in the Chicago Art Institute originally belonged to Page; https://www.artic.edu/artworks/136120/miss-expanding-universe.

18. Theater or ballet costumes are stored in costume bags much like plastic coverings from the dry cleaners. Since garments need to breathe, the fabric should have a loose weave and a drawstring that pulls the top of the bag around the coat-hanger. Hundreds of these bags might be suspended in a costume wardrobe, creating odd and mysterious shapes that shadow unknown characters or types.

19. Another Morgan photographic technique represented movement as a collage of overlapping images capturing an external dynamic as well as an internal reflection of mood.

20. No color documentation of the original *Satyric Festival Song* exists, but a 1994 company reconstruction produced the costume in yellow, black, and striped lime green stretch jersey.

21. As the Chosen One in Massine's 1930 reconstruction of *The Rite of Spring*, Graham insisted on her own practice dress and loose hair rather than the heavy original Roerich costumes (Stalpaert 2012: 62).

22. Reconstructed by costume design consultant Karen Young.

23. Knappe (2008) cites Morgan on "Dance Photography," in Andreas Feininger, *The Complete Photographer*, 1965: 1135.

24. Sabin (1927). Correspondence in Carnegie Hall Archives, New York.

25. Conversations with designers, photographers, and dancers offered these insights into Graham's process of costume construction.

26. The statuette of "Elizabeth Hawes' dress of Forstmann's fine woolen covert cloth" does not appear to have survived but was used in an advertisement in Harper's Bazaar, c. 1937. https://catalog.noguchi.org/Detail/artwork/98077. The Forstmann reputation (with German origins) for manufacturing quality wool fabric began in 1904 and endured for five decades. Now known as Victor Forstmann, the "Forstmann 100% wool" label can still be found on vintage overcoats.

27. FIT mounted a survey exhibition, *Elizabeth Hawes, Along Her Own Lines*, from March 1 to 26, 2023; the Hawes archive is housed in the Brooklyn Museum Costume Collection, Metropolitan Museum of Art.

28. In spite of Graham's bourgeois aesthetics and interest in emotional choreography, Graham and Sokolow respected each other's work (Franko 2002: 57–58).

29. Video footage of the choreography for *Chronicle* performed by the Graham Company ranges between 1938 and 2020, and the interpretation and use of costumes vary considerably.

30. In the late 1970s, Halston was at the peak of a design franchise servicing corporate partnerships that licensed hats, homewares, perfumes, luggage, and dress ranges for chain stores, as well as leading an uptown fashion house with clients such as Liza Minnelli, Elizabeth Taylor, and Marisa Berenson (Gross and Rottman 1999: 40, 49–50).

31. In a photograph featured in *Halston: An American Original*, Halston wraps a draped roll of wool jersey over the actress Carol Channing; her sculptural form bears an uncanny resemblance to the swathed body of *Lamentation* (Gross and Rottman 1999: 71).

CHAPTER 3

1. In other images of *L'Ag'Ya*, Dunham wears a cross rather than a pearl necklace.

2. The Baron Studios photographed the then Princess Elizabeth in 1947 and 1949, and later operated in Park Lane, London; Dunham was another early commission in 1948. https://www.npg.org.uk/collections/search/person/mp61466/baron-studios.

3. See also Dunham's (1959) autobiography, *A Touch of Innocence*, and her ethnographic memoir, *Island Possessed* (1969), as well as a rich collection of source materials (Clark and Johnson 2005).

4. During the 1950s, Dunham came under scrutiny from the State Department; Tayana Hardin (2016) and Constance Valis Hill (1994) examine the censorship of her work *Southland* (1951).

5. Research sources include a database of the Katherine Dunham company; see Harmony Bench, Kate Elswit, and Antonio Jimenez-Mavillard, 2022, at https://www.dunhamsdata.org/.

6. Dunham's archival footage of Haiti and Martinique is held by the Library of Congress; Fred Allsop was the cameraman. Funded by the Rosenwald Foundation, Dunham later became critical of her role as an "intruder" and acknowledged that they misunderstood local protocols: clip#34, https://www.loc.gov/item/ihas.200003813/?loclr=blogflt.

7. The dance program launched in Chicago in March 1936, with local theaters responsible for more than twenty Federal Theater Project (FTP) productions. After *L'Ag'Ya*, Dunham became prominent in left-leaning modern dance; and in 1939, she performed and choreographed for *Pins and Needles*, a musical sponsored by the International Ladies Garment Workers Union: https://www.wnyc.org/story/141815-pins-and-needles/. The FTP was shut down by Congress in 1939 following allegations about "wasteful spending," racial intermixing, and communism (Karoula 2020).

8. "Notes for Lecture-demonstrations," March 9, 1959, Box 135, Folder 2, Southern Illinois University Carbondale (SIUC).

9. "Katherine Dunham Company—Advance Requirements," n.d., Box 135, Folder 2, SIUC.

10. Son of a prominent Chicago journalist, John Pratt senior, and his wife, a musician, the younger Pratt maintained relationships with the poet Gwendolyn Brooks, the socialite Inez Cunningham Stark, and surrealist artist Gertrude Abercrombie (Aschenbrenner 2002: 116).

11. The Chicago History Museum collection includes unattributed theatrical costumes designed by Pratt.

12. Vladimir Barjansky (1892–1968), a Russian artist from Paris, was a registered "Designer and Painter of Costumes" working in Hollywood, and collaborator with the Dunham company during the 1940s. While Pratt was in the army, Dunham approached two former Chicago Art School associates, Karl Priebe, known for surrealist artworks, and John Carli Jr., an illustrator to develop designs. Signatures on random costume sketches indicate that other designers contributed to the company, although their precise role is unclear.

13. In the costume inventory, "4 Market Scene Dresses" are listed as "original" (Box 80, SIUC), possibly those with appliqued flowers in the St. Louis collection.

14. Aschenbrenner names John Pratt's mother as seamstress for Dunham's first *L'Ag'Ya* production. Those costumes were a simple skirt design with dropped waist and one layer of gathering; the men wore white shirts, loose pants, and straw hats.

15. Pratt was ever attentive to fashion trends; in the 1930s, Chanel produced a "romantic" evening dress heavy with ruffles of soft lace that was not dissimilar to the Dunham women's dresses. https://www.metmuseum.org/art/collection/search/108521.

16. For instance, Britain disrupted the supply of Indian cottons to Europe and crushed the Indian industry by using indentured labor on colonial landholdings to collect raw cotton materials, then established its own industrial centers and built new markets.

17. Edward Degas's painting *The Cotton Exchange, New Orleans* (1873) depicts the merchants at the heart of this trade.

18. Born in North Carolina in 1927, Kitt was a student in Dunham's New York school and a member of the Experimental Group in 1946 and 1947. https://www.dailynews.com/2013/07/31/kitt-shapiro-daughter-of-eartha-kitt-honors-her-mother-with-lifestyle-collection-of-home-items/.

19. In 1945, the dancers included Katherine Dunham, Lucille Ellis, Lawaune Ingram, Richardena Jackson, and Eartha Kitt. Filmed as Ballet Creole 1952. "Washerwomen," newsreel segment, reproduced British Pathé.

20. Foster's ethnography of *African American Clothing* includes interviews with formerly enslaved persons collected between 1936 and 1938.

21. "Production Notes," re. Cakewalk, Box 135, Folder 2, SIUC.

22. "Minutes of Meeting," November 27, 1973, Box 135, Folder 2, SIUC.

23. In their documentation of subaltern America during the 1930s, the journalists Evans and Agee in *Let Us Now Praise Famous Men*, mostly overlook the black population; except they note "predilections

for colors, textures, symbolisms, and contrasts" that differed from the clothing of poor white workers (1941: 238).

24. "Production Notes and Outlines," Giovanella Zannoni, c. 1970s, Box 80m FP 20-7-F1, SIUC. See Das for an assessment of how Dunham's ideas about "primitive" rituals and societies evolved in relation to her research and choreography (2017: 32–33; 129–130).

25. Universal attributes in representations of the "primitive," whether performed by white or black bodies, can be crafted via costume as much as language and must be contested.

26. For a critical account of the role of "voodoo" and exoticized notions of the black Atlantic religious system in theatrical representation, see Mazzocca and Gillman (2020).

27. William B. Seabrook's book *The Magic Island* (1929) reported on the different trance states that Haitian rituals induced, and inspired early films about Caribbean cults and magic, such as *White Zombie* (1932). With *L'Ag'Ya* (1938) and *Shango* (1945), Dunham was at the forefront in making popular shows focusing on vodou, and the region's rituals. The film-maker Maya Deren, working as Dunham's publicist, also sought to capture the exuberance and ecstasy of ritual choreography.

28. Dunham on "primitive mysteries," in "Notebook," Box 135, Folder 2, SIUC.

29. Text on postcards, "Design" folders, Box 135, Folder 2, SIUC.

30. Ornate headdresses are a dominant genre in Dunham's costume repertoire (Fensham 2023).

31. "Production Notes and Outlines," Giovanella Zannoni, c. 1970s, Box 80, SIUC.

32. There is now an extensive literature on African fashion, identifying nationally diverse cloth and dress practices as well as contemporary developments in African design (Rovine 2015: 22–24).

33. The United States occupied Haiti from 1919 to 1934; although it was nominally independent under President Vincent in 1930, there was a suppressed military coup in 1937, and the country was monitored by the US State Department into the 1940s.

34. During the 1950s, the US occupation of Haiti brought economic benefits and infrastructure such as railways and ports providing improved prices for exports, but it was vulnerable to US trade dominance.

35. After the war, Dunham purchased one of the most distinctive properties in Haiti, L'Habitation Leclerc, for her vision of a "cultural center" (Glover 2016).

36. Dunham's awareness of racism in the United States was heightened by her observations of the Caribbean. In Paris in the 1950s, she learned about decolonizing critiques through association with black scholars, such as Aimé Cesaire in his *Discourse on Colonialism* (1955), who rejected the impact of French culture in colonial outposts.

37. "Program Notes," Box 135, Folder 2, SIUC.

38. Diverse patterns and styles of Kente production confer specific status (Ross 2001).

39. Annotated in the costume drawings and inventories as "strips," suggesting a closer connection to stripped cloth than the word "stripes."

40. "Production Book and Notes," c. 1927–1960s, Box 135, Folder 2, SIUC.

41. "Production Notes," Box 135, Folder 2, SIUC.

42. Barrelhouse toured with varied explanations. Notes in foreign languages aimed to convey the deprivations of urban African Americans, "Technical Notes," p. 6, Box 135, Folder 2, SIUC.

43. Online Katherine Dunham exhibition, Missouri Historical Museum, 2009. https://mohistory.org/collections/item/2017-145-0016-001?page=2.

44. In 1943, Dunham was touring under the auspices of Hurok, and on June 3 that year, white US servicemen and police officers in East Los Angeles harassed, beat, and detained Mexican American youth that they associated with gangs wearing zoot suits.

45. Chicago photographer, Maurice Seymour, took many of the earliest photos of the Dunham company: https://ronseymour.com/the-maurice-seymour-gallery/.

46. "Production Notes," Box 135, Folder 2, SIUC.

47. Handwritten notes in "Projects," 1963–64, #5, Box 135, Folder 2, SIUC.

48. "Production Book inc. Notes," pp. 4–10, Box 135, Folder 2, SIUC.

49. "Production Book inc. Notes," pp. 4–10, Box 135, Folder 2, SIUC.

50. This shirt has a cotton lining, providing more movement flexibility than the silk, with press-stud fastenings.

51. "Diary Notes" record dancer payments, as well as mounting debts, 1953, Box 135, Folder 2, SIUC.

52. The company traveled with a sewing machine; see "Notes on Advance Requirements," undated, Box 80, SIUC.

53. The Dunham and Julot duet was labeled the "majumba" from Brazil (see "Program Notes," Box 135, Folder 2, SIUC), but the *majumba* is not a recorded Brazilian dance. In Swahili, majumba has various meanings relating to a large building, including "halls, brothels, or chapels" and "Jumba" was the name of a slavery port. Quite what the etymology represented for Dunham is lost, but the term "majumba" has entered modern dance folklore.

54. Another Comédie-Française engraving in the archives depicts Mrs. Teazle, a character in Sheridan's *School for Scandal*, an eighteenth-century farce. Far from Martinique, its comic plot revolves around a disguise created by the "teasing" corner of a petticoat.

55. "The dance is a showcase for Miss Dunham's extremely personal gift both as a dancer and as an actress," Program Notes, Box 135, SIUC. Stressing Dunham's acting skills in the role of seductress deflected attention from the erotic connotations, particularly when performing for largely Christian audiences.

56. Standard items in the account books were dressing room supplies; wardrobe costs; gloves, socks, lengths of silk, and later, a "wardrobe sinking fund," Box 135, Folder 2, SIUC.

57. "Notes of an Assistant Stage Manager," p. 2, Box 80, SIUC.

CHAPTER 4

1. Rauschenberg also identified with the Gainsborough painting of the Blue Boy, housed at the Huntington Museum, but we cannot know whether his attraction to that image was shared with Cunningham (Richardson 2008).

2. For Cunningham's late work *eyeSpace* (2006), the designer Henry Samelson created unitard costumes in a vivid electric blue, produced by an aniline dye made from coal tar, an arresting color against a solid red backdrop.

3. In *Walkaround Time* (1973), Cunningham begins in practice clothes, which are subsequently removed to reveal red tights and a long-sleeve top; the actions are a commentary on the "bride stripped bare" implied by the subtitle of "The Large Glass" (1915–1923), the Marcel Duchamp artwork that formed the basis of the set.

4. For *How to Pass, Kick, Fall and Run* (1968): "Everyone just wore black tights and the girls wore black trunks. But then Merce said, 'bring your favorite sweater or a sweater that you wouldn't mind dancing in'" (Goggans 2023).

5. Charlip was trained in dress production and textile design; he assumed responsibility for Cunningham costumes in 1952. After leaving the company in 1961, he became a children's book author and illustrator while continuing to direct theater and dance. He was known for his rainbow-colored clothing: https://www.remycharlipestate.org/about.

6. This first of Rauschenberg's "Combines" was a gaudily clad three-panel installation using found materials as collage—" China silk. . . old lace, ribbons, comic strips, patterned cloth, and newspaper" (Brown 2007: 115).

7. The Merce Cunningham Trust Dance Capsule corrects the original *Minutiae* program to acknowledge that the costumes were "by company member Remy Charlip," not Rauschenberg. https://dancecapsules.mercecunningham.org/overview.cfm?capid=46080.

8. Brown is skeptical that this eccentric work was based on Cunningham's observations of passers-by. She however recalls the humor of its dance vocabulary: "slow, repetitive slinky walks in unison with two other women; hurried movement with peculiar little hand gestures, odd jabbing with elbows: isolated head, shoulder and hand movements; a little floor duet with Merce" (2007: 113).

9. In 1946, Cage and Cunningham were invited to teach at BMC in North Carolina, and this was the first of several summer seasons. College alumni include the poet and potter, M.C. Richards, sculptor Ruth Asawa, and African American artists Jacob Lawrence and Gertrude Knight. https://jacobandgwenlawrence.org/biographies/about-gwen-knight-lawrence/.

10. Helen Frankenthaler, a soft colorist, visited BMC in 1950 to further her painting experiments with watercolor.

11. Similar effects were produced by Jasper Johns for *Second Hand* (1970): "simple tights and leotards—dyed using the full color spectrum, . . .only noticeable when we lined up to take our bows. Then, it could be noticed that the sleeve or leg on each dancer had a bit of the dominant color of the next dancer in the lineup" (Brown 2007: 539).

12. *Points in Space* (1987) is the title of a dance work, but the philosophy that dancing space-time was multi-directional appears across Cunningham's published writings, particularly *Changes: Notes on Choreography* (1968).

13. "*Field Dances* enlivened by Remy Charlip's multicolored, multi-splashed costumes" (Barnes 1968).

14. Costume preparation and maintenance was continuous in MCDC history: designers such as Lancaster, and Johns, and wardrobe managers such as Gallo were practically involved in construction and the requirement to dye costumes in "their spectrum of color" (Weill 1972).

15. Today we would be critical of the chemical toxicity, the extent of extraction, the scale of market manipulation, and the global exploitation of workers required by these new commodity forms.

16. In the theories of Deleuze and Guattari, any conflict involves an appropriation of "war" as a direct object, which makes it a supplement to the aims and machinery of the state. In so far as "war" also requires "resources and equipment" and "human variable capital," its supplementary purpose underpins state capitalism (1987: 422).

17. As discussed in Chapter 1, Capezio began working with dance companies in the 1930s to test new products and materials. The company launched "dancewear," including the first versions of the modern leotard, after learning to dance became popular in the 1950s (Dishman 2021).

18. Estelle Sommers, the former owner and manager of the New York Capezio store, was a leading figure in the American dance industry for many decades, and she is credited with introducing Spandex: https://www.capezio.com/history. A complete history of Capezio is yet to be written.

19. The Dance Capsule for *Suite for Five* includes a "Suite for Five Repertory Video" from 2005, with a short clip and interviews with dancers Andrea Weber, Ashley Chen, and Cédric Andrieux.

20. The Comenas (2004) interview focuses on Andy Warhol and the New York scene, with minimal reference to his Cunningham employment. However, Lancaster designed sets, costumes, and lighting for at least twenty major Cunningham works, including coordinating design for *Events*. A third anecdote references his first commission for *Sounddance* (1975), a work that toured widely.

21. MCDC had wide exposure and public success from the mid-1970s to the mid-1980s, not only in the United States but through performing around the world.

22. The *Event for Television* was recorded on November 8–11, 1976, and broadcast on January 5, 1977.

23. "Cunningham Dance Foundation: Basic Requirements," (Weill 1972: 4); and "Cunningham Residency" (Weil 1975).

24. In a sketch for *10's with shoes* (1981), Lancaster alternates yellow and green diagonals in ways that replicate Albers's studies of color as "quantity."

25. Dye chemicals include solvents, charmingly called hydroxybenzotriazoles.

26. In his *Trails* design, Lancaster heightened the textural contrasts between costumes and set by placing solid matte black, corrugated cardboard alongside a woven red textile and swatches of spongy pink and red spandex.

27. In the early 1980s, the short, flouncy skirt was a popular fashion trend among teenage girls. Using fabric with weight, two British designers Angela Stone and Gifi Fields adapted this type of dance skirt for day wear.

28. Retro-viral drugs became more effective in the mid-1990s, and the impact of HIV on the gay community gained greater acceptance and prominence. https://www.hiv.gov/hiv-basics/overview/history/hiv-and-aids-timeline#year-1983.

29. Lancaster's partner, David Bolger, recalls him "stirring large pots of fabric dye on the stove, with drying leotards in rainbow colors strewn all over the loft. . . a memory that is still very much with me" (Email correspondence, 2024).

30. Gallo also designed costumes for a Ballet Rambert work *Touchbase* (1992) choreographed by Cunningham, and one of them featured in a 2017 exhibition at the London College of Fashion (Connolly 2024).

31. Correspondence in the archives between Gallo and designers documents their discussion of which colored dyes achieve a desired effect. She sourced the appropriate textiles and used her sewing skills to fabricate costume details (Skinner 2023).

32. For technical discussion of the motion capture technology deployed in BIPED, see http://ivizlab.sfu.ca/arya/Papers/Dance/Biped-1.pdf.

33. This fabric, "with its tiny metallic medallions adhered to spandex," is no longer produced (Adriance 2015).

34. Before her premature death at age 46, Gallo returned from hospital to complete the BIPED costumes. In her final correspondence with Cunningham, she wrote "that heaven for her was right here, with all of you, working together for Merce" (Dalva 2024).

35. The Dance Capsule for *Ocean*: https://www.mercecunningham.org/the-work/choreography/ocean/.

36. The Cirque Royal was a tall circular venue with raked seating, and the primary design elements were a mesh disk and the clock (Riley II 1998: 252).

37. Cunningham required that "special gloves be made so the dancers could safely grip" each other (Skinner 2023).

38. Cunningham barely spoke until "after the New York premier (*sic.*) [of Enter, when] he sought me out with enthusiasm: 'So theatrical!'" (Skinner 2023).

CHAPTER 5

1. For an expanded interpretation of *Huddle*, see Lax (2018: 20–21).

2. Tate Britain lacks sufficient "art handling" staff for research visits to the storerooms of the Rauschenberg collection, so it is likely that these objects will only be seen in future as curated exhibitions (Martin 2023).

3. *Floor of the Forest* was reconstructed in 2010 at the Queen Elizabeth Hall, London, followed by a Barbican exhibition on the *Pioneers of the New York Downtown Scene* that included works by Trisha Brown, Matta Clark, and Laurie Anderson (Yee 2011). Faithful to the original, the London installation consisted of "a makeshift construction of casual wardrobe discards" (Rosenberg 2016: 89).

4. Lax also observes the proximity between ideas about "pedestrian movement" and activists' protests in "turning a contested physical gesture into aesthetic form" (2018: 21).

5. Social planners, architects, community activists, and cultural leaders opposed to the rationalization of urban space campaigned to save the "cast-iron" facades that characterized the late nineteenth-century boom years, and public spaces such as Washington Square where Judson Church was located.

6. Yvonne Rainer's rejection of spectacle in her "no manifesto" of 1965 extended to all forms of artifice, including dress (in Banes 1980: 43).

7. For dance scholar Elizabeth Dempster, Monson's exposure of the T-shirt as volume and disguise elicited questions of shame surrounding the "spectacle of the feminine and feminized place of the performer" (2015: 161).

8. Eugene Combs, a soldier who had studied Yoshinkan Aikido at Camp Drake near Tokyo, established the first commercial aikido dojo in California in 1956.

9. Accounts of Mayhew's role are limited, but she is a recognized pioneer of Aikido in the United States. She later opened the Hong Kong Aikido studio before undertaking spiritual studies in India. See Erard, https://budojapan.com/aikido/20220404vm/.

10. In her teachings, Mayhew regarded violence as a sort of "temporary insanity."

11. In an online interview, Stark Smith (2005) provides an extended account of Contact Dance history.

12. Images of Paxton doing Aikido exist but could not be sourced. Leaders at the New York dojo recall the mixture of artists and athletes who attended in these early years.

13. The Aikido jacket is durable to the needs of training, only loosely closed by the belt.

14. The cross-cultural etymology of the pajama is a garment dating back to the Ottoman Empire, for which the Hindi words are "pae" (leg) "jamas" (jacket).

15. The Australian Eva Karczag danced in a filmed version of *Spanish Dance* (1973), but this four-minute work has been performed by many generations of company dancers; see https://vimeo.com/trishabrown.

16. The scientific term "Brownian motion" was aptly applied to the "incessant variation" of Trisha Brown's choreography by Guy Scarpetta in 1979, according to Laurence Louppe (Teicher 2002: 68).

17. In 2012, a group of dancers, including Madden, reconstituted *Line Up* as a gift for Brown's seventy-fifth birthday, and this footage activates their embodied and diverse memories of its rhythmic structure.

18. Extemporary Dance Theatre Archive is located in the National Resource Centre for Dance, University of Surrey. https://www.surrey.ac.uk/library/archives-and-special-collections/our-collections.

19. The Lucy Guerin Inc. collection is located on the Theatre and Dance Platform, University of Melbourne. https://digitised-collections.unimelb.edu.au/collections/7392c640–49ce-5b2b-94d7-0fef1496767b.

20. For more on Shea's sculptural practice, see http://www.judithshea.com/.

21. Many of the performance reviews cited in this chapter were maintained by Nigel Redden, the Performing Arts Coordinator at the Walker Art Center from 1976. *Performing Arts Folders*, Box 36, folder 006a. Minneapolis: Walker Art Center.

22. Costume design drawing in a letter from Brown to Rauschenberg, undated. Robert Rauschenberg papers. Robert Rauschenberg Foundation Archives, New York.

23. For more on Razmi's film, see https://www.anahitarazmi.de/Roof-Piece-Tehran.

CHAPTER 6

1. Baker's fashion archive greatly exceeds the history of dance, but there is no catalogue of her many costumes or the haute couture dresses she wore. An anonymous French website, *Un Icône: Josephine Baker* (2021–2024), provides extensive imagery but no provenance: https://uneicone-josephinebaker. webador.fr/.

2. The provenance of the belt is connected to Pepito, Baker's husband, through his niece (de Labarre 2023).

3. Contrasting film representations with photographs of the "skirts" show either two rows of bananas or a single row on a waistband.

4. The American heiress Caroline Dudley Reagan was commissioned by André Daven in 1925 to contract a black performance troupe in New York, and Baker was a junior member of that ensemble (Bonal 2021: 37–40).

5. De Chirico married the Russian ballerina Raissa Gurievich in 1925, the year Baker moved to Paris, and she too was photographed by Boris Lipnitzki (see footnote 12). In these close-knit artistic circles, the iconographic transfer from painting to dancing body as a symbol of exotic colonial modernity seems inevitable.

6. A popular French cartoon in the 1920s depicted a Senegalese soldier to market Banania, a popular chocolate and banana-flavored drink. Unilever, its manufacturer, has made limited response to critiques of this racist and imperialist trope; see https://newpublic.co/blog/decolonizing-banania-part-1.

7. Florenz Ziegfeld conceived his "Follies" on the model of the Folies Bergère, but produced a more industrial stylization of the chorus and musical repertoire. Baker's collaboration with Balanchine was short-lived, but she later harnessed ballet as both technique and content; see Durkin (2019: 156) and Harris (2008).

8. The pejorative New York reviews of Baker's performance questioned her racialized identity and lack of skill, as well as mocking her love of France (Bonal 2021: 197–198).

9. Since the creation of the cancan in the 1890s, nightclub entertainers lifting their skirts had titillated the bourgeoisie of Paris. Images of the dancers, photographed semi-nude, were widely circulated as postcards.

10. For more on birds in fashion history, https://blog.biodiversitylibrary.org/2020/10/fashion-and-feath ers-through-books.html, accessed February 17, 2025.

11. In Baker's later years, several items of clothing not featured in this book were made of fabrics and styles suitable for domestic construction, probably made by Spiers, who also assisted Baker with her children.

12. Boris Lipnitzki (various spellings) established his Paris studio during the early 1920s and photographed many artists of the Ballets Russes and German modern dancers. His portraits were distinctive for their shadowy focus on the expressive face and gestures of his subjects, who were often also nude.

13. These images are rarely exhibited. Roger Viollet retains copyright of more than 600,000 Lipnitzki prints and negatives; see https://www.roger-viollet.fr/photographer/boris-lipnitzki-139.

14. See Durkin (2019: 40) for Baker's commentary on whitening her skin in these early years.
15. https://uneicone-josephinebaker.webador.fr/l-artiste/monte-carlo.
16. Baker became increasingly short-sighted as she aged and had to carefully navigate the stage markers before peering toward the audience.
17. Bought for personal use at a local auction; Brian Bouillon-Baker has confirmed that this dress once belonged to his mother (de Labarre 2023).
18. The French costume book, *Couturiers de la Danse*, references the fashion label, "On aura tout vu," whose 2018 Spring–Summer season was inspired by dance (Noisette 2019: 61–63).
19. Mylar is a registered trademark owned by Dupont Teijin Films that names a specific family of plastic sheet products (often shortened to PET) with high tensile strength, chemical and dimensional stability, transparency, and reflectivity. Polyester film can be manufactured in a range of different styles, finishes, and thicknesses This product is used in a wide variety of products.
20. Meadowbrook Inventions, Inc. has manufactured glitter and sequins for application and silk screening on fabrics since the 1940s: "Many glamorous gowns and dresses were created using our glitter. Modern day glitter was invented by Henry F. Ruschmann. Previously glitter was made of colored crushed glass. We started manufacturing 'slung' sequins circa 1984 and have since revolutionized the sequin industry with innovative styles, materials, and sequin products. We are the sole manufacturer of sequins remaining in the US and continue to innovate our sequin ranges" (Ruschmann 2023).
21. In 2022, a tribute show, "Josephine," premiered at the Bobino, Paris.
22. Vergès worked at Moulins Rouges as costumier, as well as managing commissions through her atelier for theater and opera companies in Paris.
23. Powell owned a Finishing and Modelling School in Detroit from the 1950s where she taught black women how to stand, to be photographed, and appear "classy."
24. "The Story of the Supremes from the Mary Wilson Gown Collection" was curated by the Rock and Roll Hall of Fame in Cleveland and toured to the Detroit Historical Museum, the New York State Museum in Albany, and the Long Island Museum. Supreme gowns have also been displayed in exhibitions at The Museum of Metropolitan Art in New York and at the Victoria and Albert Museum in London in 2008.
25. As an exception, "The beaded bikini of a Go-Go dancer, 1972," working in a New York bar was on display at the American History Museum, December 2024.
26. The Dior archive claims they have no records of the dresses that they "made" for Baker, only sample designs (Conquet 2023).
27. In addition to the Transgender Archive, a Lynne Carter collection in the New York Public Library may document these apocryphal costumes: https://archives.nypl.org/mus/18598.
28. Baker is buried in Monaco, but the French government united soil from France, the United States, and Africa when they placed her coffin in the Pantheon.

CONCLUSION

1. Elizabeth Way and Elena Romero, *Fresh, Fly, and Fabulous: Fifty Years of Hip Hop Style* (New York: Rizzoli Electa, 2023).

Bibliography

Abdurraqib, Hanif. 2021. *A Little Devil in America: In Praise of Black Performance*. London: Penguin.

Acocella, Joan. 2003. "Early Spring: The Martha Graham Company Returns to New York." *The New Yorker*, February 17 and 24.

Adorno, Theodor and Anson Rabinbach. 1975. "Culture Industry Reconsidered." *New German Critique* 6: 12–19.

Adriance, Sarah. 2015. "Dancing Cunningham and Graham." *The Juillard Journal*, March (3): https://journal.juilliard.edu/journal/1503/spring-dances-repertory, accessed May 15, 2024.

Agee, James and Walker Evans. 1960 (1941). *Let Us Now Praise Famous Men: Three Tenant Families*. New York: Ballantine.

Albers, Josef. 2006. *Interaction of Color*. New Haven and London: Yale University Press.

Albright, Ann Cooper. 2010. "The Tanagra Effect: Wrapping the Modern Body in the Folds of Ancient Greece." In *The Ancient Dancer in the Modern World: Responses to Greek and Roman Dance*, edited by Fiona McIntosh. Oxford: Oxford University Press: 57–76.

Albright, Ann Cooper. 2013. *Engaging Bodies: The Politics and Poetics of Corporeality*. Middletown, CT: Wesleyan University Press.

Albright, Anne Cooper. 2007. *Traces of Light: Absence and Presence in the Work of Loie Fuller*. Middletown, CT: Wesleyan University Press.

Allen, Zita. 2001. *Free to Dance*. Documentary TV series. Director Madison D. Lacy. New York: Thirteen/WNET.

Appadurai, Arjun. 1996. *Modernity at Large: Cultural Dimensions of Globalization*. Minneapolis: University of Minnesota Press.

Armitage, Merle. 1937. *Martha Graham*. New York: Dance Horizons.

Arendt, Hannah. 1998 (1958). *The Human Condition*. Chicago: University of Chicago Press.

Aschenbrenner, Joyce. 2002. *Katherine Dunham: Dancing a Life*. Urbana: University of Illinois Press.

Ballet, Creole. 1952. "Washerwomen" Newsreel segment, Reproduced British Pathé.

Banes, Sally. 1980. *Terpsichore in Sneakers: Post-Modern Dance*. Boston: Houghton Mifflin.

Bannerman, Henrietta. 2010. "Martha Graham's House of the Pelvic Truth: The Figuration of Sexual Identities and Female Empowerment." *Dance Research Journal* 42(1): 30–45.

Barbier, Michèle. 2022. *Joséphine Baker, Les Dernières Années: La Renaissance D'une Étoile*. Paris: Riveneuve.

Barbieri, Donatella. 2013. "Performativity and the Historical Body: Detecting Performance Through the Archived Costume." *Studies in Theatre and Performance* 33(3): 281–301.

Barbieri, Donatella. 2017. *Costume in Performance: Materiality, Culture, and the Body*. London: Bloomsbury.

Barnes, Clive. 1968. "Dance: Cunningham Finally Makes It After 24 Years, He Has a New York Season." *New York Times*, May 16: 51.

Barthes, Roland. 1990. *The Fashion System*. Translated by Matthew Ward and Richard Howard. Berkeley: University of California Press.

Barton, Chris. 2009. *The Day-Glo Brothers: The True Story of Bob and Joe Switzer's Bright Ideas and Brand-New Colors*. Watertown, MA: Charlesbridge.

Beckert, Sven. 2014. *The Empire of Cotton: A New History of Global Capitalism*. London: Penguin.

Benjamin, Walter. 1999. *The Arcades Project*. Translated by Howard Eiland and Kevin McLaughlin. Cambridge, MA and London: Belknap Press of Harvard University Press.

Bennett, Jane. 2010. *Vibrant Matter: a Political Ecology of Things*. Durham, NC: Duke University Press.

Berliner, Brett A. 2002. *Ambivalent Desire: The Exotic Black Other in Jazz-age France*. Amherst, MA: University of Massachusetts Press.

Bird Villard, Dorothy. 1984. "Interview." In *Dance On With Billie Mahoney*. Directed by William Hohauser, produced by Billie Mahoney. Kansas City, MO: Dance on Video.

Bolger, David. 2024. *Email Correspondence*. February 10.

Bonal, Gérard. 2021. *Joséphine Baker: Du Music-Hall Au Panthéon*. Paris: Tallandier.

Bouillon-Baker, Brian. 2021. *Joséphine Baker L'universelle*. Monaco: Éditions du Rocher.

Brannigan, Erin. 2011. *Dancefilm: Choreography and the Moving Image*. Oxford: Oxford University Press.

Brown, Carolyn. 2007. *Chance and Circumstance: Twenty Years with Cage and Cunningham*. New York: Knopf.

Brown, Trisha and Yvonne Rainer. 1979. "A Conversation About Glacial Decoy." *October 10*, MIT Press: 29–37.

Brown, Trisha. 2004. "A Conversation with Trisha Brown and Klaus Kertess." *Trisha Brown: Early Works 1966–1979*, DVD. Houston: Artpix.

Brunel, Lise, Babette, Mangolte and Guy Delahaye. 1987. *Trisha Brown*. Paris: Éditions Bougé.

Buckle, Richard, ed. 1989. *Dancing for Diaghilev. The Memoirs of Lydia Sokolova*. San Francisco: Mercury House.

Burt, Ramsay. 2001. "Katherine Dunham's Rites de Passage: Censorship and Sexuality." In *Embodying Liberation: The Black Body in American Dance*, edited by Dorothea Fischer-Hornung and Allison Goeller. Münster: Lit Verlag: 79–89.

Burt, Ramsay. 2006. *Judson Dance Theater: Performative Traces*. London: Routledge.

Bye, Erik. 1971. *Interview with Josephine Baker*. The Norwegian Broadcasting Corporation: https://www.youtube.com/watch?v=qMpGADWbXhY, 132, accessed November 7, 2023.

Cassin-Scott, Jack. 1971. *Costume and Fashion in Color, 1760–1920*. London: Macmillan Pub Co.

Celant, Germano, ed. 1999. *Merce Cunningham*. Milan: Edizioni Charta.

Cesaire, Aimé. 1955 (1972). "Between Colonizer and Colonized." Excerpt from *Discourse on Colonialism*, translated by Joan Pinkham. New York: Monthly Review Press: 20–25.

Chazin-Bennahum, Judith. 2005. *The Lure of Perfection: Fashion and Ballet, 1780–1830*. New York: Routledge.

Cheng, Anne Anlin. 2011. *Second Skin: Josephine Baker and The Modern Surface*. New York: Oxford University Press.

Clark, Vévé and S. E. Johnson. 2005. *Kaiso!: Writings by and About Katherine Dunham*. Madison: University of Wisconsin Press.

Coleman, Rebecca. 2020. *Glitterworlds: The Future Politics of a Ubiquitous Thing*. London: Goldsmiths Press.

Comenas, Gary. 2004. *Interview with Mark Lancaster*. New York: Warholstars. https://warholstars.org/andywarhol/interview/mark/lancaster.html.

Connolly, Mary Kate. 2024. *In Smithereens: The Costume Remains of Lea Anderson's Stage*. London: Intellect.

Conor, Liz. 2004. *The Spectacular Modern Woman*. Bloomington: Indiana University Press.

Conover, Kirsten A. 1993. "A Costume Designer Who Served as Martha Graham's Hands." *Christian Science Monitor*, July 20: https://www.csmonitor.com/1993/0720/20121.html, accessed October 26, 2025.

Conquet, Angela. 2023. *Email Correspondence with Galerie Dior*, April 25.

Coole, Diana and Samantha Frost. 2010. *New Materialisms: Ontology, Agency, and Politics*. Durham: Duke University Press.

Crooks, Mary. 2004. "Educational Resource." *National Geographic Society*, https://education.nationalgeographic.org/resource/national-geographic-society-founded, accessed July 7, 2024.

Cunningham, Merce. 1968 (2019). *Changes: Notes on Choreography*. New York, NY: The Song Cave and Merce Cunningham Trust.

Dalva, Nancy. 2008. "Episode 13: 'Roaratorio.'" *Mondays with Merce,* Merce Cunningham Trust. https://www.youtube.com/watch?v=7gtso4D1q_A.

Dalva, Nancy. 2011. "Cunningham's Dancers." *The Way of Merce: Merce Cunningham Studies,* https://cunninghamcentennial.blog/la-plus-ca-change-la-plus-ca-change/.

Dalva, Nancy. 2024. *Email Correspondence*. May 25.

Das, Joanna Dee. 2017. *Katherine Dunham: Dance and the African Diaspora*. New York: Oxford University Press.

De Labarre, Angelique. 2023. *Phone interview*. France, May 4.

De Langen, Marijn. 2022. *Dutch Mime*. Amsterdam: Amsterdam University Press & DAS Publishing.

Delezue, Giles. 1993. The Fold: Leibniz and the Baroque. Translated by Tom Conley. Minneapolis: University of Minnesota Press.

Deleuze, Giles and Felix Guattari. 1987. *A Thousand Plateaus: Capitalism and Schizophrenia*. Translated by Brian Massumi. Minneapolis: University of Minnesota Press.

Dempster, Elizabeth. 2015. "The Economy of Shame or Why Dance Cannot Fail." In *Choreography and Corporeality: Relay in Motion*, edited by Thomas De Frantz and Philippa Rothfield. London: Palgrave: 155–172.

Dickinson, Patrick. 2008. *Interview with Mary Wilson*, transcript. London: Victoria and Albert Museum. http://www.vam.ac.uk/content/videos/t/video-the-story-of-the-supremes-from-the-mary-wilson-collection/.

Dishman, Lydia. 2021. "Capezio Dances into a New Decade with a New Partner for Expansion." *CO,* online magazine. U.S. Chamber of Commerce, https://www.uschamber.com/co/good-company/the-leap/capezio-dancewear-partners-with-gbg, accessed October 27, 2025.

Dorf, Samuel. 2018. *Performing Antiquity; Ancient Greek Music and Dance from Paris to Delphi, 1890–1930*. New York: Oxford University Press.

Doyle, J. D. c.1970s. "Lynne Carter in Dior." *Digital Transgender Archive*. https://www.digitaltransgenderarchive.net/files/1r66j133h, accessed October 17, 2023.

Dudziak, Mary L. 1994. "Josephine Baker, Racial Protest, and the Cold War." *Journal of American History* 81(2): 543–570.

Dunham, Katherine. 1959. *A Touch of Innocence*. New York: Harcourt.

Dunham, Katherine. 1969. *Island Possessed*. New York: Doubleday.

Durkin, Hannah. 2019. *Josephine Baker and Katherine Dunham: Dances in Literature and Cinema*. Urbana: University of Illinois Press.

Eleey, Peter. 2008. *Trisha Brown: So That the Audience Does Not Know Whether I Have Stopped Dancing*. Minneapolis: Walker Arts Center.

English, Bonnie. 2007. *A Cultural History of Fashion in the 20th Century: From the Catwalk to the Sidewalk*. Oxford: Berg.

English, Bonnie. 2011. *Japanese Fashion Designers: The Work and Influence of Issey Miyake, Yohji Yamamoto and Rei Kawakubo*. Oxford: Berg.

Erard, Guillaume. "Aikido Pioneers: Virginia Mayhew, Founder of the New York Aikikai". *Budo Japan,* https://budojapan.com/aikido/20220404vm.

Fensham, Rachel. 2014. "Repetition as a Methodology: Costumes, archives and Choreography." *Scene* 2(1–2): 43–60.

Fensham, Rachel. 2015. "Designing for Movement: Dance Costumes, Art Schools and Natural Movement in the Early Twentieth Century." *Journal of Design History* 28(4): 348–367.

Fensham, Rachel. 2023. "Costumes as Code: Genera and Variation." In *Small Data is Beautiful*, edited by Rachel Fensham, Tyne Sumner, Signe Ravn, Ashley Branwell, and Danny Butt. Parkville: Grattan Street Press: 141–153.

Fer, Briony. 1998. "The Pleasure of Cloth." In *Liz Rideal: New Work*, edited by Briony Fer and Anna Moszynska. London: Art Books International: 10–14.

Fer, Briony. 2004. *The Infinite Line: Re-making Art After Modernism*. New Haven, CT: Yale University Press.

Fields, Suzanne. 1970. "Cunningham Aesthetic." Sunday Magazine, *The Washington Star*, February 22: 12–13.

Fink, Robert. 2005. *Repeating Ourselves: American Minimal Music as Cultural Practice*. Berkeley: University of California Press.

Finke, Anna. 2024. *Email Correspondence*. May 28.

Finlay, Victoria. 2002. *Colour: Travels Through the Paintbox*. London: Hodder and Stoughton.

Finlay, Victoria. 2023. *Fabric: The Hidden History of the Material World*. London: Profile Books.

Fitzgerald, F. Scott. 1920 (2012). *This Side of Paradise*. Mineola: Dover edition.

Foster, Helen Bradley. 1997. *New Raiments of Self: African American Clothing in the Antebellum South*. Oxford, New York: Berg.

Foster, Susan Leigh. 2011. *Choreographing Empathy: Kinesthesia in Performance*. London: Routledge.

Franko, Mark. 1995. *Dancing Modernism/Dancing Politics*. Bloomington: Indiana University Press.

Franko, Mark. 2002. *The Work of Dance: Labor, Movement and Identity in the 1930s*. Middletown, CT: Wesleyan University Press.

Franko, Mark. 2012. *Martha Graham in Love and War: The Life in the Work*. New York: Oxford Academic.

Franko, Mark. 2020. *The Fascist Turn in the Dance of Serge Lifar: Interwar French Ballet and the German Occupation*. New York: Oxford University Press.

Frost, Samantha. 2010. "Fear and the Illusion of Autonomy." In *New Materialisms: Ontology, Agency, and Politics*, edited by Diana Coole and Samantha Frost. Durham: Duke University Press: 158–177.

Garfield, Simon. 2002. *Mauve: How One Man Invented a Color That Changed the World*. New York: W. W. Norton & Company.

Geary, Christraud M. 2002, "The Image World of Casimir Zagourski." In *In and Out of Focus: Images from Central Africa, 1885–1960*. London: Philip Wilson: 69–79.

Geczy, Adam and Vicki Karaminas. 2016. "Walter Benjamin: Fashion, Modernity and the City Street." In *Thinking Through Fashion: A Guide to Key Theorists*, edited by Agnes Rocamora and Anneke Smelik. London: I. B. Tauris: 81–96.

Geczy, Adam and Vicki Karaminas. 2020. "From Harlem to Pigalle: Josephine Baker". *Libertine Fashion: Sexual Freedom, Rebellion, and Style*. London: Bloomsbury Visual Arts: 121–148.

Giménez, Carmen and Matthew Gale. 2004. *Constantin Brancusi: The Essence of Things*. London: Tate.

Glover, Kaiama L. 2016. "'Written with Love': Intimacy and Relation in Katherine Dunham's Island Possessed." In *The Haiti Exception: Anthropology and the Predicament of Narrative*, edited by Alessandra Benedicty-Kokken, Kaiama L. Glover, Mark Schuller, and Jhon Picard Byron. Liverpool: Liverpool University Press: 93–109.

Goggans, Jennifer. 2023. *Interview*. New York City, April.

Goldman, Danielle. 2010. *I Want to Be Ready: Improvised Dance as a Practice of Freedom*. Ann Arbor: University of Michigan Press.

Goodman, Elyssa Maxx. 2023. *Glitter and Concrete: A Cultural History of Drag in New York City*. New York: Hanover Square Press.

Gottlieb, Robert. ed. 2008. *Reading Dance: A Gathering of Memoirs, Reportage, Criticism, Profiles, Interviews and Some Uncategorizable Extras*. New York: Pantheon Books.

Graham, Martha. 1991. *Blood Memory*. New York: Doubleday.

Gross, Elaine and Fred Rottman. 1999. *Halston: An American Original*. New York: Harper Collins.

Grove, Nancy. 1989. *Isamu Noguchi: Portraits Sculpture*. Washington: Smithsonian Institution Press.

Hamilton, Caroline. 2023. "Fundamental Lines of Truth and Beauty." In *Dance We Must: The Art and Costumes of Ruth St. Denis and Ted Shawn, 1906–1940*, edited by Kevin Murphy and Caroline Hamilton. Williamstown, MA: Williams College Museum of Art: 34–57.

Hancock, Joseph, Nioka Wyatt, and Tasha Lewis. 2016. *Cotton: Companies, Fashion and the Fabric of Our Lives*. Bristol: Intellect.

Handley, Susannah. 1999. *Nylon: The Story of a Fashion Revolution*. Baltimore, MD: Johns Hopkins University Press.

Hardin, Tayana. 2016. "Katherine Dunham's Southland and the Archival Quality of Black Dance." *The Black Scholar* 46(1): 46–53.

Harris, Andrea. 2008. "Parody in Pointe Shoes: Josephine Baker, Ballet, and the Politics of Aesthetics, 1925–35." *Discourses in Dance* 4(2): 73–96.

Harris, Mary Emma. 1987. *The Arts at Black Mountain College*. Cambridge, MA: MIT Press.

Hawes, Elizabeth. 1938. *Fashion is Spinach: How to Beat the Fashion Racket*. New York: Random House.

Hawes, Elizabeth. 1943. *Why Women Cry: Or Wenches With Wrenches*. New York: Reynal and Hitchcock.

Henderson, Ame. 2011. "Steve Paxton: Relational Democracies of Sensation." In *Paxton Ave Nue: A Revisioning*, edited by Jeroen Fabius and Sher Doruff. *RTRSRCH* 3(1): 71–80.

Henderson, Mae G. and Charlene B. Regester. 2017. *The Josephine Baker Critical Reader: Selected Writings on the Entertainer and Activist*. Jefferson, NC: McFarland and Company.

Herle, Anita. 2016. "Anthropology Museums and Museum Anthropology." In *The Open Encyclopedia of Anthropology*, edited by Felix Stein: http://doi.org/10.29164/16museums.

Herring, Joyce. 2023. *Interview*. New York: Martha Graham Center for Contemporary Dance, April 26.

Hill, Constance Valis. 1994. "Katherine Dunham's *Southland*: Protest in the Face of Repression." *Dance Research Journal* 26(2): 1–10.

Holiday, Linda. 2013. *Journey to the Heart of Aikido: The Teachings of Motomichi Anno Sensei*. Berkeley: Blue Snake Books.

Hollander, Anne. 1975. *Seeing Through Clothes*. Berkeley: University of California Press.

Isaac, Veronica. 2017. "Towards a New Methodology for Working with Historic Theatre Costume: A Biographical Approach Focussing on Ellen Terry's 'Beetlewing Dress.'" *Studies in Costume and Performance* 2(2): 115–135.

Jacobs, Jane. 1961. *The Death and Life of Great American Cities*. Harmondsworth: Penguin Books.

James, Van. 2010. *Ancient Sites of O'ahu: A Guide to Hawaiian Archaeological Places of Interest*. Honolulu: Bishop Museum Press.

Janevski, Ana and Thomas J. Lax. 2018. *Judson Dance Theater: The Work is Never Done*. New York: The Museum of Modern Art.

Järvinen, Hanna. 2020. "Historical Materiality of Performance: On the Costumes of *The Rite of Spring* (1913)." *Studies in Costume & Performance* 5(2): 153–173.

Johnson, Deborah and Wendy Oliver. 2017. "Aaron Douglas and Katherine Dunham: The Exploration and Legitimization of African and African Diasporic Roots." *Dance Chronicle*, 40(3): 287–309.

Jowitt, Deborah. 1980b. "Before the Mist Descends." *The Village Voice*, July 2–8.

Jowitt, Deborah. 1980a. "Premiere of Dunn's 'Echo'." *The Village Voice*, May 19.

Jowitt, Deborah. 1985. *The Dance in Mind: Profiles and Reviews 1976-83*. Boston: D.R. Godine.

Jowitt, Deborah. 2024. *Errand into the Maze: The Life and Works of Martha Graham*. New York: Farrar, Straus and Giroux.

Joyce, James. 1975 (1939). *Finnegan's Wake*. London: Faber and Faber.

Joyce, James. 2011 (1920). *Ulysses: Annotated Student Edition*. London: Penguin.

Jules-Rosette, Bennetta. 2006. *Josephine Baker in Art and Life: The Icon and the Image*. Champaign: University of Illinois Press.

Jules-Rosette, Bennetta. 2013. "Spectacular Dress: Africanisms in the Fashions and Performances of Josephine Baker, 1925–1975." In *African Dress: Fashion, Agency, Performance*, edited by Karen Tranberg Hansen and D. Soyini Madison. London: Bloomsbury Academic: 204–216.

Jules, Jason. 2021. *Black Ivy: A Revolt in Style*. New York: Reel Art Press.

Jung, E. Alex. 2019. "In Conversation: John Waters; The Pope of Trash on Anna Wintour, Staying Youthful, and Why Trump Ruined Camp." *Vulture*, June 28: https://www.vulture.com/2019/06/john-waters-in-conversation.html, accessed October 16, 2023.

Kabir, Ananya Jahanara. 2015. "Plantation, Archive, Stage: Trans(post)colonial Intimations in Katherine Dunham's 'L'Ag'ya' and 'Little Black Sambo.'" *The Cambridge Journal of Postcolonial Literary Inquiry* 2(2): 213–231.

Kaiser, 1999. "On Biped." *Scena Digitale: La Nuove Media per la Danza*, edited by Armando Menicacci and Emanuele Quinz. Marsilio: http://openendedgroup.com/artworks/biped_essay.html.

Karoula, Rania. 2020. *The Federal Theatre Project, 1935-1939: Engagement and Experimentation*. Edinburgh: Edinburgh University Press.

Kaufman, S. Jay. 1930. "Round the Town." *The New York Telegram*, April 21.

Kelley, Courtney. 2018. *A Brief History of Germantown Yarns*. Kelbourne Woollens: https://kelbournewool ens.com/blog/2018/10/a-brief-history-of-germantown-yarns/.

Kinberg, Judy. 1977. "Merce Cunningham." *Great Performances: Dance in America*. New York: PBS/WNET TV, January 5.

King, Brenda. 2005. *Silk and Empire*. Manchester: Manchester University Press.

Kisselgoff, Anna. 1982. "Dance: Merce Cunningham's *Trails'Z'*." *New York Times*, March 17: C17.

Kisselgoff, Anna. 1987. "Ballet: Graham's 'Persephone'." *New York Times*, October 15: C23.

Knappe, Brett. 2008. *Barbara Morgan's Photographic Interpretation of American Culture, 1935–1980*. PhD Thesis, Kress Foundation Department of the History of Art, University of Kansas.

Kourlas, Gia. 2020. "Sally Banes, Distinguished Dance Critic and Historian, Dies at 69." *New York Times*, June 21.

Kraus, Lisa. 2011. "Learning from Line-Up." *Writing My Dancing Life: Reflections on Performances Seen, Works in Progress, and Diverse Dance Topics*, January 5: https://writingmydancinglife2.blogspot.com/ 2011/.

Landau, Ellen G. 2013. *Mexico and American Modernism*. New Haven, CT: Yale University Press.

Latour, Bruno. 2005. *Reassembling the Social: An Introduction to Actor Network Theory*. Oxford: Oxford University Press.

Lautens, Annika. 2022. "Designer Dressing RuPaul." *Fashion*, March 24: https://fashionmagazine.com/ style/zaldy-interview/, accessed October 16, 2023.

Laver, James. 1995. *Costume and Fashion: A Concise History*. London: Thames and Hudson.

Lax, Thomas J. 2018. "Allow Me to Begin Again." In *Judson Dance Theater: The Work is Never Done*, edited by Ana Janevski and Thomas J. Lax. New York: The Museum of Modern Art: 14–25.

Lehmann, Ulrich. 1999. "*Tigersprung*: Fashioning History." *Fashion Theory: the Journal of Dress, Body, Culture* 3(3): 297–321.

Lehmann, Ulrich. 2000. *Tigersprung: Fashion in Modernity*. Harvard: MIT Press.

Lehmann, Ulrich. 2007. "The Uncommon Object: Surrealist Concepts and Categories from the Material World." In *The Surreal Body: Fetish and Fashion*, edited by Ghislaine Wood. New York: V&A Publications: 19–38.

Leontis, Artemis. 2019. *Eva Palmer Sikelianos: A Life in Ruins*. Princeton and Oxford: Princeton University Press.

Lepecki, Andre. 2004. *Of the Presence of the Body: Essays on Dance and Performance Theory*. Middletown, CT: Wesleyan University Press.

Lepecki, André. 2006. *Exhausting Dance: Performance and the Politics of Movement*. New York: Routledge.

Lepecki, André. 2018. "Choreographic Angelology." In *The Sentient Archive: Bodies, Performance, and Memory*, edited by Bill Bissell and Linda Caruso Cavilland. Middletown: Wesleyan University Press: 297–319.

Lewis, Damien. 2022. *Agent Josephine: American Beauty, French Hero, British Spy*. New York, NY: Public Affairs.

Livet, Anne. 1987. *Trisha Brown/A Profile, December 4, 1975*. Reproduced in *Trisha Brown*, edited by Lise Brunel, Babette Mangolte, and Guy Delahaye. Paris: Editions Bougé: 34.

Losey, Gavrik. 2016. "FIT Talks: Gavrik Losey, Son of Elizabeth Hawes, Interview." Fashion Institute of Technology, September 12, Video. https://archiveondemand.fitnyc.edu/item/136343.

Lucas, Rosyln. 1990. "Private Gestural Language, Unfolding Poetically: Foray Forêt." *New York Times*, March 18.

Lynch, Connor. 2022. "Why Are Some Beetles Shiny, it is Not What Researchers Thought." *The Scientist*, March.

Macaulay, Alastair. 2012. "Films That Allow the Elusive to Elude." *The New York Times*, April 9.

Macaulay, Alastair. 2021. "Mark Lancaster (1938–2021), Superlative Designer for Merce Cunningham Dance Theatre, R.I.P." *Essays on Dance*, May 3: https://www.alastairmacaulay.com/all-essays/category/ Merce+Cunningham.

McCarren, Felicia. 2008. "The Use-Value of Josephine Baker," in Josephine Baker: A Century in the Spotlight. Barnard Center for Research on Women: *Scholar & Feminist Online*, 6(1–2).

Mackrell, Judith. 2006. "Review: 'Ocean.'" *The Guardian*, September 25.

Madden, Diane. 2011. *Trisha Brown Dance Company Performance 11: On Line, Dancing in Museums: A Decade of Movement*, Museum of Modern Art, New York: https://www.youtube.com/watch?v=_NSrJypk6QE, accessed July 29, 2024.

Marion, Jonathan S. 2008. *Ballroom: Culture and Costume in Competitive Dance*. Oxford: Berg.

Martin, Olivia. 2023. *Email Correspondence*. Tate Britain, June 8.

Marx, Karl. 1990. *Capital: A Critique of Political Economy, Volume One*. New York: Penguin Random House.

Matomoros, Elna. 2021. *Dance and Costumes: A History of Dressing Movement*. Berlin: Alexander Verlag.

Mazzocca Bellecci, Ann E. and Denise Gillman. 2020. "Embodiment, Reciprocity, and Reception: Shakespeare Adaptations in a Black Atlantic Context." In *The Oxford Handbook of Shakespeare and Dance*, edited by Lynsey McCulloch and Brandon Shaw. New York: Oxford Academic: 499–524.

McAuliffe, Mary. 2016. *When Paris Sizzled: The 1920s Paris of Hemingway, Chanel, Cocteau, Cole Porter, Josephine Baker and their Friends*. New York: Rowman and Littlefield.

McDonald, Felicity. 2000. "Jennifer Monson: A Review." *Dancehouse Newsletter*. Melbourne, Australia: 3.

McNeil, Peter. 2016. "George Simmel: The 'Philosophical Monet.'" In *Thinking Through Fashion: A Guide to Key Theorists*, edited by Agnes Rocamora and Anneke Smelik. London: I. B. Tauris: 63–80.

Meade, Fionn and Joan Rothfuss, eds. 2017. *Merce Cunningham: Common Time*. Minneapolis: Walker Art Center.

Meglin, Joellen A. 2022. *Ruth Page: The Woman in the Work*. New York: Oxford University Press.

Mieszkowski, Jan. 2004. "Art Forms." In *The Cambridge Companion to Walter Benjamin*, edited by David Ferris. Cambridge: Cambridge University Press: 35–53.

Miller, Daniel. 2005. *Materiality: Politics, History, and Culture*. Durham, NC: Duke University Press.

Monks, Aoife. 2010. *The Actor in Costume*. Basingstoke: Palgrave Macmillan.

Morgan, Barbara. 1953. "Kinetic Design in Photography." *Aperture* 1(4) Princeton University: 18–27.

Morgan, Barbara. 1980 (1941). *Martha Graham: Sixteen Dances in Photographs*. New York: Dobbs Ferry.

Mumaw, Barton. 1984. "Costume in Regard to Ruth St Denis, Ted Shawn, Men Dancers." Unpublished manuscript. Barton Mumaw Collection, Jacob's Pillow Dance Festival Archives.

Munro, Jane. 2009. "'More like a Work of Art than of Nature': Darwin, Beauty and Sexual Selection" In *Endless Forms: Charles Darwin, Natural Science and the Visual Arts*, edited by Diana Donald and Jane Munro. Cambridge, UK: London, Fitzwilliam Museum; and Yale Center for British Art: Yale University Press: 253–291.

Murphy, Kevin and Caroline Hamilton. 2023. *Dance We Must: The Art and Costumes of Ruth St. Denis and Ted Shawn, 1906–1940*. Williamstown, MA: Williams College Museum of Art.

National Industrial Conference Board. 1919. "Hours of Work as Related to Output and Health in Workers: Silk Manufacturing." *Research Report No. 16*. Boston, MA.

Negrin, Llewellyn. 2016. "Maurice Merleau-Ponty: The Corporeal Experience of Fashion" In *Thinking Through Fashion: A Guide to Key Theorists*, edited by Agnes Rocamora and Anneke Smelik. London: I. B. Tauris: 115–131.

Noisette, Philippe. 2019. *Couturiers de la Danse, de Chanel À Versace*. Milan: Silvana Editoriale.

Noland, Carrie. 2019. *Merce Cunningham: After the Arbitrary*. Chicago: Chicago University Press.

O'Connor, Kaori. 2014. "Anthropology, Archaeology, History and the Material Culture of Lycra®" In *Writing Material Culture History*, edited by Anne Gerristen and Georgio Riello. London: Bloomsbury: 73–91.

Olson, Liesl. 2020. "Flicker of an Eyelid: Isamu Noguchi, Ruth Page, and the Universe of Chicago." *Digital Features* 10(26). Brooklyn: Noguchi Museum.

Olson, Liesl with Eve Ewing. 2021. *Chicago Avant-Garde: Five Women Ahead of Their Time*. Chicago: Newberry Museum: September 10–December 31.

Owen, Norton. 2024. *Email Correspondence*. April 10.

Pace, Eric. 1993. "Bill Robinson, 45, Pioneering Designer of Fashions for Men." *The New York Times*, December 17.

Partridge, Meg. 2024. *Email Correspondence*. May 1.

Patel, Shankari. 2013. "Ukemi: the Bane of My Existence." *Feminist Aikidoka*, August 26, http://feministaikidoka.blogspot.com/.

Perron, Wendy. 2001. "Paying Heed to the Mysteries of Trisha Brown." *New York Times*, July 8.

Perron, Wendy. 2013. Through *the Eyes of a Dancer: Selected Writings*. Middletown, CT: Wesleyan.

Perron, Wendy. 2022. "IN MEMORIAM: Modern Dance Legend Yuriko Dies at Age 102." *Dance Magazine*, March 14.

Perry, Imani. 2022. *South to America: A Journey Below the Mason-Dixon Line to Understand the Soul of a Nation*. New York: Ecco Press.

Phelan, Peggy. 1993. *Unmarked: the Politics of Performance*. London: Routledge.

Pinasa, Delphine. 2023. *Interview*. Centre National du Costume de Scene, Moulins, France, May 5.

Pittsburgh Wool Company Documentation Project Records, 2000, MSS 700, Library and Archives Division, Senator John Heinz History Center, https://historicpittsburgh.org/islandora/object/pitt%3AUS-QQS-mss700/viewer.

Porter, Charlie. 2021. *What Artists Wear*. London: Random House.

Postrel, Virginia. 2020. *The Fabric of Civilization: How Textiles Made the World*. New York: Hachette.

Preston, Carrie. 2011. *Modernism's Mythic Pose: Gender, Genre, Solo Performance*. New York: Oxford University Press.

Purkayashna, Prarthana. 2025. *The Archives and Afterlives of Nautch Dancers in India*. Cambridge: Cambridge University Press.

Pushor, Jessica. 2020. "To Stretch and Pull and Expand a Universe." *Fashion and Style Blog, Inside the Museum*, Chicago History Museum, September 18: https://www.chicagohistory.org/ruthpage/.

Razmi, Anahita. 2011. *Roof Piece Tehran*, Video installation, 12 video loops. Frieze Foundation for Frieze Projects, in collaboration with Hasti Goudarzi: https://www.anahitarazmi.de/Roof-Piece-Tehran.

Richardson, John. 2008. "Rauschenberg's Epic Vision." *Vanity Fair*. New York, April 30: https://www.vanityfair.com/magazine/1997/09/rauschenberg199709?srsltid=AfmBOooZrsWCBRmDyxLltTZnlMo3BnWZsoYdUcJPKrE5J8Ca9mOphHXA, accessed October 27, 2025.

Riello, Giorgio. 2013. *Cotton: The Fabric That Made the Modern World*. Cambridge and New York: Cambridge University Press.

Riley II, Charles A. 1998. *The Saints of Modern Art: The Ascetic Ideal in Contemporary Painting, Sculpture, Architecture, Music, Dance, Literature, and Philosophy*. Hanover and London: University Press of New England.

Rivers, Victoria. 1999. *The Shining Cloth: Dress and Adornment That Glitters*. New York: Thames and Hudson.

Rosen, Philip. 2003. "Introduction." *Boundary 2* 30(1): 1–15.

Rosenberg, Susan. 2016. *Trisha Brown: Choreography as Visual Art*. Middletown, CT: Wesleyan University Press.

Ross, Chad. 2005. *Naked Germany: Health, Race and the Nation*. New York, NY: Oxford University Press.

Ross, Doran. H. 2001. *Wrapped in Pride: Ghanaian Kente and African American Identity*. UCLA: Fowler Museum of Cultural History Textile Series.

Ross, Nancy Wilson. 1973. *The Notebooks of Martha Graham*. New York: Harcourt Brace Janovich.

Ross, Robert. 2008. *Clothing: A Global History; or, the Imperialists' New Clothes*. Cambridge: Polity Press.

Rovine, Victoria L. 2015. *African Fashion, Global Style: Histories, Innovations and Ideas You Can Wear*. Bloomington: Indiana University Press.

Ruschmann, Roberta. 2023. *Email Correspondence*. President, Meadowbrook Inventions, Sequins Division, March 24.

Rutter, Carol Chillington, 2001. *Enter The Body: Women and Representation on Shakespeare's Stage*. London: Routledge.

Sabin, Evelyn. 1927. *Correspondence in Carnegie Hall Archives*, ALS. Martha Graham, 12 pp. 8vo, New York, January 4.

Schoeser, Mary. 2007. *Silk*. New Haven, CT: Yale University Press.

Schweitzer, Marlis and Joanne Zerdy. 2014. *Performing Objects and Theatrical Things*. London: Palgrave.

Scolieri, Paul. 2020. *Ted Shawn: His Life, Writings and Dances*. New York: Oxford University Press.

Segal, Lewis, 2003. "In Thrall to a Phantom." *Los Angeles Times*, March 20: E46.

Sekula, Allan. 1986. "The Body and the Archive." *October* 39: 3–64.

Shawn, Ted. c.1939 (remastered 1988). *Dance of the Ages*. Choreography: Ted Shawn; music: Jess Meeker; performed by Ted Shawn's Men Dancers. Jacob's Pillow Dance Festival Archives.

Sherman, Jane. 1979. *The Drama of Denishawn Dance*. Middletown, CT: Wesleyan University Press.

Sherman, Jane and Barton Mumaw. 2000. *Barton Mumaw: From Denishawn to Jacob's Pillow and Beyond*. Middletown, CT: Wesleyan University Press.

Sherman, Jane. 1984. "Notes on Costume." Unpublished manuscript. Denishawn Collection, Jacob's Pillow Dance Festival Archives.

Sherman, Martha. 2017. "Two Sides of Her Coin." *Danceviewtimes*, February 14: https://www.danceviewti mes.com/2017/02/two-sides-of-her-coin.html.

Skinner, Marsha. 2023. *Letter Correspondence*. New Mexico: April 11.

Smith, Tyler Jo. 2010. "Reception or Deception? Approaching Greek Dance through Vase-Painting." In *The Ancient Dancer in the Modern World: Responses to Greek and Roman Dance*, edited by Fiona McIntosh. Oxford: Oxford University Press: 77–98.

Smoot, D. E. 2012. "A Different Type of Oklahoma Oil Man." *Muskogee Phoenix*. September 16.

Spångberg, Mårten. 2009. "Why 'The Art of Making Dances' Now? Between? "-What is . . . " and Choreography." In *The Art of Making Dances*, edited by Chase Granoff and Jenn Joy. Brooklyn, NY: Self-published: https://martenspangberg.se/sites/martenspangberg.org/files/After_Derrida_After_Humph rey.pdf.

Spaulding, Harold E. 1990. *A Selective Guide to the Industrial Archeology of Philadelphia*. Oliver Evans Press: https://www.workshopoftheworld.com/germantown/germantown.html.

Srinivasan, Priya. 2011. *Sweating Saris: Indian Dance as Transnational Labor*. Philadelphia: Temple University Press.

St Clair, Kassia. 2018. *The Golden Thread: How Fabric Changed History*. London: John Murray.

Stalpaert, Christel. 2012. "Staging Age and Aging in 'The Rite of Spring': Reconstruction or Critical Intervention?" In *Aging, Performance and Stardom: Doing Age on the Stage of Consumerist Culture*, edited by Aagje Swinnen and John A Stotesbury. Berlin: Lit Verlag: 53–74.

Stark Smith, Nancy. 2005. "Harvest: One History of Contact Improvisation: a Talk Given by Nancy Stark Smith at the International Contact Festival Freiburg, Germany." *CQ Unbound*, https://contactquarterly.com/cq/unbound/view/harvest-a-history-of-ci#$, accessed October 27, 2025.

Starrs, Roy. 2011. *Modernism and Japanese Culture*. London: Palgrave Macmillan.

Steele, Mike. 1975. "Views and Reviews." *Tribune*, March 22.

Steele, Valerie. 2014. *Dance and Fashion*. New Haven, CT: Yale University Press.

Sweeney-Risko, Jennifer. 2015. "Elsa Schiaparelli, The New Woman, and Surrealist Politics." *Interdisciplinary Literary Studies* 17(3): 309–329.

Sweeney-Risko, Jennifer. 2018. "Fashionable 'Formation': Reclaiming the Sartorial Politics of Josephine Baker." *Australian Feminist Studies* 33(98): 498–514.

Tartz, Alexandre. 1968. *Die Star Show Mit Josephine Baker*. Olympia Theatre, Paris. Zweites Deutsches Fernsehen. https://www.youtube.com/watch?v=EfBKUKauGgc.

Taylor, Diana. 2003. *The Archive and the Repertoire: Performing Cultural Memory in the Americas*. Durham: Duke University Press.

Teicher, Hendel. 2002. *Dance and Art in Dialogue, 1961-2001*. Andover, MA: Addison Gallery of American Art, Phillips Academy.

Thanhauser, Sofi. 2022. *Worn: A People's History of Clothing*. London: Allen Lane.

The Vintage Traveler. 2022. *Blog post*. July 4: https://thevintagetraveler.wordpress.com/2022/07/04/aldrich-and-aldrich-exercise-suit/, accessed July 8, 2024.

Thomas, Helen. 2004. "Mimesis and Alterity in African Caribbean Quadrille: Ethnography meets History". *Cultural and Social History* 1: 280–301.

Thompson, Robert Farris. 1983. *Flash of the Spirit: African and Afro-American Art and Philosophy*. New York: Vintage.

Todd, Mabel Elsworth. 1968 (1937). *The Thinking Body: a Study of the Balancing Forces of Dynamic Man*. Brooklyn: Dance Horizons.

Trebay, Guy. 2013. "In Search of a Gay Aesthetic." *New York Times*, September 11.

Trentmann, Frank. 2017. "Material Histories of the World: Scales and Dynamics." In *History After Hobsbawm: Writing the Past for the Twenty-First Century*, edited by John H. Arnold, Matthew Hilton, and Jan Rüger. Oxford, UK: Oxford Academic: 200–222.

Trisha Brown Dance Company. *Spanish Dance*, video excerpt. https://trishabrowncompany.org/repertory/spanish-dance.html?ctx=date.

Ulrich, Laurel Thatcher, Ivan Gaskell, Sara Schechner, Sarah Anne Carter, and Samantha van Gerbig. 2015. *Tangible Things: Making History Through Things*. New York: Oxford University Press.

Van Gennep, Arnold. 1977 (1909). *Rites De Passage*. Translated by Monika B. Vizedom and Gabrielle L. Cafee. London: Routledge and Kegan Paul.

Vergès, Mine. 2021. *Ma vie de fil en aiguille: les mémories de la costumiére des stars*. Montrouge: Bayard Éditions.

Von Drehle, David. 2004. *Triangle: The Fire that Changed America*. New York, NY: Grove Press.

Way, Elizabeth, Elena Romero, and Slick Rick. 2023. *Fresh, Fly and Fabulous: 50 Years of Hip Hop Style*. New York: Rizzoli.

Weill, Susan. 1972. *"Merce Cunningham Residency, March 1972." Box 008 folder 011*. Minneapolis: Walker Art Center Archives.

Weill, Susan. 1975. *"Cunningham Residency, March 1975." Box 26, folder 6*. Minneapolis: Walker Art Center Archives.

Wells, Charmian. 2020. "'Harlem Knows': Eleo Pomare's Choreographic Theory of Vitality and Diaspora Citation in Blues for the Jungle." *Dance Research Journal* 52(3): 4–21.

Whitehead, Alfred North. 1920. *The Concept of Nature*. Cambridge: Cambridge University Press.

Whitted, Emily. 2020. *Made in Germantown: Production, Wear and Repair of American Frame-Knit Stockings 1683-1830*. Masters of Arts Thesis, University of Delaware.

Wilson, Elizabeth. 2003. *Adorned in Dreams: Fashion and Modernity*. London: I. B. Tauris.

Wilson, Mary with Mark Bego. 2019. *Supreme Glamour*. London: Thames and Hudson: https://www.marywilson.com/gown-collection/, accessed July 29, 2024.

Wolff, Janet. 2013. "Blue." *Manchester Review*. Manchester University Press: 1–9. https://www.themanchesterreview.co.uk/?p=2587.

Wollen, Peter. 2003. "The Concept of Fashion in the Arcades Project." *Boundary 2* 30(1): 128–142.

Wood, Betty. 1995. *Women's Work, Men's Work: The Informal Slave Economies of Lowcountry Georgia*. Athens, GA: University of Georgia Press.

Yee, Lydia. 2011. *Laurie Anderson, Trisha Brown, Gordon Matta-Clark: Pioneers of the Downtown Scene, New York 1970s*. Catalogue. London: Barbican Centre, March 3–May 22.

Young, Iris Marion. 2005. *On Female Body Experience: Throwing Like a Girl and Other Essays*. New York: Oxford University Press.

Young, Tricia Henry with Pam Killinger. 1997. *The Killinger Collection of Denishawn and Ted Shawn and His Men Dancers Costumes: Inventory by Repertory*. New York: Performing Arts Resources, 20: 93–141.

Index

For the benefit of digital users, indexed terms that span two pages (e.g., 52–53) may, on occasion, appear on only one of those pages.

Figures are indicated by an italic *f.*